The nearest I have com fluencing living things is
making seeds germinat television recently . . . done, the original idea astronaut Edgar Mitch 1972. We were sitting Franklin, when Mitchell suddenly produced a seed and asked me if I could make it germinate while he held it in his own hand. I just stared at his hand and concentrated on making the seed sprout. When it did, Mitchell and Franklin were delighted, but I was not. In fact, the experience scared me stiff . . .

By the same authors

Uri Geller

*My Story*
*Pampini*
*Uri Geller's Fortune Secrets*

Guy Lyon Playfair

*The Flying Cow*
*The Indefinite Boundary*
*The Cycles of Heaven* (with Scott Hill)
*This House is Haunted*
*If This Be Magic*
*The Haunted Pub Guide*

URI GELLER AND
GUY LYON PLAYFAIR

# The Geller Effect

**GRAFTON BOOKS**

A Division of the Collins Publishing Group

LONDON GLASGOW
TORONTO SYDNEY AUCKLAND

Grafton Books
A Division of the Collins Publishing Group
8 Grafton Street, London W1X 3LA

Published by Grafton Books 1988

First published in Great Britain by
Jonathan Cape Ltd 1986

ISBN 0-586-07430-9

Printed and bound in Great Britain by
Collins, Glasgow

Set in Times

I dedicate this book to my very close family – Hanna, Natalie, Daniel, Muti and Shipi

U.G.

'The scientific community has been put on notice "that there is something worthy of their attention and scrutiny" in the possibilities of extra-sensory perception. With those words the respected British journal *Nature* called on scientists to join – or refute – millions of non-scientists who believe human consciousness has more capabilities for real perception than the five senses.'
*New York Times* editorial

# Contents

# Part One

*by*
Guy Lyon Playfair

# 1

## In All Directions

'Look,' said Uri. 'This is what I do.'

He took the small coffee spoon I had brought with me and held the tip of the bowl between the thumb and forefinger of his right hand, with the underside of the bowl facing upwards, and began to stroke the stem lightly with the forefinger of his left hand. I looked, as instructed.

I looked as carefully as I have ever looked at anything. I had been waiting more than ten years for my first private audience with this controversial Israeli, who had divided much of the world into two bitterly opposed camps, one of which claimed him to be the greatest demonstrator of paranormal or psychic power in history, the other insisting he was just an unusually smart magician. I had never managed to decide which was right, and felt it was time that I did.

It was undoubtedly my spoon. I had received it, together with an identical one, as a free offer from a Dutch coffee company a few weeks previously, and I did not take my eyes off it from the moment I handed it to him until he gave it back to me three or four minutes later. He was not wearing a watch, I noticed, or a ring, or a belt, and the copper bracelet on his right arm was well beyond the reach of the end of the spoon. The more obvious ways of spoon-bending by sleight-of-hand were thus ruled out. There were others, and I was ready for them.

'Did you bring a camera?' he asked, after some more rubbing of my spoon with his left forefinger.

Aha, I said to myself. Misdirection. While I am fumbling in my bag for my camera and adjusting the speed and shutter opening, he is going to make some very quick movements and bend the spoon by muscle power, not psychic power. This is what sceptical friends had assured me he would do if given the chance.

I did not give him the chance. My eyes remained on the spoon as I reached down for my camera. The semi-automatic Olympus XA did not need adjusting, and at this range of five or six feet I had no need to look through the viewfinder. I held the camera in front of my nose, looked over the top of the viewfinder, and started clicking at once. The light was perfect: Uri was facing the huge window of his apartment overlooking Hyde Park at tree-top level, and there was nobody else in the room with us.

I had been warned that Uri never kept still for long, but liked to move around quickly and confuse people. However, he was certainly sitting still now, on his exercise bicycle. 'I need a heavy workout every day, or I lose my powers,' he had explained, and he had been pedalling vigorously for ten minutes or so before offering to demonstrate those powers for me. Earlier that day, he told me, he had run twice around the park as usual.

'It's bending already!' he exclaimed, after I had taken my second photograph. I said nothing, and took a third. Then he stopped pedalling, put his left hand on his hip, and held the spoon up almost at shoulder level. 'Now it'll go on bending until it has reached ninety degrees,' he assured me.

The spoon had unquestionably bent already, but I could not say for certain that he had not helped it along with his fingers. In fact I had no intention of saying anything at all for certain until I had developed my film, made enlargements and placed my protractor on them.

I took two more pictures. Uri made no suspicious movement of any kind and did not try to misdirect me in any way. Then, about three minutes after I had handed him my spoon, he gave it back to me.

Later that day, after a couple of hours in my darkroom, I was able to verify that the angle of bend in the spoon had increased from the fourth to the fifth picture although Uri's right hand had not moved and the position of the fingers of his left hand had not altered. I also noticed that the spoon had continued to bend slightly after I had taken the last shot.

I was impressed.

Immediately after his demonstration of apparent psycho-kinesis, or physical movement caused by the mind, Uri offered to show me another of his powers in action: telepathy. He asked me to draw something in my notebook, and then to try to project it into his mind. I had seen magicians do this and knew some of their techniques, so I decided to do some misdirection of my own.

I held my notebook parallel to my chest and made several movements with my pen that bore no relation to what I drew, adding a few scratches with my thumbnail for good measure. That, I reckoned, would make it difficult for him to guess what I was drawing by watching the top of my pen or by listening to the sounds it made on the paper. What I eventually drew, after Uri had become rather impatient and asked me to hurry up, was a very small head with a three-pointed crown on it. While I was doing so he turned away from me and put a hand over his eyes. Then he turned back to face me.

'Now look at me and send me what you've drawn,' he said, giving me a piercing stare with his large and almost black eyes.

I did not feel inclined to look at those eyes for long. I thought I knew a potentially powerful hypnotist when I saw one, having met several while researching the book on hypnotism I had just completed, and had no doubt that I was looking at one now. So as I mentally redrew my royal head I kept my eyes moving slowly. A sceptical magician friend had seriously suggested to me that Geller might be able to induce temporary unconsciousness just by staring at people. If true, which I am sure it is not, this would be as interesting as anything else he claims to be able to do.

'I'm not getting it,' he said, so I tried again. He then leaned forward, picked up his own notepad and made some rapid scribbles on it before handing it to me. 'I don't think it's right,' he said, 'but it's all I got.'

In this kind of experiment it is essential that you see your subject's drawing before he sees yours. Otherwise, a few quick strokes with a 'thumb writer', a tiny pencil attached to the thumbnail, are all that are needed. I had no difficulty in satisfying myself that he was not using one. I also saw his drawing before he saw mine.

As he had said, it was not right, or not completely so. There were some interesting similarities between our two drawings, though. He had drawn three circles, one with four lines protruding outwards, one with what looked like a single cat's ear, and finally one that was plainly meant to be a cat's head with two pointed ears, eyes and whiskers, and another circle below for its body.

The cat's head was remarkably similar to my human one both in size and shape. Uri took my pen and made two marks on each of our drawings, level with the top and bottom of each head. 'If you measure these with a millimetre ruler,' he said, 'you'll find they are exactly the same size.'

I did measure them later, and they were. Again, I was impressed. If this was sleight-of-hand, it was close-up work of a very high order.

'You see,' he said, 'what I do is real.'

I had no reason to disagree. Whether what he did was conjuring or psychic interaction with a spoon and a mind – both mine – it was evidently real. A spoon had bent (upwards, incidentally) and a drawing had been at least partially reproduced without any obviously normal methods being used. Nor had he used any of the magicians' tricks that are just as obvious to somebody who knows what to look for. His psychic powers looked real enough to me.

And yet . . .

Although Uri and I had first corresponded with each other more than ten years previously, and we had several friends in common, we had never actually met. I had followed his career fairly closely since he had first become well known outside Israel in the early seventies, and I had put together a large file on him in the hope that I would be able to write something about him one day. It was clear to me by the middle of the decade that he was either the world's greatest psychic or its greatest magician. Like many people, I was not sure which.

Before I could try to find out, I lost touch with him, and the past few years all I had heard about him were rumours, most of which were not very complimentary: he had lost his powers, he had been unmasked, he had gone into hiding, he had fled to Mexico, and so on. At the same time, he had somehow or other made a lot of money, it was said.

When I heard early in 1985 that he had come to live in England, I was a little apprehensive about approaching him directly. The only thing I had ever written on him, which will be mentioned later, was not very flattering. Then one day in April he telephoned me out of the blue, or, rather, from his rented apartment just a few minutes' walk from mine. I was, to say the least, surprised. Here was the world's most controversial celebrity on my doorstep – and inviting me to come and see him.

I accepted gladly, though a suspicion lurked in my mind. Did he need publicity so badly that he had to ask writers to come and see him, I wondered? Had he really lost his powers, and was he now trying to make a comeback?

A brochure on the porter's desk at his apartment block informed me that apartments were available for rents of '£800 a week' and more. The porter buzzed a number, received no reply, and remarked, 'I'll try the other apartment.' Yes, Mr Geller and his family had rented two of them! His weekly rent came to about the same as my total outgoings for a year, and he had already been there for two or three months. As I swished upwards in the lift, after running the gauntlet of the security guards, I reflected that there had to be something Uri could do, and do very well.

He greeted me like a long-lost brother, and immediately wanted to know how my books were doing, what I was working on then, and where I lived. We discussed our mutual friends and brought each other up to date on their activities. I felt he was genuinely interested and not merely curious. At length I asked him, 'What have you been doing lately?'

'Right now, I'm looking for gold,' he said, 'and before that . . .' He went on to fill in the gaps in my file, bringing in one name after another, of a multinational corporation, an intelligence agency, and even one or two heads of state. Before very long, I had reached what the writer Renée Haynes has called the boggle threshold, the point at which the mind cannot handle any more information on a given subject, and instead begins to reel.

'People always used to ask me, "If you're so psychic, why aren't you a millionaire?"' he concluded. 'Well, now I am!' He was not showing off, I felt, but merely stating a simple truth.

He did not have to be telepathic to learn that I was indeed interested in writing something about him. I had heard, over the literary grapevine, that he was preparing a sequel to his 1975 autobiography *My Story*.

'Maybe you and I should work together,' he said.

After a brief discussion, we agreed on how we might arrange the book. Although English is only his third language, he expresses himself very fluently and precisely in it, with only occasional lapses into the syntax of his first two – Hungarian and Hebrew. It was settled. He would tell his story, in his own words, to a tape recorder, while I acted as questioner, editor and research co-ordinator. He would then read the transcripts and amend them where necessary. I would write a separate section in which I put Uri's story into the context of current psychical research and dealt with the questions he could not answer impartially, such as 'Is he genuine? If he is, what then? Why do so many people insist that he is not?' and, I would hope, 'What does it all mean?'

The last question could, of course, only be tackled if I was satisfied that Uri's psychic abilities were indeed real. As I made clear to him at the start of our collaboration, I had not made up my mind, when we first met, whether they were or not, or whether perhaps some were and others were not. In view of this, I felt it was a considerable act of faith on his part to ask me to work with him, especially since I made it clear that I could not allow any censorship of my part, although he was welcome to correct errors of fact. (In the event, he contributed as much to my part as I did to his, even correcting my typographical and spelling mistakes as meticulously as any copy editor I have known.)

'I can't come to a conclusion after a single demonstration of spoon-bending or mind-reading,' I told him, 'except that I want to know more about you. I want to go right through your files from start to finish, and read everything the debunkers have said as well as the opinions of your supporters. Then I'll be able to form a conclusion. At least, I hope so.'

If this fellow is a magician, I thought to myself when I had said this, he's going to show me to the door right now.

'Go ahead,' he replied immediately.

Then I had to eat my words, or most of them. Uri showed me one of his spare bedrooms, which was jammed from wall to wall with packing cases. There were newspapers, magazines, books, audio and video tapes, film cans, huge index files, posters, and heaven only knows what else. It was like the end of *Citizen Kane*, when the contents of Xanadu are arranged on the floor for that classic travelling crane shot. To go through it all, I reckoned, would take me at least a year.

'The rest of it is coming over in the container,' said Uri, helpfully.

I decided that the time had not yet come for the full authorized biography of Uri Geller. When it does come, perhaps twenty or thirty years from now, it will need a whole team of writers and researchers, and several years of work. By then, maybe, the material will be housed in a library department of its own, like the Harry Price Collection at London University. It could already fill one, and Uri has not even reached his fortieth birthday.

He was born on 20 December 1946 in Tel Aviv, Israel (then Palestine). His parents had fled their former homeland, Hungary, shortly before the Second World War, in which Itzhak Geller served with the Jewish Brigade of the Eighth Army. Uri's unusual abilities showed themselves at a very early age; his mother recalls a soup spoon bending and breaking in his hand when he was four, and there were many occasions on which Uri seemed to be able to read her mind.

He went to school in Tel Aviv, and after a year on a kibbutz he entered Terra Santa College in Nicosia, Cyprus, where his mother took him following her separation from his father. He spent six years there, returning to Israel at the age of seventeen. He served as a para trooper during his military service in the Israeli Army and fought in the Six Day war of 1967, during which he was wounded in action. He then worked as an instructor in a youth camp, where he met Shipi Shtrang. This enterprising youngster, then aged fourteen, arranged Uri's first public performance of psychic powers in a Tel Aviv school hall in 1969. He went on to become a combination of manager, agent, business adviser and partner, professional colleague and eventually brother-in-law.

In little more than a year, Geller had become one of the most sought-after entertainers in the country. He even received an unexpected testimonial from Prime Minister Golda Meir. Asked by a reporter what she saw for the future of Israel, she replied, 'I don't know. Ask Uri Geller.'

Controversy surrounded him almost as soon as he set foot on the public stage. On 20 October 1970, the popular weekly magazine *Haolam Hazeh* printed his photograph on its cover beside the headline URI GELLER A CHEAT. Readers were told that 'all of Israel's magicians have assembled for a witch-hunt', their quarry being 'this telepathic impostor'.

In August 1971 a researcher as controversial as Uri himself arrived in Israel after hearing from a friend, the late Itzhak Bentov (who was killed in the 1979 Chicago air disaster), about Uri's purported psychic skills. This was Dr Andrija Puharich (MD), an inventor and medical researcher with impeccable scientific qualifications and a long string of patents to his name, one of his specialities being the development of miniature deaf-aids. Another was the study of unusually gifted people, including the clairvoyants Eileen Garrett, Harry Stone and Peter Hurkos, and the Brazilian healer Arigó.

As he described in his book *Uri* (1974), he was sufficiently impressed by what he saw in Israel to arrange for Geller to visit the United States, with the support of the Apollo 14 astronaut Edgar Mitchell, and to undergo a lengthy series of scientific tests in a number of laboratories in the USA and Europe.

The most exhaustive of these took place at Stanford Research Institute in California (later renamed SRI International, and referred to in this book as 'Stanford' or 'SRI'). There, laser physicists Dr Harold Puthoff and Russell Targ carried out six weeks of tests at the end of 1972 and a further eight days in August 1973. Some of these were documented live in the SRI film *Experiments with Uri Geller* (1973) and were later published in the leading scientific journal *Nature* (18 October 1974). Detailed popular accounts of them can be found in Targ and Puthoff's book *Mind-Reach* (1977) and in John Wilhelm's *The Search for Superman* (1976). Each of these books contained first-hand accounts of the controversy that surrounded the SRI research even before it was made public, and which was still continuing more than twelve years later.

Also in 1972, the late Dr Wilbur Franklin, chairman of the physics department at Kent State University, Ohio, carried out the first study by a professional of Geller's metal-bending (and metal-fracturing) abilities.

In October 1973, further laboratory experiments in metal-bending were carried out by US Navy research physicist Eldon Byrd of the Naval Surface Weapons Center in Maryland. Although the research was not conducted on Center premises, Byrd's highly positive report was reviewed by his peers at the establishment, and became the first paper of its kind to be released with the approval of the Department of Defense. Byrd later learned to bend metal paranormally himself, and to teach others to do the same.

Geller spent much of the year 1974 as a laboratory guinea-pig. His investigators, all of whom produced positive reports on their findings, included: Dr Thomas P. Coohill, associate professor of physics at Western Kentucky University; Professor A. R. G. Owen, now head of the department of mathematics at Toronto University; Professor John B. Hasted, head of the physics department of Birkbeck College, University of London, which Uri visited on three separate occasions during that year; Professor John G. Taylor of King's College (also London), who later retracted his positive findings; and Ronald S. Hawke, research physicist at the Lawrence Livermore Laboratory, California.

In July and August 1974, Geller toured South Africa, making numerous public appearances and four radio broadcasts. Dr E. Alan Price, a former senior radiologist at Johannesburg General Hospital, carried out a field study of the already famous 'Geller Effect', whereby Uri would act as a catalyst for all kinds of strange occurrences in people's homes. After following up a total of 137 case reports, Dr Price wrote a lengthy report that included a mass of documentation and statistical analysis, and concluded 'that there is enough evidence to suggest that the Uri Geller Effect exists and is genuine'.

In 1974 and 1975, Geller found time to be personally tested by four magicians, all of whom concluded that his psychic powers were real. Their findings will be discussed later in this book. In the latter year, he was also studied by psychologist Dr Thelma Moss, of University College at Los Angeles, and by Dr Albert Ducrocq, a researcher at the INSERM Telemetry Laboratories at Foch Hospital in Suresnes, France.

All of the above research was collected and published in *The Geller Papers* (1976) edited by Charles Panati, a qualified physicist from Columbia University and author of three textbooks and a number of popular works, who for a time was science writer for *Newsweek* magazine.

Throughout this period, the Geller Effect was making itself felt all over the world. It began on Uri's visit to West Germany in 1972, during which he was credited with such feats as bringing an escalator in a department store to a standstill, and even halting a cable-car in mid-air. There were also countless examples of what was to become his standard repertoire of cutlery-bending, causing broken watches to start ticking, and both transmitting and receiving drawings or words by telepathy.

It continued in England, with appearances on the BBC's Jimmy Young (radio) and David Dimbleby (television) programmes in November 1973 leading to a spate of media publicity of the kind given a decade earlier to the Beatles. Gellermania replaced Beatlemania. Even the normally sober and sensible *New Scientist* joined in the fun, devoting no less than sixteen pages of its 17 October 1974 issue (and its cover) to a feature on 'Uri Geller and Science' that was plainly timed to coincide with the paper already mentioned, which was published in *Nature* the following day. On 22 March 1974, the *Daily Mail* published the results of a poll in which its readers had been asked, 'Does Uri Geller have psychic powers?' Ninety-five per cent replied YES.

The Geller Effect spread to Scandinavia, where it was a case of more of the same. There were lively news conferences at which reporters would see spoons bending in their own hands, feel keys curling up inside their closed fists, watch Uri reproducing something they had just drawn (or mcrcly thought of), and thcn rcturn to thcir desks in a state of mental turmoil only to find that they could not unlock them because their keys no longer fitted, although they were certain that Geller had never touched them. There were equally lively radio and television programmes during which switchboards would jam as listeners or viewers phoned in to report yet another case of a long-dead watch or clock coming back to life, or of a spoon or a fork suddenly performing a spontaneous twist. There were furious debates between scientists who thought the Geller Effect deserved further study, and sceptics who insisted with increasing desperation that Uri was just a naughty magician pretending to be psychic. In short, Geller displayed an ability unmatched since the films of the Marx Brothers for inducing instant chaos, and he plainly loved every minute of it.

Gellermania swept on, like a psychic hurricane, through South Africa, Australia, New Zealand, Japan, Latin

1 The *Daily Mirror* reflects the wave of Gellermania that swept Britain in 1974.

THE WORLD OF KEITH WAITE

"If Uri comes on again, missus, switch off"

America and also every major country in Europe. Even the appearance of a book by a magician named James Randi, entitled *The Magic of Uri Geller* (1975), had little effect except to add to his publicity. It failed to demolish the Geller legend, as it was clearly meant to do, just as it failed again when it was revised and reissued in 1982 under the title *The Truth About Uri Geller*.

Uri's own book *My Story* was translated into thirteen languages, and led to requests from all over the world for promotion tours, and by the end of the year in which it was published (1975) there was no knowing when Geller-mania would come to an end, if ever.

Yet it did end, almost as suddenly as it had started three or four years previously, and until now we have never known why. One possible reason was suggested by Colin Wilson in *The Geller Phenomenon* (1976):

In a life of constant travel and performance, he has had no opportunity to try to explore that inner space in which his powers probably originate. The next stage of his career, the stage of self-exploration, will provide him with that opportunity . . . Uri Geller is in an ideal position to test the truth of the assertion that psychic powers can be increased by inner discipline.

Wilson was right. There was to be a period of self-exploration, though it was not to come for another three or four years. By 1976, Uri's career had already changed course. Indeed, for a time it appeared to follow the example of Stephen Leacock's character who 'flung him-self upon his horse and rode madly off in all directions'.

We have both done our best to arrange the following account of those years from 1975 in chronological order, while at the same time attempting to sort it into chapters that concentrate on certain features of it. Inevitably, there has been some overlap, since throughout the period covered, Uri was often almost literally in several places at once. We have both provided all the dates and references we could find, although we have to confess that we never did get through all those boxes.

'What was it that sent you off in new directions?' I asked Uri on our first joint working day.

He thought for a moment. 'It was a telephone call, really,' he replied.

'That's as good a way as any to start a book,' I said. 'Go on . . .'

# Part Two

*by*
Uri Geller

# 2
## *This is Mexico*

The porter had already started to take our luggage out to the taxi that was waiting to drive us to the airport. A few minutes later, Shipi and I should have checked out of the Camino Real Hotel in Mexico City and been on our way back to New York after an extensive book promotion tour for the Spanish-language edition of *My Story*. I was having a final check through the drawers and wardrobes in my room when the telephone rang.

The caller was Raul Astor, the head of Televisa, the television company for which I had done a major broadcast the previous evening.

'Uri,' he began, 'I'm calling you to tell you something very important.'

I looked at my watch. 'Well, you'd better tell me very quickly,' I replied, 'or I'll miss my flight.'

'Please,' he went on, 'don't leave the hotel, because there is a very important person coming to see you.'

'Look, Raul,' I said, 'I'm sorry, but I can't wait for anybody. I can't cancel my flight now.'

'Uri, listen to me very carefully. You have to do what I tell you. This is a serious matter.' I wondered what on earth he was talking about. 'The wife of the president-elect of Mexico saw you on our programme, and one of her aides just called me to say that she would like to meet you.'

I made some hasty excuse or other, but he would have none of it.

'You'd better stay,' he interrupted sternly. 'This is

Mexico.' He went on to explain that in his country it was the president, and the president's wife, who made the decisions. A president-elect was equally important, and you did whatever he – or his wife – told you.

Shipi and I had the fastest conference of our lives. He quickly checked the diary, and found that my next engagement was not for ten days.

'Look,' he said, 'we'll meet her and we'll take a flight tomorrow. So we stay another day – what's the big deal?'

I had loved my first trip to Mexico. There was a nice swimming pool at the hotel, and I had developed a taste for tortillas and guacamole. (I was not a vegetarian in those days.) I had visions of what might happen if I disobeyed Raul's order. I decided to agree with him. I had better stay.

Almost as soon as Raul hung up, the telephone rang again, and a voice told me in broken English that Señora de López Portillo was in the hotel, and was on her way to see me.

It had all happened so quickly that I had still not fully realized who my unexpected visitor was when I heard the rhythmic thump of feet – *whoomp, whoomp, whoomp* – in the corridor. I peered round the door, and saw what looked like a military parade heading for me. It was a solid mass of army and police uniforms, crash helmets and walkie-talkies. There must have been at least twenty of them.

They marched up to my room and halted. Then they stood aside, like the Red Sea being parted by Moses, to leave me face to face with Señora Carmen Romano de López Portillo.

She was not at all what I had been expecting. I had seen her husband's photograph on enormous posters all over the city put up by the Partido Revolucionario Institucional (PRI), the party that had effectively run Mexico and chosen its presidents for nearly fifty years. I expected the wife of this distinguished and intelligent-looking man to be elderly, grey-haired and discreetly dressed. Instead, I saw a very exotic and beautiful woman.

With her curly black hair, huge green cat's eyes and dazzling smile, she might have been a mature but well-preserved actress. She wore a very colourful and sexy dress, with high-heeled shoes and plenty of make-up. She held out her hand towards me, and only then, after all the commotion of this military-style invasion, did it dawn on me just who she was and what she represented.

We shook hands, and she came into my room. To my surprise, one of the men promptly stepped forward and closed the door behind her, leaving her alone with Shipi and me. Through the window, I could see that the area around the pool was already swarming with yet more uniformed men. We were surrounded.

She ignored the chair I offered her, planted herself on my bed, and lost no time in letting me know why she had come to see me.

'I saw your television show,' she began excitedly, in good English. 'It was incredible! You know, I was holding my watch and it started working, and my son – his spoon bent – and oh, you were *fantástico*! My God, all my life I've wanted to meet somebody like you. I'm so interested in these things, and I believe in them. You *must* stay in Mexico!' It was an order, not an invitation.

We talked for two hours. She wanted to know everything about me, and she wanted me to know all about her, her family, her background, and her feelings about God, religion and just about all the mysteries of life from flying saucers to bent spoons.

At last, she got up. I expected her to say goodbye and

leave, but instead she gave me another order.

'You come to my house. Now.'

Driving through the streets of Mexico City with the wife of the president-elect was an experience unlike any I had previously had. We tore through the traffic, surrounded by motorcycles with sirens wailing, while she sat back calmly with her walkie-talkie, constantly sending out messages, firmly in command of her entourage. Her Ford LTD had been fitted with all kinds of special compartments for radios, tape recorders, music cassettes, notepads, pens and pencils and make-up boxes, many of which were also strewn over the rear window-ledge. When I got my custom-built Cadillac later, I had it refitted in the same way, to remind me of hers.

Our presidential motorcade swept out of town and into the suburbs, finally pulling up at a modern art-deco villa standing in about an acre of land and surrounded by a high fence. Several police cars were parked by the gate.

When she led me into her living-room, all I could see at first was a mass of pianos, of all shapes and sizes, modern and antique. There were more of them all over the house, and later I counted at least twelve. She was a pianist, she told me, and had studied with a well-known American.

I told her that my best friend was the distinguished American concert pianist Byron Janis, who had studied with the great Horowitz.

Her gorgeous cat's eyes lit up. 'Oh,' she exclaimed, 'you know Byron Janis? He must come and play for Mexico, at the Bellas Artes.'

She showed me around the whole house, and introduced me to her mother, a most lovable lady who received me very graciously. Then she showed me her husband's private study, which was crammed with books. He was not at home, but at his office where he was serving the outgoing president, Luíz Echeverria, as minister of finance.

Although I stayed with her all afternoon, we had little opportunity for more than polite conversation, for we were constantly interrupted as officials and servants hurried in and out with papers and documents. Eventually, she announced that we were to go out to dinner with some of her friends.

As we walked into the restaurant, the clatter of cutlery stopped and there was dead silence. To describe Señora de López Portillo as having a strong personality would be an understatement. It was not that she was the wife of the president-to-be; she simply had that kind of power. As I already knew, whatever she wanted, she got.

Before the end of that long and bewildering day, I learned that she had plans for me and, looking back today on what they led to, I realize how lucky I was to have missed that flight to New York.

Some Latin Americans forget their promises the day after they make them, but she was not one of them, and the following day she duly introduced me to her three children: her teenage daughters Carmen and Paulina and her son José Ramón – known to his family and friends as Pepito. He was a very bright and intelligent young fellow in his early twenties, an amateur astronomer with a keen interest in the scientific research that had already been done into my abilities.

Arrangements were promptly made for me to visit the president-elect. José López Portillo, then aged fifty-five, had had a distinguished career as a lawyer and professor of political science at Mexico's National University before taking charge of the country's finances. Despite his age, he kept in good shape by running a mile a day, swimming, and battering his punch-bag. As Pepito took me into his office, I was struck by the contrast between his elaborate security system, with guards and policemen all over the place, and the simplicity of both his personal appearance and his furniture. He was sitting at an ordinary table, wearing a typical Mexican embroidered white shirt, with no tie.

'Don't bend anything in this office,' he said with a laugh as we shook hands. We made polite conversation for a few minutes with Pepito, whose English was perfect, occasionally helping his father to find the right word. Señor López Portillo said he was very pleased that I was in Mexico; he had not seen my television show himself, but he had heard a lot about it and gathered that it had made quite an impression on a number of people in addition to his own family. He hoped we would meet again, he added, but in his home rather than here.

Despite his initial order to me not to bend anything, I had a feeling that this was what he rather hoped I would do, and when I offered to give him a demonstration there and then, he promptly sent for a spoon. Secretaries and bodyguards then crowded into the office for a little light relief from the cares of state.

I held the spoon and stroked it, just as I always do, and before long it started to bend, much to everybody's surprise and pleasure. The president-elect sat and stared. Then he told somebody to go and fetch another spoon.

I wanted to explain to him that I could not bend one after the other, just like that. Once I have done one, I am not in the right psychological state to do another. I believe that the physical and mental energies that I need are stored, and I use up nearly all of them every time I bend something. It takes at least half an hour for me to refill my energy pool. On the rare occasions when I had been obliged to bend several things in a short time, I had noticed that the first one would go to ninety degrees as usual, but the second would only go to sixty, the third to thirty, and the fourth would not bend at all. With me, a bent spoon is a kind of visiting card or proof of identity, and normally I produce it only once.

'Excuse me, Señor Presidente,' I began, 'but I cannot . . .'

'No, no, no,' he interrupted. '*I* will do it!'

I have noticed several interesting things in connection with my spoon-bending. If there are negatively-minded people around, I often fail to oblige – not because I cannot, but simply because I feel I do not have to prove anything to anybody. Even if they do not tell me they are sceptical I seem to pick it up telepathically, and then usually nothing happens. If it does, sometimes one of them will take the spoon and immediately bend it back into shape by normal means, as if trying to pretend that it never happened.

On the other hand, every time I have bent a spoon in front of people who are at the top of their professions, whether they are presidents, prime ministers, generals or chairmen of boards, their reaction is quite different. They always want to do the same themselves straight away. I'm the top man around here, they seem to be thinking, so why can't I do this too?

López Portillo was no more successful than any of the others. He kept stroking his spoon for several minutes until he gave up, with a good-natured laugh. I think he really wanted that spoon to bend.

\* \* \*

I was duly invited to his home for the second time in as many days, and on this occasion my new friend Muncy, as she asked me to call her, made two more promises. One was to send me an invitation to her husband's inauguration, on 1 December 1976, which she subsequently did; and the other was to introduce me to President Echeverria. So before I had fully recovered from my surprise at being taken to meet a man who was to be head of a major state, here I was on my way to meet a man who already was one.

I was treated once again to one of those hair-raising motorcades, and this time my destination was Los Pinos, the Mexican White House. I was shown into the huge and spotlessly clean vestibule of this magnificent building, with its shining floor and elegant but unpretentious Mexican furniture and decor. It was absolutely silent, which was a welcome contrast to the noise of the journey.

Suddenly, I began to feel a bit under-decorated myself, realizing that I probably ought to be wearing a tie. Like most Israelis, I am an anti-tie person, and at that time I do not think I even had one. I did not even own a suit. Well, I thought, López Portillo had been wearing an open shirt, so perhaps this was considered an acceptable form of dress even in the presence of the head of state? I hoped so.

The silence was broken as the huge wooden door swung open, and I was ushered into the presidential office. There, I had another uneasy moment. There were several men sitting around, but none of them sat behind what looked like the presidential desk. I had never seen a photograph of Echeverria, and had simply no idea which of them he was.

Okay, Geller, I said to myself hurriedly, use your psychic powers, and for heaven's sake go up to the right man. This seemed to work, for I did manage to get it right, telling the president through his interpreter how honoured I was to be invited to see him, and how much I had come to like his country in the short time I had been there. I expected some equally formal reply, but the first thing he said to me was, 'Could you find oil for us?'

He said it with a smile, and I thought he must be joking. He probably thought I was also joking when I replied, 'Of course, Mr President. At least, I can try, though I can't guarantee anything.' As I will explain later, neither of us was in fact joking.

I spent about twenty-five minutes in the president's office, during which time I managed to bend a spoon, demonstrate some telepathy, and also perform an unexpected service for him. At one point, he suddenly handed me an old watch, telling me that it had not worked for ages and asking if I could make it tick. I managed to do so, and left him and his colleagues with plenty to think about after my brief audience.

Shortly after this, I was contacted by René Leon, one of Mexico's top impresarios, who arranged for me to do a show at very short notice in the largest theatre in town.

On the morning of the day the show was to take place, there was an unpleasant incident of a kind that people who become well known have to learn to live with. Somebody telephoned me at my hotel and spoke in rapid Spanish, ignoring my protests that I hardly knew a word of the language. I promptly called Muncy, who sent a couple of her security guards over straight away with strict orders to look after me. When I repeated the few words I had been able to catch, including *brigada* and *bomba*, they turned rather pale.

Anyway, they obeyed their orders. The show went ahead as planned, but when I walked on to the stage all I could see at first was a mass of blue uniforms. There must have been two or three policemen for every member of the public, and there was even a line of them in front of the stage, facing the audience and holding their machine-guns in a way that suggested they were quite prepared to use them. I was later told that there were even light tanks patrolling the streets outside while I was giving my show, which I managed to do successfully in spite of the heavy police presence for which Muncy had been responsible.

She was delighted by the show, and soon afterwards she made it clear to me that she would like me to settle in Mexico for good. I told her I was honoured and grateful to her, for I already felt at home in her country and would like to spend as much time there as I could, but there were problems. I had several commitments, for my book was due to be published in a dozen languages, and promotion tours in a number of countries had already been arranged. Moreover, although I would come back to Mexico as soon as I could, I could not yet afford to hop on a plane every time I felt like it. I was making a reasonable living with my demonstration-lectures and television shows, and my book was selling well, but I was no millionaire, as yet.

Muncy, as I knew by now, had a unique way of solving problems. On this occasion, she simply ordered me to go along to the offices of Aeromexico, where I would be given a card entitling me to free travel – first-class, of course – on any of their flights to anywhere in the world.

I didn't believe it. Nor did the person I spoke to at the company's headquarters. 'Only the chairman of the board has that kind of card,' I was assured.

Muncy was not satisfied with that explanation. 'Come with me!' she said. She got into her car and drove me back to the office, where she expressed her wishes in eloquent Spanish, and I duly received the precious card. In exchange, I signed a contract whereby I was to promote the airline worldwide, which I did with the help of T-shirts I had imprinted with the slogan 'Uri Geller Flies Aeromexico' and later wore on several major television shows.

Mexico is a democratic country. Even so, as is the case in every country I know of, democratic or not, it does help if you know the right people.

Word soon spread around that I was a close friend of the López Portillo family, and this led to the opening of all kinds of doors. For example, I was offered the free use of a really splendid triplex penthouse in the plush Zona Rosa district, with swimming pool and all. The owner, I believe, felt that by being nice to me he was setting up a useful hot line to the president's ear. If I was corrupt by nature, I could certainly have celebrated my thirtieth birthday by retiring to a life of luxury, privilege and wealth. Luckily, however, I did not, for I like to go to sleep with a clear conscience.

All the same, I seemed to have become a fairly influential person in Mexico, without trying at all. In fact within a very short time of my first arrival in the country I had things that some people have to work all their lives to obtain, such as unlimited air travel facilities and a free home, not to mention what to almost any Mexican is the ultimate status symbol: direct access to the First Family.

For some time to come, I was to shuttle back and forth between my new home and my professional commitments in other countries, and although I have never established permanent residence anywhere since I left Israel in 1972, flying into Mexico City's Benito Juarez airport came to feel like returning home. It was somewhat different when

I arrived in December 1976 for the inauguration of President López Portillo: on that occasion I was given the full red-carpet treatment as soon as I stepped off the plane, and I will never forget how I felt when Muncy spotted me in the audience at the ceremony and waved at me from her seat beside the man who was about to take over the country's highest office.

Shortly after the new president and his family moved into Los Pinos, I was invited there again, to meet the entire cabinet and give a demonstration of my abilities. So I came to know personally everybody who was anybody in the top echelon of national government. It soon became clear that, like Muncy, I was in a position to get anything I might want.

One morning, I had a very disturbing dream. It was of a huge fire breaking out somewhere, and I had the strong impression that López Portillo was nearby and was in danger. I telephoned Pepito right away, told him about the dream, and begged him to ask his father to take extra care. I do not think he took me very seriously, although he did pass on the information. The very next day, a major fire did break out in a hall shortly before the president was due to speak there. Pepito was more impressed by this episode, I think, than by all my demonstrations of metal-bending and mind-reading.

On another occasion, I gave the president himself a spontaneous demonstration of mind-power at work. One of his favourite ways of relaxing was to shoot his bow and arrow on the lawn at Los Pinos, and one day he asked me if I could direct an arrow into the bull's eye by psychic means.

'I certainly can't do it any other way,' I replied truth-fully, for I had never fired a bow and arrow in my life and could not even hold the thing properly. However, my attitude was much the same as it always is when I am faced with a new challenge, such as when ex-president Echeverria had asked me if I could find oil: 'I can try.'

I took the bow and arrow and tried, using all the power of concentration I could manage. My mind went back to my schooldays in Israel, when for a time I had become quite famous for my skill at basketball: I was a terrible player, in spite of my height, but my speciality was to throw the ball right into the net, time after time, from the half-way mark. I could do this only if there was nobody near me, though, so I was fairly useless as a team player.

Wham! The arrow slammed right into the centre of the target. I was as amazed as the president was. Spontaneous incidents of this kind have happened all my life, and still occur regularly today, as they have done and do in the presence of most of my close friends. They always make a more lasting impression than anything I do in public or in a laboratory, where there always seems to be somebody around who says (later) that I must have been cheating. I could fill the rest of this book with accounts of these incidents, if I could remember them all, and a selection of them will be mentioned in due course.

As far as Muncy was concerned, I had no need to convince her of anything. We became real friends, and she began to tell me about her most intimate troubles and worries, of which despite her wealth and position, she had her fair share. Like anybody else, she needed somebody to confide in, and it is not surprising that rumours gradually began to spread that I was something more than a family friend.

I could hardly blame the rumour-mongers. I went around with her quite openly all the time, and wherever she went she was surrounded by official photographers working on behalf of the National Archives. No relationship could have been less clandestine than ours, and we were both fortunate that the Mexican press treats its public figures with considerably more respect than is the case in most countries.

When we went out to a restaurant, as we did regularly, she would have her bodyguard ask the band to play one of those romantic *mariachi* numbers, or our special private song which went 'That's the way – aha, aha – we like it'. As it did so, she would sit and gaze at me as if trying to tell the world she was in love with me. One evening, I felt she was overdoing it.

'Look, Muncy,' I said, 'if you want me around you've just got to stop acting like this.' I had noticed more jaws dropping than usual at nearby tables.

Her reply was typical of her. 'I don't care!' You did not argue with Muncy.

She knew where to draw the line, however, for she was too proud of her family, her husband's position and her country to risk a major scandal. After becoming First Lady, she tackled her responsibilities, especially in the field of welfare, with her usual enthusiasm, and as she saw it she had a right to enjoy herself in her own way after a hard day's work. So she did.

One day, she invited Shipi and me to join her for a flight on the presidential Sabreliner jet. I loved flying in those days, and a trip on a Sabreliner is something few people get a chance to enjoy. During the flight, I went forward to talk to the two pilots.

'You know,' the chief pilot remarked casually, after giving me some technical details, 'these planes are built like fighters. I've heard of American pilots making a slow barrel roll in them.'

I thought it would be fun to do one, but he said it was strictly against aviation regulations. I went back to sit beside Muncy, who was making notes on her pad for her next public speech, and waited for her to pause and look at me.

'How would you like to make a slow barrel roll?' I asked her. She looked puzzled, so I explained that it was a kind of 'wall of death' routine in which we would be flying upside-down for a time as the plane made a full rotation on its longitudinal axis.

Muncy also thought it sounded like fun. 'Let's do it!' she said at once.

'Is that an order from you to the captain?' I asked.

'By all means,' she replied imperiously. I passed on the order, which the chief pilot felt obliged to confirm personally, whereupon he pulled up the nose and over went the twin-engine Sabreliner on its back, which I am sure its manufacturers never intended it to do. Muncy enjoyed the experience as much as I did, and when we were flying the right way up again I noticed that one of the pilots had taken the opportunity to give us a physics lesson: before going into the roll, he calmly poured himself a glass of water and held it in one hand throughout the operation without spilling a drop.

Not all my experiences in that Sabreliner were as enjoyable as this one. On another occasion, Muncy was away from home and decided she wanted to see me right away. She called me and announced that the plane was waiting for me.

Shipi came along for the ride, and during the flight we ran into a sudden hailstorm. The plane began to leap up and down like a leaf caught in a gust of wind, and then, to my total horror, lights started flashing and alarm signals ringing. Two large red squares lit up to show the words ENGINE INOP – that is, both engines had become 'inoperable' and had stopped.

The pilots just sat there without saying a word.

I turned round. 'Shipi, we're going down,' I said. 'We're dead.' I really believed it. For some reason I never understood, I tried to put on my shoes, which I had taken off during the flight. I closed my eyes and prayed as hard as I could. This is it, I said to myself. God, help us!

It was all over as suddenly as it had started. We were out of the storm, both engines came back to life and the pilots regained control, apparently quite unaware of my state of panic. I will never underestimate a Mexican pilot.

Inevitably, I saw less of Muncy after her husband's inauguration than I had before it. She had become involved in a number of social and welfare committees and projects that kept her fully occupied during the daytime. We could only meet in the evenings, when she liked to relax at the ballet or a concert or enjoy a slap-up meal in a restaurant. This in turn meant that I was seen less often with her, so the rumours surrounding our supposed relationship began to die down, although, as I was to discover to my cost, they did not die out altogether.

I was frequently out of the country on book promotion tours or television engagements, and when I was back in Mexico I liked to take things easy. My bank account was growing nicely, and I did not have to work every day as I had during the first two or three years of my career. So I began to slow down.

I suppose I was ready for a change, and although the local gossips no longer seemed interested in my connections with the presidential family, I was soon to learn that these had come to the attention of at least one person who took a serious professional interest in them.

So it was that, one sunny morning, Mike strolled into my life.

# 3

## A Shopping List

I was doing some lazy window shopping in the Zona Rosa, not far from my borrowed penthouse, and peering at some phoney-looking jewellery, of which there is plenty to be found in Mexico City, when a man came and stood beside me.

'Hi,' he said, pleasantly. 'You're Uri Geller.'

I assumed he had recognized me from one of my stage or television shows. He was in his mid-forties or fifties, I guessed, and looked harmless. I said yes, I was.

'Well,' he went on, 'I really would like to talk to you about something you might find interesting. I know about the work you did at Stanford Research Institute. Can I invite you for a drink?'

His attitude was friendly and relaxed, and not in the least pushy. He struck me as a knowledgeable man with a genuine interest in parapsychology. I told him that I did not drink, but would be happy to have a cup of coffee with him.

We headed for the nearest coffee shop, and sat at a table. When we had ordered, he took off his Ray-Ban Pilot sun-glasses and put them carefully in their case. Then he was silent for a moment, and I felt there was something on his mind that was important to him. People often expect me to know everything about everybody I meet, but telepathy does not work like that, at least not with me. I was curious.

I asked him how he knew about my work at SRI.

'Oh,' he replied, 'we know a lot about you.' I wondered

who 'we' might be, and why they found me of such interest. I waited for him to get to the point, which he soon did. He was, as I should have guessed, involved in intelligence work. I forget his exact words, but 'intelligence' was definitely one of them. He offered to show me some identification, but I said that was not necessary. (It would also have proved nothing – there is a store on 42nd Street in New York where you can buy all the identification you like.)

He went on to talk about my usual repertoire, from bending spoons, reading minds and seeing inside sealed boxes to erasing computer tapes. Then he casually dropped a couple of remarks that seemed to establish his credentials better than any card would have done. The first was a reference to a videotape made during my stay at SRI, on which a watch can be seen materializing out of the air. This sequence was not included in the film of some of my work that was shown publicly, and not many people knew about it. Then he mentioned, equally casually, that 'we' even knew about some work I had done some time previously, of which there has never been any mention in public and never will be. (In 1985, I learned for the first time that SRI scientists had been given an Israeli intelligence report on me. There must have been some very high-level pressure to release or obtain any such report, and no doubt there was an exchange of favours involved, although it could be that Israeli intelligence simply wanted to be kept up to date on the latest research into me.)

We went on chatting for an hour or so. Mike, as he asked me to call him, made a note of my home telephone number and said he would like to meet me again some time. Nothing specific was said, but what I felt he was trying to convey to me was 'Maybe you can help us, and maybe we can help you.' I was definitely intrigued.

He telephoned me about ten days later and asked if we could meet, at a fast-food place not far from my apartment. I had an engagement that evening, and told him I would not be able to stay for long.

'What I'm asking you for is your help, Uri,' he said as soon as we met. 'There are certain fields in which we are interested where we are always coming up against brick walls. So we thought perhaps you might be able to help us with your powers, by accomplishing certain things that we can't do.'

'Like what?' I asked.

'Wait a minute.' He held up a hand, as if I had interrupted a well-rehearsed speech. 'Another thing,' he went on, 'quite apart from your psychic powers, do you realize just how influential you have become in this country?'

It was no time for false modesty. 'Yes,' I said.

'Well, I could also use you in that capacity. There are other fields in which we could use your help. I can list a few . . .'

'Give me your pen, then, and I'll write them down,' I said.

'No, no. Don't write anything down.'

I asked him to give me an example, but instead he launched into a classroom lecture on communism, capitalism, the strategic importance of Mexico, Cuban influence in Central America, and the special part played by the Soviet Embassy in Mexico City. It was, he said, one of their largest anywhere in the world. It was a leading centre of espionage against the United States and Canada, and it was reckoned that at least half of the 300 people who worked there (six times as many as the number of

Mexicans in their Moscow embassy) had received special KGB training in the stealing of secrets, both military and industrial, from the USA. The current KGB boss, Mikhail Muzankov, was believed to be in charge of revolutionary and terrorist activities in the whole of the Americas.

'There are a good many things we would like to know that we don't know,' he concluded, again without being more specific. I asked him how my influence with the president's family could be of any help.

Again he held up a hand. 'Oh no, no. Now we're talking about your powers.'

I was beginning to wonder just what we were talking about, in fact. 'You mean you want me to help you with my influence, and also with my psychic powers?' I asked. 'Which is more important to you?'

'Both,' he replied. 'And Uri, don't discuss what I am telling you on the telephone, and don't let your friends know about it either. Now, let me tell you something about the Central Intelligence Agency, or "the Company", as we call it.' It was the first time either of us had mentioned the CIA by name, and I noticed that he did not use the initials, but spelled it out in full.

'There are a few people in this community who are totally devoted to going all the way in intelligence gathering. Most of us ridicule the whole psychic scene, because we've had bad experiences in the past with people like you.'

'What makes you think I'm different?'

'We know more about you.' Again, he said there were certain things I could do for him, but before I could ask what they were he was off on another lecture.

'Israel has the finest intelligence service in the world,' he began. 'It finds needles in haystacks. How? Because it tries everything. Its people can be ninety-nine point nine per cent sure that there's nothing in so-called psychic functioning, but they leave the possibility open: what if it's real? That's why the Mossad is what it is.' He paused, perhaps to see if I had anything to tell him about the Mossad. Then he mentioned that he had an older friend who had been a member of Haganah, the Jewish self-defence organization, and that he had pro-Israeli sympathies himself. He then changed the subject abruptly.

'There are people in this community who would like people like you to work for them,' he said. But, he explained, this was an individual matter and no such orders had come from the top. There was a very small group of CIA agents who were well informed on para-psychological matters, believed in its potential, and were quite prepared to make use of it on their own account. There was no need for their superiors to know, and no official 'agency authorization' involved.

'If it works, it works,' said Mike, 'and if it doesn't work, all that was wasted were a few hours.'

Time was running short, and I had no intention of showing up late for my engagement. We arranged to meet again soon, when we would get down to the details of this famous shopping list.

Although I did not know it at the time, I had already had direct contact with a member of the CIA. One day, not long after my arrival in the USA in 1972, I received a telephone call in New York from a man who introduced himself as a scientist from Washington, DC, and wanted to know if I could demonstrate my telepathic abilities right then, over the long-distance phone. I gave him my usual answer to this kind of request: I didn't know, but I could try. He then said he had drawn a picture on his pad and was looking at it. Could I tell him what it was?

I immediately told him what I thought it was, which made him sound quite pleased, and I never heard from him again. I cannot remember what the picture was, having done thousands of experiments of this kind.

Several years later, a friend of mine happened to meet the man concerned. My friend was given an account of the experiment by the 'scientist', who by then had left the CIA. The former agent said that he had no doubt that my abilities were genuine, and several of his colleagues who had been keeping a close watch on my career agreed with him.

At our third meeting, Mike at last got down to business.

'I'm throwing the ball into your court, Uri,' he said, in his usual relaxed and friendly way. 'You choose what you can do best, and what you would like to do first. We're not pressing you.'

Had either of us written down the shopping list he then read me, it would have looked something like this:

If I was to be driven round the block where the Soviet Embassy was located, would I be able to describe certain things in certain parts of the building? Could I locate the computer room? Could I erase certain tapes there? Could I 'read' the number of a combination lock? Could I name the ranks and duties of people seen entering or leaving the building? Could I crack codes? Could I predict espionage drops? He seemed particularly interested in the last item.

It was quite a list, and there was even more of it to come. The next item struck me as exceptionally optimistic.

'On certain dates that we know, and some we don't,' said Mike, 'two Soviet diplomats board a certain Aero-mexico flight with diplomatic pouches handcuffed to their wrists. Could you tell us what's in those pouches – whether it's papers, computer parts, software or whatever? Would you be able to switch the bags for us?'

I told him I thought this was completely crazy and unnecessarily dangerous as well. Mike did not seem offended. He just laughed and moved on to yet another item: could I make a drone (a small remote-controlled pilotless aircraft) go off course? I said I thought that sounded like something I was more ready to try.

'Let's drive out to a field one day and do it,' he said eagerly. I wondered for a moment if he really meant it, and as we shall see later, he did.

Then he came to his second shopping list. This was of the things he wanted me to do by normal rather than paranormal means, that is to say, by making use of my access to the president.

He prefaced the list with another of his mini-lecture-briefings. This was the Mexican one, and it began by stressing that although Mexico was a democracy, it was not as anti-communist as it could be. Its neutral position had become somewhat distorted, and the American government was becoming increasingly concerned at the Soviet presence in a country the other side of the world from the Soviet Union, with which it did virtually no trade at all, a country that also shared more than 1,000 miles of frontier with the United States and was in addition located right on the back doorstep of Latin America's first communist state – Cuba. Mike was unhappy about this state of affairs, and wanted me to do something about it.

'Get real close to the president, Uri,' he said earnestly. 'Talk to him as much as you can, philosophize with him, try to make him appreciate that he is allowing his country to be used as a base for hostile operations against the United States.'

He became more specific. 'The president's wife has a close friendship with a certain person, and we would really like that friendship to be terminated.' He named the man, whom I knew as one of many who seemed anxious to cultivate relations with Muncy. He was not a Mexican, and had a Russian or at least a Slavonic-sounding surname. He was in some kind of import-export business, and was based in Europe.

Mike then asked me if I could obtain invitations for him to attend receptions and parties at the Eastern bloc embassies. Failing that, would I be prepared to take as my guest a certain girl to whom he would introduce me, if I managed to get myself invited?

I told him to cross that item off his list right away. I could just imagine Muncy's reaction if I had shown up with a 'girlfriend' on my arm at a function to which she had secured me an invitation! That was not very smart thinking on his part.

Having delivered his shopping lists, and asked me again to take my time before attempting to deliver any of the items, Mike returned to a topic that was clearly of great personal interest to him: parapsychology. He seemed genuinely concerned by the fact that his own government had no serious commitment to research into it, whereas the Soviets were known to take the subject very seriously indeed, as they had done ever since the dust had settled after the Bolshevik revolution of 1917. He hoped that I could be instrumental in correcting this imbalance to some degree, although he did not go into any detail.

All this time, there had been no mention of payment for my services by either of us. Mike knew that I was earning a good living, and he had probably guessed, correctly, that I could hardly refuse a few favours to a country that had done so much in the past to help my own homeland.

'What kind of US visa do you have?' he asked, just as I thought our meeting had come to an end. It was clever timing on his part. Maybe he was psychic himself? He had certainly mentioned something that was often on my mind. As an Israeli citizen who made frequent visits to the United States, I had spent several whole mornings of my life standing in line at US consulates all over the world in order to obtain a re-entry visa. An 'indefinite multiple' stamp in my passport would mean an end to that for ever.

'If there's anything you need from us, feel free to call this number,' said Mike, without waiting for me to reply. It was not his own – I never did know either his number or even his real name – but that of a man at the American Embassy whom I will call Tom Morris.

Shortly afterwards I went up to the Marine guard and said I had an appointment with Mr Morris. Behind him, I could see those familiar lines of applicants for US entry visas snaking around the huge hall of the Consular Section, and I wondered if it was really possible that I would never have to join them again.

To my astonishment, I recognized one of the people standing patiently in line. It was the son of ex-president Echeverria, who now had to wait his turn just like anybody else. When you are out of office in Mexico, you really are out, and I could understand why Mike was so anxious to make use of my relationship with the family of the current president. He would not be at the top for ever.

The Marine directed me to a desk at the side of the hall, where the secretary immediately recognized me and asked me to come with her to the main embassy lobby, which was wonderfully quiet and empty. After a short wait, I was in Tom Morris's office.

He seemed very pleased to see me. He had heard a lot about me, he said, and had bought a copy of *My Story*, which he had found very interesting. Without further delay he helped me fill in a form, and handed this and my passport to an assistant, who took them away.

Then, just as Mike had done, he started to give me a talk. This one was on the Mexican system of government, the presidency, the powerful Partido Revolucionario Institucional, and the subtle interrelationships between them. I learned a good deal about how things were run in a country that, though ostensibly a Western-style democracy, was to all intents and purposes a one-party state in which the president of the day had the powers of an absolute monarch – but only as long as he remained in office. (As I had just seen, once out of office he had next to none.)

The assistant returned with my passport. I could not wait to find the page with the fresh stamp on it: 'Valid for Multiple Applications for Entry Until Indefinitely'. Yes, there it was. The Americans had done me a 'favour', so now I would do one for them.

I turned down the offer of a car and driver, explaining that I could not work properly with somebody breathing down my neck. Anyway, I preferred to walk whenever I could, as I still do. So Shipi and I set off for a stroll along the Calzada de Tacubaya on the western edge of town, where the Soviet Embassy was located.

I had never tried to obtain information from the inside of a building before, but I saw no reason why it should be more difficult than any other exercise in either telepathy or clairvoyance. I had done plenty of each, and my usual practice was to visualize a blank screen in my mind and wait for a word or an image to take shape on it. Sometimes these impressions are very clear, and stay on my screen for several seconds, and when this happens I know I have picked up the right message. Sometimes they come and go, or fade, and in this case I can be either right or wrong.

On this occasion, and on a number of similar strolls around the large block over the following couple of weeks, I picked up a good many impressions. I noted them down as they came, making hasty scribbles and sketches on pieces of paper and stuffing them in my pocket without trying to figure out what they might mean. I passed these on to Mike, with such explanation as I could provide.

He was particularly interested in what I had to tell him about espionage drops. He did not tell me, of course, that I had strolled into centre stage of one of the major spy dramas of the century, in which one of the chief actors was a Californian drug-pusher named Daulton Lee, who is now serving a life sentence for his part in selling details to the Soviets of the ultra-top-secret Rhyolite and Argus communications satellites. Lee had made several visits to the Soviet Embassy in 1975 and 1976, and on 6 January 1977 he made his last, on which he foolishly threw a piece of paper through the railings and was promptly arrested by the Mexican police.

According to the official version, he was arrested on suspicion of having murdered a Mexican policeman some time previously. An American Embassy official just happened to be in the Soviet Embassy at the time on a courtesy call, and was able to alert the US authorities. They soon found out who he was and what he had been up to. Whether my information had anything to do with this episode or not, I cannot say, although it did strike me as odd that the Mexican police seemed to be ready and waiting for the spy who could not of course be arrested by the Americans in a foreign country. Officially, however, I was told nothing at all, as is invariably the case with an affair of this kind. As one of my friends in the intelligence community put it later, 'If you're any good, there's no need for you to know how you're doing. If you're no good, then we don't use you any more.'

There was at least one occasion, though, when I was able to see immediate results. Mike had brought up the subject, already mentioned, of whether I could make a drone go off course. This seemed to be a pet project of his, and I thought it sounded like more fun than gazing over the high wall of the Soviet compound at a row of barred windows, so we agreed to try it.

One morning, Mike picked me up in a large station-wagon, the back of which was crammed with all kinds of boxes and packages. He had a colleague with him, who was introduced to me as 'Jack'. We drove out of town and stopped beside a large empty field, where the two Americans unpacked their gear. If there had been any children around, they would have been fascinated to see two grown-ups putting together a huge model aeroplane with bright red and yellow lines painted on it. They would have envied the fellow who held the little black box and turned knobs to make the plane take off, turn in a wide circle and then come in to land right beside him. They would probably not have known that RPVs (remotely powered vehicles), as they are known, are already in use by the military of several countries. What we were playing with was no toy.

Jack and Mike held several more test flights to make sure everything was in order. They had it make a number of straight passes directly over our heads, from one side of the field to the other, so as to make sure that it flew in a straight line when required. When Mike was satisfied that the drone was performing as it should, he turned to me.

'Now,' he said, 'knock it off course – to the left.'

I concentrated hard and shouted out loud 'Go left!' Immediately, the little plane began visibly to drift off course by several degrees, maybe between five and ten – quite enough to make it miss its destination. Mike, who never let go of his control box and never allowed me anywhere near it, stared first at his knobs and switches and then at the drone in disbelief. Then, both he and Jack began to jump up and down like high school kids at a ball game.

'Hey, there you go! Whoopee, you've done it!' they cried. I was as pleased as they were, as I always am when I succeed in a new type of task.

They immediately wanted me to do it again, of course. Mike had the drone make another overhead pass. I repeated my shouted instructions to go left, and once again it went left.

'Now make it go to the right,' said Mike.

I repeated my procedure as requested, but nothing happened. The plane flew on in a dead straight line until it was almost out of sight. Mike brought it back and we tried again. Still no luck. I was equally unsuccessful in getting it to go up or down, yet I succeeded again and again in making it drift to the left.

We all reckoned that our outing had been a partial success, and it reminded me that the only way to see if something can be done, however unusual it may seem, is to go ahead and try. It was also reassuring for me to get instant confirmation that I had done exactly what I had been trying to do.

I was never invited to go drone-flying again. Had Mike simply been putting my powers to a simple test? I suspect that he was really more interested in what my counterparts in the Soviet bloc were capable of.

Tom Morris, on the other hand, seemed more interested in my normal talents. He was particularly curious to know what the president of Mexico and his wife were doing and saying, and what countries they were planning to visit. This led to a conflict of interests. I had no intention of spying on a family that treated me as a friend, and I never passed on any personal information about any of its members.

I saw no harm, however, in bending the president's ear whenever I had the chance about the Soviet presence in Mexico, and as it turned out my next intelligence assignment came not from the Americans, but from a Mexican member of the president's security corps. His briefing was very vague. All he wanted me to do was visit a certain street market and try to locate a stall that was thought to be connected with illegal political activity of some kind, and was dealing in more than fruit or vegetables. I duly went to the market and strolled around it several times, and I kept coming back to one particular stall, which looked just like all the others. I had a good look all round it and caught sight of a large pile of books under the counter, one of which I could see was the famous 'little red book', *Quotations from Chairman Mao Tse-tung*, required reading in those days for followers of the Chinese form of communism.

This was intelligence-gathering at a very low level, and it was nothing compared with what was to come. It may, however, have had something to do with the next request for my services, which also came from the Mexicans. As for the Americans, before I received any more requests from them, I was suddenly asked by Tom Morris one day if I would like to stay in his house on my future visits to Mexico, instead of in my borrowed penthouse. He had a fairly modest rented house that was nothing like the place I was living in, and since he had a wife and a servant there was not much room for me, not to mention Shipi or any friends I might want to invite to stay. Yet Tom was quite insistent, explaining in a rather imprecise way that the time might come when I would need a safe place to stay, and the home of a foreign diplomat was as safe as you could hope for in Mexico City.

Tom also asked me if in future I would send him postcards whenever I travelled anywhere, just any card with a simple message of greeting and no more. I should send them to the APO, the Washington department that handles all diplomatic mail. Later, I found this to be standard practice in intelligence circles (although I do not know that Tom had any connection with the CIA). It is a fairly simple way of knowing who is where at a given time.

Tom struck me as somebody who had a good reason for whatever he did or whatever he wanted me to do, so I agreed to both his requests. After all, it was him I had to thank for that 'indefinite multiple' stamp in my passport, which had made life so much easier for me.

So I took a last dip in my private rooftop pool in the Zona Rosa and packed my belongings. From then on, the Morris family residence became my new home base whenever I was in Mexico.

# 4

## New Directions

One day I received a social invitation from Jorge Diaz Serrano, director-general of the state-owned oil company Petroleos Mexicanos, or Pemex, whose job made him one of the most influential people in the country. It also gave him cabinet rank, and he had been present when I was invited to Los Pinos to give my demonstration to President López Portillo and his colleagues in the government.

It was more than a social event, however, and before I describe it I have to go back a few years and introduce the man who was originally responsible for setting my career on its new course. His name was John Norman Valette Duncan, but all his friends called him Val, and when he was knighted he chose to be known as Sir Val Duncan. He was born in 1913, and served in the Second World War on the staff of General (later Field Marshal Viscount) Montgomery, for whom my father also served in a more humble capacity as a sergeant in the Jewish Brigade attached to the Eighth Army. After the war, he joined the Rio Tinto-Zinc Corporation, of which he eventually became chairman and chief executive, also finding time to become a director of both British Petroleum and the Bank of England.

We met at a party in 1973, one of many to which I was invited after my appearances on the Jimmy Young and David Dimbleby shows for the BBC had splashed my name all over the British newspapers. Soon after we had been introduced, he took me aside for a private chat.

'How much longer are you going to run around the

world performing in front of audiences?' he asked. 'Why don't you start making money?'

I was surprised. I thought this was what I was doing. If you come from a family as hard up as mine was, a five-figure bank account makes you feel fairly secure, and the way my lectures and television shows were going led me to think that my fortune might even reach six figures one day. I asked Sir Val to tell me what he had in mind.

'Do you know anything about dowsing?' he asked. I was not even sure what the word meant. I had a vague idea that dowsers were crazy people who wandered around with bits of wood in their hands, looking for water.

'I think you could be a dowser,' he went on. He explained that I had already shown that I could dowse on a small scale when I had identified objects inside closed boxes and cans at SRI, and that dowsers did not look only for water. They looked for whatever they were asked to look for, and quite often they found it. He was a dowser himself, he told me, and he would like to show me how it was done. He promptly invited me to come and stay at his home on the island of Majorca: the company jet was at my disposal.

Sir Val and I soon became good friends. He had lost his wife about ten years previously, and as far as I know he had no children. At his beautiful house in the Mediterranean, he began to pass on what he knew as a father would to a son. He showed me how to hold a forked twig or a pendulum, and then he said he was going to test me, by hiding something or other in one of the rooms in his house, then bringing me in to see if I could find it.

I had done this once before in Israel at the request of General Moshe Dayan, but I had never thought of it as dowsing. Then, I had just used my bare hands, so when

Sir Val came to fetch me, I put aside the pendulum and the twig and walked up and down the room where the hidden object was with my hands outstretched, palms down, like a kind of human Geiger counter.

Soon, I felt something on the palm of one of my hands. It was rather like the effect you get when you try putting two magnets together with similar poles facing each other, which you cannot do because they seem to bounce off each other. My hand felt like one of those magnets, and this feeling meant that I was getting warm. Then I closed my hand and pointed a finger downwards, moving it around until I felt that bouncy resistance again. I then followed the line in the direction it was pointing and found the object behind, inside or underneath whatever my finger led me to.

It worked almost every time, and Sir Val was very pleased and impressed. He explained that there was no reason in theory why, if I could find his wedding ring, or whatever he had hidden in his house, I should not be able to find hidden natural resources, such as oil or gold. And that, as he made clear to me, was where the real money was to be made.

We met on several more occasions in 1974 and 1975, and he told me that he had tried to interest the board of Rio Tinto-Zinc in making use of my services, but had been turned down. We also discussed a number of projects in areas other than mining in which he thought I might have a useful part to play, but sadly nothing was to come of any of them, for the man I had come to regard as my adopted uncle died suddenly in December 1975, at the age of sixty-two.

A few months after my first meeting with him, I had to go to South Africa for a lecture tour. Before I went, I happened to be chatting with my friends Byron and Maria

Janis about my recent trip to Majorca, and what Sir Val had taught me there. Maria, who, by the way, is the daughter of Gary Cooper, promptly telephoned a friend of hers named Clive Menell, who was chairman of the board of Anglo-Vaal, one of South Africa's leading mining companies, and told him she thought he should get in touch with me.

He duly did so, and when I had finished my tour he invited me to come and see him, first at his home and then in his office in Johannesburg. He would, he said, like to test my powers. There were a couple of somewhat sceptical geologists present as well.

I was asked to leave the office for a few minutes, while they hid a small piece of gold somewhere in it. Then I was brought back and asked to find it, which I soon did, using the method I have already described. This made their attitude a little less sceptical. Next they rolled out a huge map on a table, asking me to have a look at it and tell them which was the area with the best coal deposits. Sir Val had already explained to me that some dowsers could work just as well from maps as they could on site, so I spread out my hands and moved them around in the air above the map until I felt that magnetic sensation on one of my palms. I then scanned the area directly underneath with a fingertip, and pointed to one specific location, which the geologists marked.

It never occurred to me to ask for a contract or any form of payment. I was merely doing a favour for the friend of a friend, and I never heard any more about this episode until several years later, when I was being interviewed by a reporter from *Newsweek*. I told him about this early attempt to find minerals by dowsing, and suggested he should contact Mr Menell and see if my suggestion had been followed up.

Evidently it was, for the magazine reported in its issue of 28 January 1980 that Menell confirmed that I had pointed to a strip of land near the border with Zimbabwe and insisted that something was down there. 'Since then, notes Menell, miners have discovered large deposits of coal in that area,' *Newsweek* wrote.

This was my background in the dowsing business when I was invited to the home of the head of Mexico's oil industry.

Former president Echeverria may have been joking when he had asked me if I could find oil for him, but when one of Jorge Diaz Serrano's colleagues asked me the same question, he sounded extremely serious.

'Why don't we try it, right now?' I replied. 'Do you have some oil in the house?' I thought he must have a can of lubricating oil, at least, and it made no difference to me what kind of oil it was. Eventually, all that could be found was a big bottle of olive oil from the kitchen, so I told Serrano to pour some into a small liqueur glass and hide it wherever he liked. We were in a large room that was filled with splendid furniture, and there were maybe a hundred places where the thimble-sized glass could have been concealed.

Somebody took me out of the room to one of the bedrooms, which was a good distance away, well out of earshot. The aide stayed with me until Serrano himself came to fetch me and asked me to do my stuff, which I began to do in my usual way. The atmosphere was more relaxed and friendly than it had been in Menell's office in South Africa, and before long I felt I was on the right track. As soon as I felt the signal on my fingertip, I followed the line, without noticing at first that it led me to – of all things – a flower pot. My finger headed for it like a guided missile, went through the earth and landed right inside the glass, which had been buried in the pot and now contained a lump of oily mud.

There was a burst of applause, and all kinds of Spanish expressions of surprise and pleasure. Serrano, however, said nothing. He glanced quickly at one of his colleagues, who was also sitting very still, and I saw their eyes glitter. They seemed to be saying to each other, 'Geller doesn't know what he has done, but we do. This is the jackpot!'

The subject of oil-dowsing came up at another social gathering a few days later, and I remember somebody remarking how fantastic it would be if Mexico could fully exploit her oil resources. This was desirable for both economic and political reasons: Mexico had a huge foreign debt problem (as it still has, with the figure moving steadily towards the $100,000 million mark), and as the United States was the main purchaser of such oil as Mexico was already producing, an increase in output would give her considerable clout in negotiations over a number of important issues that affected the two neighbouring countries.

Soon afterwards I was asked to go out into the field and look for some real oil, in its natural setting. I flew to an airport in a small provincial town, where a helicopter was waiting, with a couple of geologists on board, to take me first to an area where there was already known to be oil. They were testing me, reasonably enough, by seeing if I could confirm what they already knew.

We then flew around for at least an hour over both land and sea. The geologists marked their maps whenever I held out a hand and called to them 'here, yes' or 'there, no'. I used the same method as before, although obviously I could not go down and stick my finger in the sea or the ground. Finding oil is a slow business, and even slower if you do not know exactly where to start looking. All I could do was show them where to start, and if I was right I would be saving the company tens of millions of dollars.

I was given no feedback, although some time later Serrano was kind enough to tell me that my hand-waving from the helicopter had been 'very precise'. It is on record that in 1978, about a year after my trip, López Portillo and Serrano jointly announced that Mexico could become the world's leading oil producer, even bigger than Saudi Arabia, thanks to a number of recent successful strikes. It was now reckoned that just one of the country's many oil-bearing regions had reserves three times the size of all the North Sea fields put together.

Again, I received no money and never asked for any. If I had been greedy in those days, I hate to think what my fate might have been. Serrano was the favourite for a time to become the next president, but he never made it to Los Pinos. Instead, one of his former employees, Miguel de la Madrid, became president in 1982. Four years later, I learned from the *International Herald Tribune* (29 October 1986), Serrano was then 'in prison in connection with accusations involving a $34 million fraud in the sale of oil tankers'. The total embezzled from Mexico's long-suffering people during the oil-boom years has been estimated at more than £6 *billion*, a fair percentage of the country's foreign debt.

Some of that would have come in handy while I was repaying the $40,000 that Byron Janis had lent me to help set myself up in New York. However, I paid him back every cent, with interest, out of my earnings as an entertainer. And I still sleep soundly every night.

For any ambitious Mexican, the ultimate prize is a personal link with the president, preferably in the form of a photograph or a visiting card with an autograph and a dedication. The importance of a document of this kind may be difficult to appreciate by those who are not familiar with the way things are done in Latin America. If you have one, you can use it as an 'Open Sesame' credit card to open any door you choose. I mean any door.

A card or a signed photo from the president's wife was just as valuable, and the lengths some of Muncy's hangers-on were prepared to go to in order to get one were quite remarkable. It was a sign that you were close to the presidential family, and this in turn signified almost unlimited power, and also security long after the president of the day was out of office. As I was soon to find out, one of Muncy's cards with the right inscription on it was literally worth more than its weight in gold.

One evening, I was invited to dinner in a very smart restaurant by one of these power-seeking individuals and a group of his friends. They all immediately began to talk about Muncy, what a wonderful person she was, and how they were having a special gift made for her – some elaborate piece of jewellery costing tens of thousands of dollars.

I listened without much interest. I could have told them that Muncy and her husband had received so many gifts from visiting heads of state and other dignitaries (and who knows who else?) that they had to store them in a special warehouse. Muncy had taken me to see it, and it was crammed to the ceiling with paintings, dinner services, carpets, clothing, stereos and so on. She did not have everything, she had two or more of everything, but she did not really care for them.

I excused myself, and went to the toilet. I did not need to, but I did need a break from all the hypocritical praise of Muncy that was clearly meant for my ears, and then hers. As I was going through the motions of relieving myself, my host came in carrying his briefcase, which struck me as an odd thing to take into a toilet. Seeing that we were alone, he waited for me to zip myself up, then opened his case and took out a leather pouch like those you see pirates use in films for keeping their loot in. He thrust it towards me.

'This is from me, to you,' he said, as he turned to leave. 'Look at it later.'

I took it without thinking, and nearly dropped it, for it was unbelievably heavy for its size. As I made my way back to the table, I took a peep, and nearly dropped it again when I realized what was shining at me out of the darkness. It was a bar of solid gold. It even had the mark of a Swiss bank stamped on it.

I knew what was needed in exchange: Muncy's card, with her signature and an appropriate message. For the rest of the meal, I was fighting with my conscience and my host looked very pleased with himself, as if he already had one in his pocket. As we were leaving the restaurant, however, I took him aside, heaved the pouch into his hand and told him I did not want it. He never spoke to me again.

At about this time, I was able to make myself useful to the presidential family in a way I would never have expected, by giving some practical advice on personal security. I knew something about this, thanks to my army training in Israel, where security is taken very seriously, and I was becoming quite alarmed at how sloppy it was in Mexico, in some areas. Muncy's bodyguards, for example, were fine and loyal men, but they would frequently fly around in her aeroplane with their guns cocked and safety-catches off. Thank God we never hit any hailstorms with them on board. Airport security for the presidential plane was particularly bad: it was often left unguarded, and seldom checked thoroughly before a flight. Pepito was more security-conscious than his father, and he listened carefully whenever I suggested something that needed tightening up. His father in turn listened to him, and I noticed several changes following my recommendations.

One day there was a terrible tragedy that made the family, especially Muncy, realize how careful one should be in matters of security. Her brother Sergio, a wealthy businessman in his own right, had a real obsession with personal protection, and there were guns lying around all over his house. One day, his teenage son picked up one of these and shot himself with it, fatally. It was, I gathered, suicide and not an accident.

Every time I catch myself going on a toy-shopping spree for my children, I think of that unfortunate boy. He showed what money, power and influence can do to a child: they can lead to depression, misery and a final desperate act of rebellion against the world his parents created for him. I try to make my children appreciate what they have, to explain how fortunate they are and to make them understand that there are still children who starve to death in this unjust world. The terrible scenes of famine we all saw on our television screens in 1985 gave me the chance to illustrate this to them very vividly.

In the course of a conversation with the president one day, he showed me something I had not noticed on my previous brief visits to his office. It was a Colt semi-automatic plated in gold and silver with the emblem of Mexico engraved on it. I am not particularly fond of guns as weapons, having been wounded by one, but I cannot help admiring fine craftsmanship of any kind, and this was the most magnificent hand-gun I had ever seen.

Seeing the look on my face, President López Portillo took the Colt out of its leather box and handed it to me. 'It is yours, Uri,' he said.

I was thoroughly confused, and made the first excuse I could think of for refusing the gift. 'Señor Presidente,' I stammered, 'I – I can't accept this . . . I could never take it to America with me.'

In reply, he simply took out one of his personal cards and wrote something on it. 'With this card, Uri, you can do anything. If anybody questions you about your gun, you show them this.'

I could not believe it. Having turned down a chunk of gold in exchange for a card like this, here I was being given both at once, without asking for either. Life does have its ironies. Yet even with my precious card I had to obtain more formal authorization to carry arms, so I did the rounds again and eventually obtained an official identity card as Agent of the National Treasury.

Some time before this, one of my American friends had suggested that it would be useful if I could somehow obtain an official position of some kind in the Mexican government. I thought he was being rather optimistic, yet now I was at least nominally a member of one of its security services. One way and another, my progress up the ladder in Mexican society was exactly what Mike had hoped for, and I had not had to betray the trust and friendship of the president's family in the process. After all, nobody had asked me to steal any Mexican state secrets, merely to give them something in the form of pep talks about Soviet aims, of which they already seemed to be well aware. At one of our meetings, Mike broke the no-feedback rule to the extent of mentioning that my remarks on this subject seemed to have been well received.

On that same occasion, Mike brought out a large book with a plain blue cover which he opened and placed in front of me.

'Would you tell me what impressions you get about this man?' he asked.

It was a black and white photograph of Yuri Andropov, of whom at that time I had never heard. The first thought that came to me was that he had some connection with my father's native land, Hungary, and Mike told me that he had been Soviet Ambassador there at the time of the Soviet invasion in 1956, since when he had become head of the KGB.

'This is quite a nice fellow, on the outside,' I went on. 'Very low-key, rather pleasant in some ways, but ruthless inside. He's doctrinaire, very loyal to his beliefs, and he's inflexible.' All of this is now common knowledge, and I am sure Mike knew it then. He told me a little about a remarkable new technique that CIA psychologists had developed, whereby they could learn a good deal about a man's character and even his future prospects just by studying a photograph of him. Then he began to ask me some very strange questions.

'Can you read somebody's mind even if they are thinking in another language? Do you have to be near them? Does this man have any serious diseases? When do you think he will die?'

I was silent for a moment, and before I could say anything Mike continued with a question that really shook me.

'We know you can affect computers, Uri, and we know

you can do telepathy.' He leaned forward in a caricature of a conspiratorial gesture. 'Do you think you could – uh – induce sickness in a person's body? Could you maybe, like, have his heart stop?'

I said nothing, and began to come out in goose-pimples. Mike went on to talk about voodoo, black magic, and reports of people sticking pins in dolls. Eventually, he must have realized that all this kind of thing was turning me off completely, and he switched into another of his little talks. This was one of his own, I felt, and not one of those that he had been trained to deliver.

'You know, Uri, both the United States Congress and the military ridicule the whole psychic scene,' he began earnestly. 'This is partly because of the negative results we've had with psychics, but there's more to it than that. How do you study a subject thoroughly unless you're prepared to put money into it? The Soviets are doing this, and there's enough in the open literature to indicate that they've been doing it for over fifty years, if you read it carefully. They've gotten themselves a head start, because they've been spending the money, and we haven't even begun on a serious level. Even if we had, the press would have picked it up and torn it apart, and the grants would have been cut off. It's the non-believers in key positions in the media whose open ridicule influences the scientists, and they in turn influence government thinking. It's a vicious circle, and it can only be broken from the top.

'Now for the good news: our next president, Jimmy Carter, is a believer. At least, he's a religious man, and his sister Ruth is a faith healer. He's sighted a UFO and said so publicly. He's also a trained scientist. He could be receptive to the idea of research in new areas.'

\*   \*   \*

New Directions 73

I might already have had something to do with that interest. When Rosalynn Carter, wife of the American president-elect, visited Mexico together with Henry Kissinger, it was Muncy, as Mrs Carter's counterpart, who gave a formal banquet for the visitors. López Portillo himself was not present, but I was, and Muncy sat me right next to her two distinguished visitors. Pepito and the American ambassador were also at our table, together with the son of President Ford.

Mike had specifically asked me to do some demonstrations for them, such as bending a spoon for Mrs Carter and reading Mr Kissinger's mind, and during the meal I made polite conversation and waited for the right moment. Rosalynn Carter was very natural and unaffected, and seemed quite open to the idea of such things as telepathy and psychokinesis. So, to my surprise, was Kissinger, although he was more cautious.

'It would be very unwise for people not to accept certain phenomena that cannot be explained,' he said to me at one point. Perhaps he was just being polite, for he was after all one of the most experienced diplomats in the United States.

When coffee had been served, the atmosphere became less formal, and at last I felt it was time to do my stuff. I took a pretty solid dessert spoon and handed it to Mrs Carter, asking her to hold it in one hand, by the bowl.

'Now let me put my hand over yours, so,' I said, 'and I'll just stroke it with this finger.' I particularly wanted her to feel it bending in her own hand.

I stroked away for a while, and it soon began to curl upwards in the usual way. Mrs Carter looked both astonished and pleased, and she began to laugh.

I took my hand away. 'Now, you hold it and watch as it goes on bending.'

She did so, and watched wide-eyed as the spoon curled slowly upwards in her own hand until there was a right-angle bend in it.

'Oh my!' she exclaimed. 'I wish my friends at home could see this. I must show this to Jimmy.' This she may have done, for as I recall she kept the spoon as a souvenir of our first meeting.

Several of the guests had left their tables to come and watch, and I have a photograph taken by the official American Embassy photographer showing Mrs Carter still clutching her souvenir after she and I had changed places so that I could sit next to Henry Kissinger.

'Now, Mr Kissinger, I'd like to do something totally different with you,' I said.

He recoiled slightly, and even moved his chair back a little. Then he raised a hand. 'No, no,' he said. 'I don't want you to read my mind. I know too many secrets.' He really looked quite apprehensive. I told him all I wanted him to do was draw something while I was looking the other way and then cover it with his hand. All eyes were on us by now, and he generously obliged.

'Now,' I said, as I looked into his eyes behind their wide spectacles, 'start sketching it over and over in your mind.' I have done so many of these things that I cannot recall what it was he drew, but I do remember that this was one of my better efforts. What I drew was not only the same shape as his drawing, but exactly the same size.

Kissinger went a little pale. 'What else did you get from my mind?' he wanted to know.

'Oh, I'd better not talk about that here,' I replied.

He looked at me sternly. 'Is that so,' he growled in his guttural voice. 'Are you serious about that?' Everybody around us became suddenly quiet, and I was reminded of the time not long before when I had been having a meal with the top brass of Paraguay during my tour there, and had asked if it were true that the country was a refuge for some well-known Nazis. I have never seen so many forks freeze in mid-air as on that occasion. (President Stroessner, by the way, was another one who wanted to bend a spoon himself after I had bent one for him.)

'No, Mr Kissinger, I was only joking,' I said, to break the tension. 'I just got your drawing, that's all.' I had in fact picked up something else, but this was not the time to mention it. He looked relieved, and I do not know what he would have said if I had told him that I had just been carrying out a private request from a CIA man.

'So all I've heard about you seems to be true,' he concluded. 'I've heard a lot about the powers of the mind, but I never realized they could be so precise, and that you could demonstrate them just like that, at parties. I thought you had to concentrate, and you didn't even do that.'

'Oh, I did,' I replied. 'While you were sketching your picture over in your mind, that was the crucial moment of concentration for me.'

'Amazing,' was his final verdict. It may not have been a scientifically controlled experiment, but it gave him something to think about.


Mike was clearly very pleased at the way things had gone at the banquet. He thought for a moment, then he asked me, in his usual relaxed way, 'You can draw something and project it into somebody's mind, can't you?'

'Sure, I do it all the time.'

'Let's try it, now?'

I hesitated. I had still not recovered from all that talk of black magic and heart-stopping, which had really scared me. Then I decided to forget it. After all, he had not actually asked me to bump off Andropov. So, while he looked away, I drew something he was not likely to guess: the flag of Turkey with its moon and star. I put the pad face downwards and pushed it to him.

Mike immediately took the pen and drew a rectangle with a crescent and a star-shaped blob inside it. Then he turned the pad over and stared for a moment at our two almost identical drawings.

'That – is – incredible!' he declared. People are always amazed to find that they can do what I do, whether it is bending spoons or sending and receiving messages, if they stop worrying about whether it is possible and just do it.

Then he became serious again. 'Listen, Uri. You have just put something into my mind, haven't you? Could you, in the same way, put something – an idea – into the mind of somebody in such a way that you make him act on it? Even if he may not want to? Even if he doesn't know what he's been asked to do?

'I'm talking about the President of the United States.'

# 5
## Getting the Message

The inauguration of Jimmy Carter was to take place on 20 January 1977, and Mike told me that somehow or other I would have to attend. It was the only way, he said, that I could get close enough to the president and deliver the message that he, Mike, had in mind. He doubted whether an official meeting could be arranged because of what he called the 'ridicule factor': for a new leader to be seen publicly associating with psychics would inevitably undermine his image right at the start of his term of office. In any case, there would be observers, and that meant there would be leaks to the press. Washington was not Moscow, where the rulers did what they liked and the press did what it was told.

'Don't worry, though,' he assured me. 'You'll almost certainly get an official invitation.'

The year 1976 was a very active one for me. Requests for my performances continued to pour in, and I was able to raise my fees. My tour of Brazil, for example, grossed almost a million dollars. I was originally invited there to do two television shows, but thanks to my enterprising and efficient agent Marcos Lazaros I ended up with a nationwide tour involving forty performances, one of them in a football stadium in front of an audience of 12,000.

One of my television shows was seen by the wife of a distinguished diplomat, Ambassador Vasco Leitão da Cunha. She had been suffering from arthrosis for some time and was unable to walk unaided. As I was doing my usual stuff – bending spoons and telling people to get their old clocks and watches going – she thought to herself: Why can't he do something for my legs? The following morning, she leaped out of bed and danced around like a twelve-year-old, according to columnist José Carlos Oliveira of *Jornal do Brasil* (26 July 1976). As he pointed out quite rightly, she was responsible for this 'miracle cure' and not I. Something similar had happened in Denmark in 1974, and it made up for the case of the Swedish woman who tried to sue me for bending her intra-uterine device so that she had an unwanted pregnancy after watching me on television!

Another of my Brazilian viewers was Lucita Crespi, whose uncle Nino Crespi had been a famous racing driver. He had been killed in a crash during a race in Rio de Janeiro forty years previously. His family had kept the chronometer he had been using at the time, which had never ticked again although several attempts had been made to have it repaired. It started up again during my show, however, and went on working perfectly for several days. Oliveira's conclusion was that 'we are all Uri Gellers'.

One way and another, I had forgotten all about Mike's promise when I received a telephone call in my Manhattan apartment towards the end of the year from a girl named Lucy. She just introduced herself, giving her full name, and asked if we could meet. I could think of no reason why not, so we did, and I found her to be an attractive and intelligent young lady with as much interest in parapsychology as she seemed to have in me. We went out together several times and got along very well. Her face seemed familiar, and it turned out that she had accompanied Rosalynn Carter on her visit to Mexico, though we had not spoken to each other on that occasion.

One day, she surprised me by mentioning that she was a close relative of the Carter family. She had told Jimmy all about me, she said, and his reaction had been one of open-minded interest. Then, before I could make the obvious connections in my mind between her, me and Mike, she asked if I would like to come and attend the inauguration ceremonies in Washington.

I had said nothing to her, or to anybody else, and was certainly not fishing for an invitation. A presidential inauguration is a major social event, to which everybody in the country would like to be invited. What chance did I have? I was fairly well known as a somewhat unusual entertainer, but I was no big star, and I was not even an American. The thought of receiving such an honour had slipped from my mind once again when the envelope appeared one morning on my doormat.

I could not believe it. Mr Uri Geller was formally invited to attend the inauguration of President Carter in Washington. So was Mr Shipi Shtrang. We just looked at each other in sheer bewilderment. We had come a long way.

What a week it was! Lucy, or at any rate somebody, had arranged the full treatment for us. Out of all the hotels in Washington, we found that our reservations were in the one where the president's close relatives were to stay. Some of them were even on the same floor, and the first person I met when I stepped out of my room was Carter's brother Billy.

'Hi there,' he boomed, 'You're Uri Geller – I've heard so much about you.' He wanted to find out for himself right away if any of it was true, and in his book you will find a double-page photograph of the two of us sitting in that hotel corridor and doing a telepathy experiment.

Lucy was the most efficient of escorts. She gave me a whole stack of invitations, not only to the VIP podium on the inauguration route, but to any number of balls, parties and receptions, one of which was to be in the White House.

The parade was a fairly uncomfortable affair. It was freezing cold, and President Carter insisted on making the long journey from the ceremonial stand to his new home on foot, which must have alarmed his security advisers. As I sat and shivered, I wished I had brought some warmer underwear with me.

When the entourage came in sight, the whole affair struck me as absolutely ludicrous. I am always ready to try something new, yet Mike's plan – to beam a telepathic message into the mind of the chief executive of the most powerful country in the world – was going a bit too far.

The new presidential couple were waving and projecting their warm southern smiles to the crowd. One smile came in my direction, and although Mrs Carter could not have recognized me from that distance, it was personal contact of a kind. So, as they passed in front of me I took aim, so to speak, and fired off a sort of compressed thought-capsule containing the images of psychic phenomena, Soviet superiority, and money.

'It's all a question of money,' Mike had told me. 'Money for grants to research institutes.' He had not mentioned any figures, but the sum I had in mind for some reason was that of $6 million. So I added that figure to my message, which I delivered as well as I could in view of the distance between me and my target.

I still had to make more direct contact with the president. There is much argument as to whether telepathy is more effective at close range; Russell Targ and others have shown that it can operate at very long distances, even from Moscow to California, but I would imagine that the kind of thing I was trying to do would be more powerful at close range. I could be wrong, but in any case Mike's suggestion had been for me to get as close to Carter as I could.

I had to wait for a while. There was no chance of getting anywhere near him at the first event, a formal affair in a big convention hall. There, I only recognized two people: the actor Jack Nicholson, one of a number of celebrities from all fields who had come to pay their respects to the new president, and a very familiar figure I spotted on my way into the hall. I sneaked up behind her and called out, 'Muncy! Turn around!'

She really fell apart when she saw who it was, and I could see her wondering how on earth I had got myself invited. However, this was no time for explanations.

At last it was time for the main event of the week-long celebrations, and I found myself inside the most famous home in the United States. It was not exactly a private visit, as there were several hundred other guests, and after my initial excitement at setting foot inside the White House, my spirits sank again. Security was tight, to say the least. Lucy shepherded me around and introduced me to several people, including one of Carter's close advisers, but my mind kept wandering. I knew this was probably the only chance I would ever have to meet the president, and at the same time I saw that not even Lucy with her family connections could penetrate the wall of protection around him – in his own home.

Then, all of a sudden, the guests began to form a line to pay their personal respects to the Carters. I doubted whether the secret servicemen would let me even get into the line, let alone actually speak to them. The next thing

I knew Lucy was literally grabbing hold of me and shoving me to the back of the line, leaving me there behind what looked and sounded like the whole of the population of Georgia.

I was reminded of my first parachute drop. I remembered the green light that meant I was next in line and there was no turning back. It went on again now, inside my head, and I summoned all the concentration I could manage. I felt this was an assignment I had to get right first time.

Much sooner than I had expected, there was suddenly nobody in front of me except Jimmy and Rosalynn Carter and their personal entourage. This is it, Geller, I thought.

Mrs Carter recognized me at once, and broke the tension. 'Oh, Jimmy,' she exclaimed, 'this is Uri Geller. You remember, that young Israeli I told you so much about?'

The president's expression barely altered, and there was a brief silence as I stepped forward and grabbed hold of his hand. I held on to it for a good six seconds, looking down into his eyes – he was shorter than I had expected and I am six feet one inch – and forcing that same message through them, this time really putting everything I had into it.

*Psychic phenomena are real. Open your mind. Put money into research. Six million dollars. Catch up with the Soviets.*

The tension and urgency I felt must have made my grip even firmer than usual, for Carter winced slightly and I felt him trying to withdraw his hand. Don't overdo it, said the voice in my head. Then his well-known smile beamed at me.

'Are you going to solve the energy crisis for us?' he asked. It was the second time a head of state had asked

me much the same question. I forget what I replied, but I
had a strong feeling that my message had been received.
There are times when I feel certain, rather than merely
confident, that I have done something right, and, thank
God, this was one of them. Rosalynn Carter said a few
kind words to me and that I must come and meet them
again, and then it was all over. Mission accomplished. I
am sure one of the photographers immortalized this event
and the photo is somewhere in the Washington archives.

There was no direct feedback. Lucy telephoned me once
or twice, but we never met again and I never knew if she
had been manipulated into meeting me without knowing
who was behind it. Or was it a coincidence? As for Mike,
he simply disappeared from my life as suddenly as he had
entered it.

A report appeared nearly seven years later in the *New
York Times* (10 January 1984) in which it was stated that
President Carter ordered 'a high-level review of Soviet
psychic research' in 1977, following what was described as
'a private audience' with me. (No information about any
such meeting has ever originated from me.) The secret
review was completed in 1978, according to the newspaper, and although 'it found no evidence of the "psycho-
warfare" project such as Mr Geller had warned of, it did
find definite Soviet interest'. White House officials 'could
neither confirm nor deny' that such a review existed.
Neither can I.

When I celebrated my thirtieth birthday in December
1976, I had reason to feel fairly pleased with myself. I had
made my name a household word over most of the world,
I had visited almost all the countries I had always dreamed

2  A cartoonist's view of White House interest in psychic
matters that appeared in *Science Digest*.

of visiting, I had made several good friends and my bank
account was well into seven figures. The attacks against
me by sceptics and magicians only made people more
eager to come and see me or watch me on television.
Several books had been written about me, in addition to
literally hundreds of newspaper and magazine articles. I
had attended the inauguration of one head of state, and
was just about to attend another. Everything seemed to
be going my way.

Psychologically, however, it was not. To begin with, I
began to feel constantly unwell, and the cause was easy to
find. I had always been a hearty eater, and now I had
become a compulsive one, suffering from what is called
bulimia, or insatiable appetite. I would gobble up every-

thing put in front of me, and dining out regularly with Muncy in all the smartest places in Mexico City only provided more temptation to overdo things. Fortunately we were both teetotallers, and I hate to think what might have happened otherwise, but we were both developing some rather extreme eating habits.

Few of the restaurants we visited ever produced a bill. The publicity that arose from the fact that the president's wife had dined somewhere was usually thought to be worth more than a handful of pesos. I even paid for meals now and then by bending some spoons, and one restaurant framed one of my impromptu metal sculptures and hung it on the wall! Waiters would do their best to tempt us with their specialities of the day, and we invariably gave in. When the dessert trolley was wheeled over after a huge meal, Muncy was quite capable of ordering one of everything and devouring half of each.

I was just as greedy, and often I would have to excuse myself to go to the toilet and force myself to throw up, to make room for yet more excessive food intake. At home, it was much the same, and I would even stick my toothbrush down my throat to induce vomiting. Eventually, I found I could no longer keep anything down, so that the more I ate the thinner I became. I tried to fool myself into thinking that this was due to the exercise I continued to take, running up to five miles a day even in the thin atmosphere of Mexico City, but I failed to fool those nearest to me.

On one of my visits to New York, Shipi's sister Hanna came over from Israel to be with me, as she often did, and she told me I was looking really terrible. Back in Mexico, Muncy said the same. Tom Morris told me I reminded him of an inmate of a concentration camp. One day as I was getting out of a car, I suddenly found I had lost all my strength. I had to grab the edge of the roof and pull myself up. It was a brief, unexpected and very frightening moment of truth, and the truth was that I was slowly killing myself.

The fact of realizing this seemed to awaken some remote area of my unconscious mind, where the decision to do something about it at once was taken. It was powerful enough to produce immediate results, with a good deal of help and support from Hanna, and from that moment on I began to eat normally, as I have done ever since.

Almost immediately, I had to face a potentially far more serious problem. The president of Mexico had clearly become concerned at the impression Muncy was making when she appeared with me in public, and in due course she received an official order from him to step into line. She was not to wear such sexy clothes, or so much make-up. She was to try to enter a restaurant without turning all eyes in her direction as she swept in with me on her arm. She should, in short, remember who she was and what she represented.

I had been worried myself for some time. I had seen plenty of jealousy on nearby faces in restaurants and theatres, all the more, no doubt, because I was an outsider. I began to feel more and more uncomfortable, but neither I nor her husband, it seemed, could change Muncy's ways. Her inevitable reply to any comment on her behaviour was 'I don't care!', and if I or anybody else cared there was clearly nothing we could do about it. That was the way she was.

One day, Pepito took me aside. There was something he clearly had to get off his chest. I did not have to be psychic to recognize that expression on his face.

'Listen, Uri,' he said. 'There is talk. There are rumours. Don't go out with my mother any more, it's not good for us.'

There was no trace of a threat in his voice, but even so, warning bells began to sound in my ears. Pepito was telling me, in effect, that although both he and his father knew that Muncy and I were just good friends, the family could not tolerate any hint of scandal. And such hints were already being dropped.

At this time, I should add that tongues were also wagging about the president. Like most public figures in Latin America, he was widely assumed to have a mistress hidden away somewhere, though I have no evidence that he had. From what I could see, his relations with his wife were entirely normal. If they seemed a little distant at times, I put it down to his intellectual side. He worked very long hours, and would spend such free time as he had in keeping himself fit and then retiring to his study to read, write, or reflect on the history of his country, on which he is a recognized authority. He did not seem to have enough time to chase after other women, and he was always most hospitable and courteous to me. Never did he even suggest that he objected to my keeping Muncy company while he was occupied with other matters.

He must have had words with her, however, since our relationship gradually became a good deal less public, although we continued to see a lot of each other. One day early in 1978, she invited me to join her and the children for a short holiday in the seaside resort of Cancun. It was a romantic spot, and strolling along the beach by the Caribbean in the moonlight was an experience I will never forget. However, even there I knew that Muncy's vigilant bodyguards were not far away, so I can hardly claim that we were alone together. I am also sure that the president was kept informed about all his wife's movements.

We were also, it seems, still in the sights of the gossip-mongers.

On 10 February 1978 the (London) *Daily Express* printed a short item under the headline BENDING THE RULES FOR URI. It contained a small photograph of me and only three column-inches of text, and had no dateline or byline. It began:

There is startling news from Mexico about spoon-bender Uri Geller. The Israeli psychic superstar has struck up a warm friendship with President López Portillo's lively wife Carmen. A friendship which, according to some observers, might precipitate a 'Mexican Watergate'.

The article went on to reveal that I and my 'clever assistant' Shipi Shtrang had managed to become Mexicans thanks to the First Lady's good offices. It added that this 'saves Señor Shtrang from Israeli military service'. It then announced that 'Geller and Carmen, who is buxom and in her late forties, have surprised Mexicans by taking holidays together' at Cancun, where 'at one hotel, reports a member of staff, they were behaving rather intimately'. The member of staff was quoted as saying, 'We did not know where to look.' I myself, according to the paper, said, 'It is true I am fond of her – and her husband and three children.'

This article was fairly accurate. I do recall speaking on the telephone to somebody at the time and confirming what most of Mexico already knew: that Muncy and I were good friends. I am sure some waiter or waitress *was* startled by her behaviour. As I have indicated, it often used to startle me.

Yet how did that article find its way into a London

newspaper? What was all the talk about a Mexican Watergate? Why include the gratuitous smear against Shipi? A minimum of checking would have established that he left Israel quite openly and legally before he was liable for military service. In any case, he would almost certainly have been exempted from this, since he suffered in his teens from Ménière's disease. He has since visited Israel without any problems at all.

It must have been a plant, and I wondered who might have planted it. The mention of the Watergate affair suggested that it might have been the inner circle of the PRI, the party that really runs things in Mexico. It may have decided that enough was enough, for which I could hardly blame it. My relationship with Muncy might well have been misunderstood, although, as I have said, it was the most public of friendships, and if the president had wanted it terminated he had only to let me know, which he never did.

It could also have been a leak sprung deliberately to embarrass me by one of my witch-hunters, who must have known very well that in Mexico an innuendo of this kind could be enough to put my life in danger. In view of some of the dirty tricks they were to play on me later, I definitely cannot rule this out.

I was due to visit Los Pinos on the evening of 10 February, but I never got there. A copy of the *Daily Express* was on the president's desk that morning, presumably having been telexed from the Mexican Embassy in London. Things then moved very quickly.

The telephone rang in Tom Morris's house, where I was still staying on my visits to Mexico. It was for me, and the caller was Pepito.

'Don't come to Los Pinos today, Uri,' he began.

'Something very bad has happened.' His father, he said, was very angry. In fact, he was furious. 'There was something in a newspaper,' he went on.

I tried to get some details out of him, but all he would tell me was that people were saying bad things about his mother and me. His tone of voice was serious and, as he went on speaking, the distant warning bells started up again. It became clear that something was under way that Pepito could not control, and this telephone call was a friendly warning and no more.

Suddenly, everything seemed to collapse around me, and it was the tone of urgency in Pepito's final words that made me realize that it was time to plan my exodus.

My precious Aeromexico card gave me the right not only to free first-class travel, but also to turn somebody out of a seat to make room for me if necessary, and even to keep a plane waiting on the runway. I had never needed to resort to such measures before. Now, I did.

Tom Morris drove Shipi and me to the airport, and were it not for the diplomatic plates on his car I am sure he would have ended up in jail for any number of motoring offences. We shot through red lights, down one-way streets, and over pavements. Traffic cops waved and yelled at us. Passers-by stopped and stared at what must have seemed some unusual driving even by Mexican standards.

Somehow or other, we made it to the airport. There was no time to thank Tom properly for all that he had done for me, and at last I flopped into my seat on the flight bound for New York.

I had originally stayed in Mexico as the result of a direct order from the wife of the nominated president. Now I was leaving, just as unexpectedly, on the advice of her son. Even after we had taken off, Pepito's final words to me rang louder in my ears than the jet engines that were lifting me from what could have been imminent danger: 'My suggestion is to get out of Mexico – quickly.'

# 6
## Successes and Failures

The house telephone rang in my New York apartment. There was a man downstairs from the US Customs who wanted to see me. His identification looked kosher. Could he be sent up?

You have to be careful in New York, but I trusted the concierge's judgment. Besides, although the visit was quite unexpected, I had an idea what it might be about. Some time previously, I had flown in from Mexico bringing the precious Colt that President López Portillo had given me. I had already brought it into the United States several times, openly and legally, and had never had any problems at customs after producing my documents as an accredited agent of the Mexican security services. On the last occasion, however, the official took the gun away, returning after a long delay to explain that he would have to retain it. There was something that needed checking, and I would be notified later of the outcome.

The customs agent, whom I will call Carl, looked authentic enough, as did the badge he showed me. He was carrying a small package.

'Mr Geller?' he said when I opened the door. 'I have your gun to return to you. Special orders from the United States Attorney-General to release it.' How the Attorney-General became involved, and whether it is normal for confiscated goods to be returned by personal delivery, I have no idea. Nor do I know if Carl was acting under orders or if he was just curious to meet me. Anyway, I invited him in and we had a pleasant chat, during which it emerged that he was interested in psychic matters. As he got up to leave, he told me where I could reach him, and asked me to let him know if I ever needed help of any kind.

There was, as it happened, something I needed very badly. My mother was then living on her own in Israel, and I wanted her to come and live in the USA so that I could see more of her in between my engagements. I had no intention of becoming an American citizen myself, or of establishing permanent residence there. Indeed, it was not practical for me to establish permanent residence anywhere, since I was constantly travelling all over the world fulfilling my professional engagements. New York was only one of my temporary home bases, and my status of non-resident alien required me to spend no more than six months (183 days, to be precise) of each year in the USA, a condition I obeyed scrupulously. However, New York was the base I visited most often, and it was where I wanted my mother to be.

Carl promised to see what could be done, and shortly afterwards he came to see me again together with a man I will call Don. He, I gathered, was a counter-intelligence agent with the Federal Bureau of Investigation.

We had a long and informal conversation, with Don doing most of the talking. He was fascinated by the whole paranormal field, especially telepathy, and was keen to see for himself what I could do. We did some of my usual drawing experiments, and he was delighted to find that, like many people, he was just as good at receiving and transmitting images as I was.

'Look,' I said to him at one point, 'if I can be of any assistance to you in any way, I'd be happy.' I had no hesitation in making the offer. The FBI is one of the most respected law-enforcement agencies in the world, and its image is a good deal cleaner than that of the CIA. I was sure that nothing they might ask me to do would conflict with my own interests or principles. If they wanted to return any favours I might do for them, that was up to them. There was no mention of payment by either of us.

Don looked very pleased, as if he had been hoping that I would say that.

I had in fact had dealings with the FBI before. This is what happened:

On 9 August 1975, a young man named Samuel Bronfman was kidnapped close to his father's home near New York, and according to press reports his father was asked for 'a substantial sum' for his safe return. Edgar Bronfman was the head of the huge Seagram whisky empire and, as his eldest son, Samuel was due to inherit a good deal of the billion-dollar business.

The Bronfman family had apparently been contacted by both mail and telephone, and a tape of Samuel's voice had been delivered to them. The written message told Mr Bronfman that his son had been buried in an underground cave somewhere in Westchester County, and left with enough food for ten days at the most. Negotiations were said to be under way for his release in exchange for a seven-figure sum, but there was no mention of what steps were being taken by either the police or the FBI. Also unreported (until now) was the fact that a member of the Bronfman family put through a call to me from his home in Toronto to ask if I could help locate Samuel before it was too late.

This was not long after Sir Val Duncan had told me I could use my natural gift for dowsing to find just about anything, and as I have said, my usual reaction to a challenge is to have a go. I agreed to do what I could at once, for I knew Edgar Bronfman was a generous contributor to Jewish causes and a strong supporter of Israel. The necessary arrangements were quickly made, and a private helicopter flew me from New York to the area where Samuel was thought to be in his underground prison.

First, I was taken to the palatial Bronfman home and shown a number of Samuel's personal possessions in order to establish some kind of link with him. Then I climbed back into the helicopter, and we flew up and down over a wide area of Westchester County, but I received no impressions at all. Apparently, my first assignment of this kind was a complete failure. Edgar Bronfman was in his Manhattan apartment, so I decided to go along and admit my defeat to him.

The luxurious town residence had been turned into a command centre, and among those present, in addition to the desperate father, was the chief of the New York FBI. As I was shown into the living-room, the first thing I noticed was a large map of New York City attached to an easel. Suddenly, before I had even been properly introduced to anybody, I had one of those moments of super-confidence. I walked over to the easel and jabbed my finger into the map, somewhere in the Brooklyn area.

'That's where he is,' I stated, with complete certainty.

That is exactly where he was. I cannot claim to have located Samuel Bronfman single-handed, because it was one of his kidnappers who eventually provided the police with the exact address. The FBI then moved in, recovering Samuel, who was unharmed, and a reported $2.3 million stuffed into rubbish sacks. It was revealed that the FBI had been staking out the area for some time after watching the hand-over of the money and following the very careless extortionist back to his home. The kidnappers, two Irish-Americans thought to have been involved in fund-raising for Irish terrorists, eventually noticed that they were under observation. For some reason, they became convinced that the Mafia had sent a hit-squad to get their money and, believe it or not, one of the kidnappers then sent his daughter along to the local police with a note asking for protection! Both kidnappers were later jailed.

That is the story as it was reported in the press, although it is one you might not believe if you read it in a crime novel.

Although I had not made any contract with Mr Bronfman, after the happy ending to this affair I sent him an invoice for $25,000, which I reckoned he could afford. I was then receiving fees of up to $5,000 for my ninety-minute lecture-demonstrations, and I felt this was a fair sum for two or three days of hard work, especially since I had at least provided evidence for the accuracy of my impressions. I have a strong suspicion, incidentally, that at the moment I put my finger on that map, it was not known that Samuel was in Brooklyn. Not surprisingly, however, nobody told me.

I received a cheque in due course for the sum asked – minus one zero! I decided to let go at that, however, since there had been no written contract and $2,500 was better than nothing.

Several years later, there was a curious sequel to this episode. I was in a hotel in Europe, discussing an assignment about which I cannot give details here except that my client was somewhat secretive, as European business-men tend to be. When I brought up the subject of my fee, the man wrote something on a corner of his napkin, tore it off and rolled it into a tight ball, then handed it to me. I smoothed out the tiny piece of paper to find the figures

2.5 written on it. That was all, and I assumed they meant $2,500. I accepted with a nod, and the man asked for the address of my bank. He would pay at once, he assured me.

I called my bank a day or two later to check that he had kept his word. A puzzled clerk told me that there had been no recent payment of $2,500.

'There has only been one entry in your account in the last few days,' he added, 'for two hundred and fifty thousand dollars.'

As soon as Don heard that I was willing to offer him my services, he said, 'I understand you're in need of some help yourself, concerning your mother?' Carl, the customs agent, had evidently briefed him well.

Both Don and Carl soon became regular visitors to my apartment, and they would sometimes bring their wives or their colleagues with them. The table in my living-room was often piled high with handcuffs and bundles of keys, which they would remove in order to be able to relax in comfort. We often went out to eat together, and my relations with the FBI men became more informal as well as more frequent than they had ever been with the CIA agents I met in Mexico.

One day, Carl came to see me with a colleague from the US Drug Enforcement Administration. They showed me a stack of photographs of some very ugly-looking characters, and another one of a ship. A major drug delivery was expected soon, I was told, and they were wondering if I could learn anything from these photographs? I did my best, and passed on the impressions that came into my mind, although as is usual in this kind of work I heard no more.

This must be as disappointing to you as it always is to

me, but you have to understand that a golden rule of any kind of police or intelligence work is that nobody is ever told anything at all except on the 'need-to-know' principle. If there is no need for you to know something, you are not told it. As several of my clients have put it, there was only one way I would ever know if I was delivering any information of value: I would be asked for more.

As in Mexico, I was asked for more. One day, Don asked me a question very similar to one of the first that Mike had read out from his shopping list.

'If I drive you around the block where the Soviet Consulate is located,' he said, 'could you tell me something about what's on one of the floors of the building?'

The consulate was only ten blocks away on East 67th Street, so we went for a ride. All the windows on the floor in question, I noticed, had been blacked out. I saw with some amusement that there was a police station right across the street.

I returned to the area several times on foot, taking care to keep out of the range of the camera slung over the front door, and as in Mexico I simply passed on whatever I had picked up with my psychic antennas, and heard no more.

Next, I was invited to a party in an isolated house out on Long Island Sound, where the host was an intelligence agent whose speciality was Soviet affairs, and one of the guests was to be a Soviet official he very much hoped could be persuaded to defect. I was asked to do two things: demonstrate my abilities to the man if I had the chance, and send him an unspoken message to defect. I found both requests somewhat unusual, potential defectors usually being much more useful if they stay put and keep up the flow of information, but it was not for me to ask questions.

Don came along with a woman who was not his wife, whom I had met, but a counter-intelligence agent. They soon arranged for me to meet the Soviet guest, a short and stocky man whose hair was white, although he was not more than middle-aged. I was not told his name. I bent a key for him, which he seemed to find intriguing, and gave him my telephone number, inviting him to get in touch if he wanted to. (He never did.) All the time I was sitting beside him, I punched out my silent message as hard as I could: *Defect, defect, it's good for you, defect . . .*

It was at about this time that Arkady Shevchenko, the Under-Secretary-General at the United Nations, defected after passing information to the US authorities for more than two years. In his book *Breaking With Moscow* (1985) he says: 'I was grateful that even in the age of technological miracles no one could yet read thoughts.'

Some of his former colleagues at the Soviet Mission now probably know better. In 1980 I received a telephone call from a man with a thick Slavonic accent asking if I would come and give a demonstration-lecture to the Parapsychology Society of the United Nations, in the Dag Hammarskjöld Auditorium.

I was surprised to learn that there was such a society, but there was – I have the printed announcement of my performance – and the evening went very well, although the lights were uncomfortably bright.

The small auditorium was well filled, and although the UN is as multinational an organization as you can find, a good many of the faces looked distinctly East European. At least one member of the audience, I believe, was an intelligence agent sent along by one of my friends – not to see my show but to check out his fellow spectators.

Cameras clicked all through my performance, and

questions in a variety of Slavonic accents were asked afterwards. I was probably filmed as well, for when the lights were finally dimmed, I noticed a man in the back row packing up a very large camera-case. I posed for some informal group photographs afterwards, and a newspaper reporter who was present later obtained a copy of one of them for me, with the names on the back. Several of them were Russian.

Several months after my show at the UN I was booked to take part in a 'psychic cruise' to Bermuda on board the SS *Britannis*. As engagements of this kind usually are, it was a welcome combination of well-paid work and relaxing leisure. To my great surprise, I immediately recognized several faces in my floating audience. The last time I had seen them had been in the Dag Hammarskjöld Auditorium. Later, I chatted informally with some of them, and the trip passed off without incident, although I did have an uneasy feeling of being watched all the time.

Perhaps they were wondering if there would be a repeat of the incident I described in *My Story* when I was on another cruise, a musical one this time, as a guest of one of the artists, Byron Janis. There were also some Hungarian musicians on board, and they had the bright idea that we should all concentrate on stopping the ship! We did, whereupon the engines suddenly stopped humming and the ship, the *Renaissance*, gradually slowed to an almost total standstill. Byron, with his best innocent expression on his face, went to ask the captain what had happened.

'We just have a little problem,' he was told. 'The propeller drive shaft seems to be in a very contorted shape, and the fuel is not getting through properly.' It took a couple of hours to get the engines started again. I felt like a naughty schoolboy and have never tried anything like that since.

\* \* \*

Later in this book, I will be telling you about some of my most successful undertakings. In the rest of this chapter, I am going to describe a few of my less successful ones. I am doing this for two reasons: I do not want to give the impression that I can do anything on demand at any time and always get it right, and I hope that the serious student of the mind and its powers will be able to learn as much as I think I did from those failures.

As an investigator for the FBI, Don sometimes became involved in the hunt for kidnappers and their victims. Once, he telephoned me from Arizona to tell me that the father of a boy who had disappeared had offered to pay my expenses if I would fly out and help look for him. I agreed at once, and travelled all over the area concerned, but was unable to receive any impressions except that the boy had been killed and buried in the desert. I never heard if his body was found.

The last request I ever had from Don could have led to my greatest success if I had been proved right. It was like something out of a second-rate thriller, although from Don's tone of voice as he briefed me I could tell he was not playing games. Nor was he merely testing me – he had done that often enough already. No, there was a major problem: what it amounted to was that there was evidence, presumably from an Eastern bloc defector, that a member of the topmost layer of the US administration in Washington was a longtime Soviet mole, a 'sleeper' who had been trained to remain in place indefinitely.

'Could you just come up with a name, an initial, a general impression – anything at all?' Don asked.

I had very little to go on, but I did what I could, and a few weeks later I did come up with a name. When I passed it on to Don, I could see he thought either that I had gone out of my mind or that I was kidding him. He just would not take me seriously, and I am sure that he never passed on the name I gave him to his superiors. So it will probably never be known if I was right or wrong. Evidently, Don thought that I had lost my touch, for he never asked me to do anything for him again.

The FBI, as you might expect, does not say much about its involvement with people like me. The only mention of it in print that I have seen was in the 27 January 1986 *International Herald Tribune*, in which the deputy assistant director of the bureau's records management division, Thomas H. Bresson, was asked if it was normal for the FBI to deal with psychics. He replied, 'I wouldn't rule it out.'

Nor, as I know, would some of his colleagues.

In June 1978, a twenty-five-year-old New Yorker named David Berkowitz was sent to prison after being convicted for the murder of six people, and for wounding another seven, most of them attractive young girls. Sentencing him to a total of 315 years in jail, the judge expressed his 'earnest desire that this defendant remain in jail for life, until the very day of his death'. I doubt if a single New Yorker felt otherwise, for there has never been a killer as feared and hated as the individual who terrorized the city throughout much of 1977 and became known as the 'Son of Sam'.

It was Carl who persuaded me, without difficulty, to become involved in the case. He introduced me to a New York police officer who was clearly ready to try anything, and one evening we drove to the scene of Son of Sam's latest murder, a lonely 'lovers' lane' spot near the Verranzano Bridge. Before we set out, he showed me some police photographs of previous victims. They turn my stomach over even today when I think of them, and I could not have been more strongly motivated than I was after I had seen them. If there was anything at all that I could do to catch the maniac responsible for what I had seen, I was going to do it.

I strolled around the area, concentrating as hard as I could – maybe too hard. I began to pick up impressions, and gave the policeman a verbal description of a man. I also gave him the only word that really came in strongly: Yonkers.

I felt that I had not been much help. Yonkers is a large area of upstate New York, and there was probably thousands of men living there who fitted my none too precise description. So I cannot claim to have contributed anything useful to the solution of this case.

Later, it became known that the police had caught Berkowitz after checking all vehicles that had been given parking tickets at or just before times when there had been a murder in the area concerned. It was after tracing one car back to its owner's Yonkers address that they finally moved in and made an arrest. It was no consolation for me to know that the limited information I had provided was correct. Correct it may have been, but it was not specific enough to save the life of at least one more innocent young girl.

To add to my feelings of frustration regarding this case, I learned later that several other psychics were called in at various stages, some of whom provided information that, had it been co-ordinated at the time with my modest contribution, might well have led to an earlier end to this dreadful case.

A more recent case on which I seemed to do everything right except solve it took place in Rome in the winter of 1983. Two members of the wealthy Bulgari family were kidnapped from their home in November, and released on Christmas Eve after a ransom had been paid. During the search a relative of theirs asked me to come and help locate the victims, a woman and her seventeen-year-old son, and with the co-operation of the Italian police I searched all the areas involved.

At first, I drew a complete blank. Then, one day as Shipi and I were tramping the streets of Rome, I received a sudden and very strong impulse to go at once to a certain piazza on the other side of town. We got there as fast as we could, whereupon a Mercedes screeched to a halt beside us, and a woman got out and rushed to a public telephone. I recognized her as a member of the Bulgari family, and she recognized me, since we had already met briefly. It turned out that she had just received a telephone message to come to this call-box and wait for another message. This was in the early stage of the case, when the poor woman was being given repeated instructions to dash from one call-box to another to receive ransom demands.

Something very similar happened again a couple of weeks later. Once more, I felt a strong compulsion to go to a certain place. I felt something was about to happen there, as before, and indeed it did. There was no telephone in sight this time, so I just stood on the pavement for a few minutes, wondering what I was supposed to be looking for.

Everybody tends to look suspicious in circumstances like these, but I did not receive any definite impressions from passers-by until a man wearing a white sweater walked right past me and tossed something into a metal litter bin. I had a good look at him, and passed on a description of somebody I felt sure was involved in the case. Had I remained on the spot, I would once again have run into a member of the victims' family, who had been summoned by a telephone call to retrieve a package from the bin in question. It contained the boy's ear, hacked off by the sadistic kidnappers in an attempt to force the payment of a large ransom. Evidently, the attempt was successful, for a week later the two victims were released, and the family lawyer confirmed that money had changed hands. By yet another 'coincidence', I had already marked the exact spot where they were found on a map, without knowing why it was to be significant.

Why had my powers led me to the exact spot at the right time, drawn my attention to an ordinary-looking fellow doing something that looked quite natural and harmless, and then let me down when it came to the information that really mattered? This kind of thing seems to happen again and again when I am dealing with dangerous people, whether kidnappers or murderers. Are my survival instincts somehow suppressing my psychic ones?

If it became generally known that I could solve any problem on demand, my name would be at the top of every hit-list in the world of organized crime, and it would not be there for long. I would have to be eliminated. Perhaps it is in my own interests not to solve major crimes?

I have had some success, however, with minor crimes. A wealthy client of a world-famous jeweller had left some priceless object at one of its branches to be altered. While the craftsmen were working on it, it was stolen. The manager was extremely upset. He did not want to call in the police, fearing that the publicity would damage him even more than the financial loss. So instead he called me.

I went to the store, scanned it in my usual way, with my hands, and told the manager that the object had been stolen by a former employee, whom I described, who was now living in a town several hundred miles away in an area I mentioned. The manager confirmed that just such a man was already on the list of suspects. To make sure, he persuaded me to fly to the town in question, where I rented a car and prowled around the area in which the suspect lived and had recently bought a restaurant. My initial impressions were confirmed, and the case was then handed over to the well-known criminal lawyer Roy Cohn. I heard no more about it.

I dislike working on kidnap or murder cases. The pressure is very great, and the feeling that desperate people have pinned their hopes on me makes it harder for me to work successfully. Another problem is that I have usually had no direct contact with the person I am supposed to be looking for. In the case of a kidnap or murder victim I might be able to make indirect contact by handling some personal property, as I did on the Bronfman case, but this is not the same as personal contact. Sniffer dogs can only find what they are looking for if they recognize its scent, and it is possible that telepathists work in a similar way.

One of my clients may have found a simple but ingenious solution to this problem. He is the head of a large chemical company with interests all over the world, and a spate of kidnappings in his country led him to take the question of personal security very seriously. Would I agree, he asked me, to enter into a contract whereby if he were to be kidnapped, he would concentrate his mind at certain precise times of the day and try to send out a 'distress signal' that would help me find him?

This struck me as a very sensible idea, and I accepted

his proposal. Since then I have had several others of this kind, some of them also from the heads of major corporations, including one of the best-known Hollywood film studios. Naturally I hope that none of my 'insurance' clients will ever have to send me a telepathic claim, but if they do I am sure the fact that I have made personal contact with them will make things easier for me. Some of them have even given me such personal items as scarves, combs and old toothbrushes as additional aids to establishing contact. Once again, I cannot help wondering why it is the people at the top of their professions who are the most receptive to the kind of thing that I do. Could it be that they know, even if only subconsciously, that they would not have reached the top without using their own psychic powers?

One of my clients telephoned me at the end of 1985 to wish me the compliments of the season. I told him I was working on this book and asked how he felt about having his name mentioned in it.

He laughed. 'If you do that,' he replied, 'then they'll kidnap me – and they'll kill you.' So I will not mention the name of this chairman and principal stockholder of a very well-known international corporation.

Then I mentioned an idea that has occurred to me more than once recently.

'How would you feel,' I asked him, 'if I were to give a news conference and confess that I was a total fraud who had been fooling the world all these years?' I sometimes feel like doing this just to see what would happen, and I am sure I could get a huge advance for a book about my 'tricks'. The problem is that I would never be able to explain how I did them!

He laughed again, a little more warmly this time. 'I'd

go on hiring you,' he said. Coming from him, that was a real compliment.

Now I come to an episode of which I feel thoroughly ashamed. I have never mentioned it before in public, and I include it here as an example of what can happen when psychic powers are misused. It answers the question I have often been asked: 'If you're so psychic, why don't you go and break the bank at Monte Carlo?'

I came to England in 1975 to promote the Polydor album *Uri Geller*, on which Maxine Nightingale – a singer I helped to launch – sang some lyrics I had written to music composed and arranged by Byron Janis and Del Newman. One evening, Shipi and I went along to a London casino near Marble Arch to try our combined skills at the roulette table.

A couple of years previously we had tried to make some quick money by psychic methods at a casino in Las Vegas. We had ended the evening so broke that we could not even afford a hotel room, but had to spend the night in our car wrapped in newspapers to keep warm.

This time it was different. Whether I was using my powers to make the ball land where I wanted it to, or whether I had precognition of the number, as I had had eight times out of ten tries in one of the Stanford experiments (which was filmed), I do not know. All I know is that our earnings rose steadily. It was more than a lucky break; it was one of those occasions when nothing can go wrong, and you know it.

We deliberately made our pile slowly, in order not to attract too much attention and risk being 'asked to leave', as they say. We stayed very late, then made our way back to the Churchill Hotel with all our pockets crammed with banknotes.

In the small hours of the morning, we counted our takings. We had made just over £17,000. In our excitement, we made immediate plans for a trip to Monte Carlo.

Later, after what was left of a sleepless night, a huge Daimler arrived to take me to Liverpool for a radio programme. I decided to take my bundle of banknotes with me, and as we drove out of London I kept opening my briefcase to make sure it was still there. Then something very strange and frightening happened, which is as hard for me to describe as it may be for you to believe. There was a sudden explosion in my head, and a loud cry, followed by a long echo and the building-up of a pressure that became unbearable. My mind was filled with a single thought: *why had I used my powers for my own gain*? I felt both hot and cold, and began to tremble. My mouth went dry. I thought I was going insane. This, I said to myself, is the end of Uri Geller. I'm about to explode because of this – thing in my head.

I yelled at the driver to stop, but he could not hear me through the glass partition. I pounded on this so hard that I cracked it. He heard that all right.

'Stop! Stop!' I shouted, shaking him by the shoulder.

He calmly explained that he could not stop on a motorway, but would turn off at the next exit. Mercifully, this appeared almost immediately, and he pulled up. I suppose he thought I wanted to be sick.

The door opened, although I have no recollection of opening it myself, and I was literally pushed out of the car as if by a blast of wind. The next thing I remember was lying flat on the ground with what felt like a ton weight on top of me, pressing my face into the pebbles. This is it, I thought. I'm dying. I'm dead.

Then, as if an electric switch had been turned off, it stopped as suddenly as it had started.

'Are you all right, Mr Geller?' said a voice above me. It was the anxious chauffeur. I looked up and saw that we were at a service station, and one or two people were staring in our direction.

'Just leave me alone for a minute,' I replied. I got to my feet and went over to the newspaper stand, where I started to flip through magazines compulsively, trying to hide the humiliation I felt. Then I went back to the car, like a dog with its tail between its legs, and told the driver we could go on.

When we were back on the motorway, I opened the left window, took the bundle out of my bag and threw it as hard as I could. It was well secured with several stout elastic bands, and it landed intact by the side of the road. If it was found later by a police patrol and assumed to be some stolen money that the thief had dumped, that is what it was. If the finder happens to read this I hope he will get in touch. I do not want the money back, but I would be interested to know where it ended up.

I have learned to listen to distant early warning signals in my head. I have heard them once or twice on subsequent occasions when I have been asked to do something unethical, but I have learned my lesson. Since that dreadful morning on the motorway, I have preferred to earn my living by working hard for it.

# 7
## Small Business

Ever since I can remember, I have been inventing things. For the child of a family like mine, life in Israel in the fifties was hard, and although my parents were not exactly penniless, they had no money to spare for all the toys I would have liked. I remember pressing my nose against the window of a toyshop in Tel Aviv, gazing longingly at a jeep on display and knowing that my mother could not afford it. Today, when most families can afford some kind of electronic gadget for their children to play with, the time seems to have passed when boys and girls had to make their own toys.

When I was about six or seven, my father came home one day with some old bullets, probably blanks used in weapons training. Although it was long before the beginning of the space age, I soon converted the bullets into little moon rockets, building a launching pad with bits of wood and elastic bands and firing them off into space one by one. They all probably ended up in the bushes or in the garden next door, but in my imagination they headed for the moon, the stars, and all the other worlds of which even then I seemed to be unconsciously aware.

My next invention was more practical, one that many children have invented for themselves and probably still do. It was a wind-up alarm clock attached to a piece of string that pulled a box off my bedroom shelf when the bell rang, so that the box landed on my head and gave me an extra reminder to get up.

Before long, I had moved on to more sophisticated

projects. Watching my mother pedalling away at her old Singer sewing-machine, I felt it was time to introduce some modern technology into our home, so I took an old electric motor that had been part of a ventilating unit and adapted it to drive the pedals. The result would never have won any design awards, but it worked, as did my next invention: a bicycle powered by an outboard motor. This was the heaviest and most awkward-looking bicycle imaginable, but it took me to and from school every day. (Licences were not needed for mopeds in those days.)

Although I have never had technical training of any kind, except in the army, I always seem to have had an understanding of the way in which things work, and of ways in which new things could be made to work. In my early twenties, after I had completed my military service and begun to work as an entertainer, I kept up my habit of inventing things in my mind even though I had neither the means nor the know-how to manufacture them.

In the late sixties, I was earning a modest living as a photographer's model and demonstrating my telepathy and metal-bending at private parties in the homes of my friends, and it was at one of these informal gatherings that I met a young fellow named Meir Gitlis. He had a small workshop in his back yard, and was apparently able to repair just about anything that had broken down. He was the electrical genius I needed, and we soon became good friends.

He was as interested in my abilities as I was in his, and he was in fact the first person ever to make any kind of scientific study of me. One of the first things he asked me, the first time we met, was whether he could wire me up to an electro-encephalograph (EEG) so that he could have a look at my brain waves while I was doing a demonstration of telepathy. I do not remember what he discovered, if anything, for we both soon became more interested in all the gadgets and machines I was carrying around in my head but did not know how to put together.

Our first joint ventures, naturally enough for a couple of Israelis, were in the field of security and alarm systems. As I knew even then, security is taken very seriously in Israel and the absolute minimum is left to chance. (Anyone who has flown on El Al will know what I mean.) There is none of the casual attitude towards the protection of life and property that I have come across in many other countries, both on the premises of major companies and in the private homes of their directors, and even, as I have already described, in the personal security system of a head of state.

My army service had given me plenty of first-hand experience of security of all kinds, from self-protection to the defence of the country, and I was able to feed Meir with enough ideas to keep him busy for years. A good many of these have taken shape over the years and are now in production by Meir's small company, Nachshol Electronics. He and I have never had a written contract or a formal agreement of any kind. We have just become firm friends, who seem to share a mind. If my career had not taken other directions, I might be working today as a full-time industrial designer, with my drawing-board on a screen inside my head, and I might also have spent much more time than I have in promoting our designs and inventions.

In the early days, I said little about these because there was not much to show for them. Most of them existed only in my mind, and no inventor likes to say too much about his projects before they are patented. Later, when I became well known, I had another reason for keeping a low profile as an inventor.

In October 1974, the *New Scientist* published a huge cover story on me, a whole page of it being devoted to the suggestion that I was doing all my feats in the laboratories at SRI with the help of a radio receiver embedded in my teeth! I suppose this made sense, to some, at the time. Dr Andrija Puharich, who had helped set up the experiments, was the holder of many patents for miniaturized hearing aids, including one that could be embedded in a false tooth; and since what I was doing with my telepathic skill was clearly 'impossible', it had to be explained in terms that a scientist or a magician could understand. The suggestion was that it involved some kind of signalling between me and my sinister accomplices, Shipi and Hanna Shtrang. Although a New York reporter promptly arranged for me to be examined by a dentist, who found nothing in my mouth apart from perfectly normal teeth, I felt that it might not be a good idea to become known as an inventor, so I have never discussed this side of my career in any detail. However, now that a number of Meir's and my inventions are on the market and have been demonstrated to members of the media, I see no reason not to mention them.

It may strike you as curious that some of our first inventions to go into production were designed to detect fraud. One of these is called the Diamontron. It is about the size of a small pocket torch, and instead of a bulb it has what looks like the tip of a ballpoint pen protruding from it. The operator switches it on, allows it to warm up until the 'ready' signal lights up, then places the tip on a diamond and presses it gently. This must be done carefully, but it only takes a few minutes to learn how to do it. If the diamond is a real one, a light then comes on accompanied by the sound of a buzzer.

The secret of this little device is quite simple, although the electronic and metallurgical technology and ingenuity that went into its construction are far from simple. The principle on which it works is that a diamond has unique crystalline properties, with the highest thermal conductivity of any gem-stone. When you press the tip of your Diamontron on your stone, you are heating it and at the same time measuring the heat flow into it. If the stone's heat conductivity is characteristic of that of a diamond, then the light comes on and the buzzer sounds. If not, then what you are examining is not a diamond.

Another of our inventions enables anybody to distinguish at once between real and forged banknotes. This one is known as the Moneytron, and although it looks something like the diamond-tester, it works on an entirely different principle. Instead of a ballpoint-tip, it has a small roller which is passed over the banknote. This does not transmit any heat, but scans the banknote for a certain chemical with which it is impregnated and which cannot be detected visually. The original model was designed for American paper currency, which does not contain the thin strip of silver which you can see in English banknotes, for example, just by holding them up to the light. Other models have been adapted to the individual requirements of various countries – for Bank of England notes, the Moneytron scans the ink used to print the serial number and responds accordingly, and again the light and buzzer only come on if the note is a real one.

One of our favourite inventions is the one I call the Electronic Canary, although it is sold under several names. Its purpose is to detect the presence of gas, and when it does, its red light starts blinking and it emits an alarm signal louder than any real canary could manage. I hope the days are over when these unfortunate birds were taken down mines to warn when gas levels had built up to dangerous levels, which they could only do not by sounding an alarm call, but by dropping dead.

The Electronic Canary is about half the size of a brick, and is another tribute to Meir's skill at packing a lot of advanced technology into a small space. This sensitive bird works on the principle of semiconduction, and responds to as little as five per cent of the lower explosive limit of certain gases, including those most commonly in commercial and domestic use. It will, I hope, help save human lives as well as those of canaries.

Another of our recent inventions is a miniaturized radiation detector. Following the disaster at the Chernobyl nuclear power station in 1986, we received large orders for this from several countries.

Meir has also manufactured a number of sensor devices that respond to sound. I cannot give any details of these, for obvious reasons, except that they are designed to provide what is known as a pre-entry alarm. That is to say, they detect the presence of intruders before they have actually intruded. The familiar home burglar alarm goes off when somebody tries to force a window or a door, whereas with one of the devices made by the General Sensor Division of Nachshol installed, you can be creeping up behind your intruders before they get within reach of your building, or in a military context you can be lining them up in the sights of your rifle.

One of our most ambitious and successful inventions to date has been the GS Inertial Sensor, which can be used on installations large or small, from a warehouse to a state border hundreds of miles long. Like many of our products, it has been sold to several countries, in some of which it is also made under licence. From a distance, it looks like an ordinary chain-link fence, but by the time you get close enough to have a better look at it, it has already taken a good look at you and the duty operator monitoring the central control unit will have taken appropriate action.

Some time ago, a company based in Helsingborg, Sweden, bought the distribution rights for the Inertial Sensor in that country. Naturally, we did not ask what they or their customers might be planning to use it for – in the security business nobody tells anybody anything they do not need to know. I should also mention that none of our inventions can be used for aggressive purposes, but are all made to improve security and defence systems.

In October 1982, there were numerous reports in the media that a Soviet submarine had been located in Swedish territorial waters, close to the secret naval base at Muskö, twenty miles south of Stockholm. It was a most confusing affair, to judge from reports. Some said there were two submarines, not one, and that they had been bombed with depth-charges to force them to the surface. Others said they (or it) had escaped, and later in the month it was even suggested that no Soviet submarine had ever been there in the first place. One report I found particularly interesting, in the *Daily Mail* (6 October), stated:

The intruder is believed to be penned inside Hörsfjärden Bay at Muskö by anti-submarine netting and thick metal chains which were put into position when its periscope was first spotted five days ago.

The same reporter, Christopher Mosey, seems to have covered the story more thoroughly than most. On 5 February 1983 he reported in *The Times* that the Swedish

Defence Ministry had confirmed the discovery and filming of caterpillar tracks on the sea-bed, which had been made by 'a four- to five-metre-long robotlike, previously unknown vehicle'. The same reporter had speculated at the time of the incident that the 'trapped' vessel was in fact a robot sent from a submarine. I can merely speculate that such a robot can only have been sent to test Sweden's defences, which it seems it did very successfully from the Swedish point of view.

I could only speculate further when I received a copy of the promotional material issued by Stängselnät AB of Helsingborg, distributors of the Israeli-made system known in Sweden as Direkt-Larm. On the cover of the colour brochure was a photograph of a Soviet submarine half out of the water and alongside two Swedish naval vessels. The flags of the two nations were clearly visible. In the lower part of the picture, there was a section of our fence, which may have been superimposed. The picture itself could have been taken during an earlier incident in which another Soviet submarine ran aground near another Swedish naval base. Anyway, the brochure specifically referred to the fact that 'Direkt-Larm has protected and saved everything from human lives to major valuables at airports, military installations, ports and harbours, industrial areas, yes, even war zones.'

There were a lot of rumours around in the early seventies that both the Americans and the Soviets had been doing experiments in telepathy between a submerged submarine and the shore. The original story in a French science magazine was almost certainly a 'plant' designed to test official reactions from both sides, though 'remote viewing' experiments from a submarine were later carried out and published by scientists from SRI International. I have done some underwater telepathy experiments myself (not at SRI) which have never been made public, and all I can say about them is that they were very successful.

There was no telepathy involved in the Swedish incident, as far as I know, and if it was one of our Inertial Sensors that helped locate (or trap) a Soviet submarine (or something) then it was only doing what it was designed to do.

There are still things that machines cannot do, and in my time as a freelance business consultant I have been given some fairly strange assignments. I always insist on a down payment in advance for my services, as a guarantee that the client is not going to waste my time, and I always make it clear that I cannot guarantee results. When I am asked to do something I consider unethical, the client is in effect fined on the spot, because my down payment is not returnable.

On one occasion, I was hired by a European company that was in the process of negotiating a very large deal, involving the purchase of land for the building of town houses with landscaped gardens. It stood to make a handsome profit, but the price being asked by the seller seemed excessive to them, and I was asked to attend a conference in order to find out, by mind-reading, the lowest price the seller was willing to accept – whatever he might say it was.

When I arrived at the company's headquarters, I was surprised to find myself being shown into a small room next door to the conference room, which was completely empty except for a chair beside a large window that overlooked the conference table. The window turned out to be a two-way mirror, and may have been installed especially for the occasion. I cannot imagine why a firm of this kind would normally need a two-way mirror in a conference room.

The meeting went ahead as planned, with figures being hurled from one side of the table to the other. I did what I was supposed to do, and the deal was signed in due course to the buyers' satisfaction. I did this job with a clear conscience, reckoning that the seller could make a lot of money even if it was less than he hoped, while the buyers were only doing what anybody would gladly do if they knew how: finding out the lowest offer they could get away with.

Once or twice I have been asked to do things that were definitely unethical, if not illegal. I was once hired by an aircraft company that gave me few details until I had accepted, subject to my usual conditions, and received my advance. There have been several well-publicized instances of aircraft companies bribing senior members of governments and even, it is said, a member of a royal family in their eagerness for business. It soon became clear that this particular company was thinking of something even more contemptible than bribery – and expecting me to do it for them.

It was hoping to sell one of its products to an African country, whose representative was rather smarter than it had bargained for. He had done his homework thoroughly, and concluded that the aeroplane in question was quite unsuitable. The salesman knew this, and wanted me to change the African's mind for him – forcibly. I replied that this was the kind of thing my powers would not allow me to do, and that was the end of that assignment.

A word of warning to anybody with psychic gifts who may be tempted to use them in order to do things that should not be done: your powers are not entirely your own, and if you disobey what seems to be a natural law, you may be tried and punished sooner than you think. I learned that lesson after my night at the roulette table in London.

My attitude towards the use of psychic powers is the same as it is towards the inventions. Either can be used for defence, or for espionage, which is an essential part of any defence system, since without adequate intelligence there can be no secure defence. Neither can be used for offence.

Some of my inventions come into my mind spontaneously, often during my daily run. Some, however, are born in other ways. They can result from suggestions made by others, who may not take them seriously themselves. Here is a recent example of how a potentially useful invention can come about:

In May 1985, Meir was staying in my London apartment on a visit, and on 26 May I invited a dozen of my friends round for dinner. My guests included a Member of Parliament, Clement Freud, and my co-author Guy Play-fair. The subject of chemical warfare came up and somebody, I think it was Guy, suggested that there should be a form of chemical 'peacefare' involving the use of pheromones, or biologically active chemical substances. There had been a radio programme a few days previously on possible uses of airborne pheromones, and the speaker, a scientist named Dr Bill Fletcher, had suggested they might be used to control potentially violent crowds.

Clement Freud liked the idea. It would come in useful in the House of Commons, he said with a chuckle. Neither he nor most of my other guests seemed to take the idea very seriously, and the conversation moved on to another subject.

Meir, whose English is not perfect, was not laughing,

and nor was I. Later that evening, I had a few words with him in Hebrew and asked him to get to work right away. Afterwards, Guy gave me more details of the broadcast, which fortunately he had taped.

According to Dr Fletcher, pheromones are known to play an important part in animal life. They cause ants to scatter in the face of danger, and bees to muster for an attack on an enemy. Even trees communicate by means of them, sending out chemical messages that warn of an invading virus. They affect human beings in a number of ways.

It was possible, Dr Fletcher said, that pheromones of human origin might have helped create the atmosphere at the Hitler rallies, at which a single emotion came to dominate the minds of huge crowds. It was also possible, he added, that there might be a chemical component as well as a social one to the crowd violence that was becoming such a problem in English football games, where it had already led to serious incidents. Yet even he did not seem to take his ideas very seriously, and he ended his talk by suggesting the search for a pheromone that would make men and women more sexually attractive to each other.

On the evening of 29 May, just three days after my party, English and Italian football teams met at the Heysel Stadium in Brussels. Before the game even started, there was an outbreak of senseless violence on a scale never seen before even in a crowd of English 'football support-ers'. A large group of young people went on the rampage, and as a result of their blind stampede thirty-eight people died, most of them Italians.

In all the discussion that followed this horrendous incident, there were plenty of suggestions on ways of stricter control of potential hooligans, and steps were taken to ban English spectators from attending any games abroad. Less attention was paid to possible causes of such crowd behaviour.

Perhaps Meir and I were responding to our Israeli conditioning – to look closely at anything at all that might help improve defence and security, however crazy it might sound. He and I are now looking very closely into the biologically active human pheromones, and ways of temporarily suppressing them.

As for Dr Fletcher's reference to chemicals that do something for the sex life, this is something I have been working on for some time. Now that the active ingredient of musk has been isolated and synthesized, it is no longer necessary to kill animals in order to obtain it, and it may be that an aerosol-borne aphrodisiac is on the way at last.

On the commercial side, I have created a new collection of cosmetics, colognes and perfumes which in my opinion have a fantastic scent and hopefully attract both sexes, and which will be available to the public soon.

Not all my inventions are as complicated as those I have mentioned. A recent one is a pair of sun-glasses that enable you to see out of the back of your head. Well, not literally, but when you wear them you can see who or what is behind you. I originally thought of these 'spy sun-glasses' as useful for women who are afraid of being followed by strange men, though they might also come in useful for espionage purposes.

Then there is my line of games and toys for children and adults being manufactured, marketed and distributed by Matchbox Toys. The first three are: 'Uri Geller's Strike!', which gives players the chance to win 'millions' in gold bars, or just a collection of my bent spoons, by discovering treasure and minerals hidden in the map of

Europe; 'Spoon Bender', a game which tests your guessing skills; and 'Blow Your Mind', a mind-boggling memory game.

I have also begun to think of ways in which computers can be used in psychic experiments, both for home entertainment and more serious purposes. These are based on my own experience of many years as a somewhat unconventional computer 'operator', which I will tell you about in more detail in the following chapter.

I never know which of the many ideas that tend to come to me during my daily run are going to work in practice. That is for Meir to decide. My job is to capture whatever comes into my mind and pass it on to him.

I do not want to give the impression that I am a natural genius who simply waits for inspiration to descend from the blue. Inventing and creating are not all inspiration; an inventor has to have a reason for wanting to find new ways of doing things, and a good knowledge of the need for new discoveries in the area in question. All my successful inventions have come about as the result of a good deal of thought beforehand about the genuine necessity for something or other; whether serious, like a defence system, or less serious, like a perfume that makes you sexy, or toys and games. There are two or three areas that I have been thinking about a good deal recently.

One is the ocean. It has always seemed strange to me that we have probed so far into outer space and landed men on the moon, yet we still know very little about three-quarters of the surface of our own planet, and the mass of water that covers it. The recent rapid growth of the offshore oil industry gives some idea of what should be possible in the fields of marine agriculture and mining of precious minerals once the formidable technical problems have been overcome. Did you know, for example, that the sea is full of gold? Not only the sea floor, but the water itself? In some parts of the world, such as off the coast of Brazil, you can actually see it with your own eyes. Yet there is still no economically feasible way of getting it out. Some day, there will be.

Some day, we will also invent ways of making the sea itself work for us, by harnessing the tremendous natural power of its waves and tides. We will follow the lead the Japanese have taken in harvesting the crops that grow naturally and abundantly in sea-water, such as the many varieties of kelps and seaweeds that are a standard part of their daily diet. We will learn to develop the surface of the sea, instead of destroying more and more of our landscape, to make way for factories and airports that could be anchored off our coastlines, where they would interfere with the environment to a far lesser extent than some of them do today.

Another subject in which I have a special interest, and have already invested money, is that of medical technology. I have never gone in for any form of psychic healing myself, for several reasons, chiefly because the force involved is too erratic and unpredictable. I have always been very reluctant to use it on anything living.

The nearest I have come to influencing living things is making seeds germinate, which I have done twice on television recently: on the BBC children's programme *Roland Rat* (4 October 1986) and the West German show hosted by Thomas Gottschalk and watched by seventeen million people (10 January 1987).

As with so many other things I have done, the original idea was not mine. It came from the astronaut Edgar Mitchell, shortly after we first met in 1972. We were sitting and chatting with Dr Wilbur Franklin, when Mitchell suddenly produced a seed and asked me if I could make it germinate while he held it in his own hand. As you can see in the photograph, I just stared at his hand and concentrated on making the seed sprout.

When it did, Mitchell and Franklin were delighted, but I was not. In fact, the experience scared me stiff. I felt I had been tampering with life, something I should not do, and I tried to tuck it away in the back of my mind. I did not try anything of this kind again for more than ten years, until my visit to Japan described in the following chapter.

I have often been told that if I can make a seed grow much faster than normal, I should also be able to heal people by speeding up natural regenerative processes. This may be so, and I have recently been in touch with some medical researchers who are anxious to have me do some experiments of this kind, although I do not feel I am yet quite ready for them. One day, I hope I will be.

I once saw a photograph in a magazine of a little Korean eating-place in France called Restaurant Uri. I cut it out and framed it, to remind myself of another of my long-term plans: for a chain of 'fast health food' bars where people can enjoy some real nutrition instead of junk. Having seen what a change in eating habits did for me, I would like to encourage others to find out what it could do for them.

I met two people, Craig Sams and George Schrenzel, who are already in the health foods field. Together we are creating a range of healthy foods that I enjoy eating myself which will sell under the label 'Truly Healthy by Uri'. The range will be produced to the highest standards with no artificial ingredients, animal products, added sugar, or preservatives and will be marketed worldwide.

For the present, I will continue to research for beneficial ideas, and my team will continue to look for ways of making them work. It may be that only one out of ten proves to be successful. Behind every successful creation there are any number of failures, and this explains why I may seem to be jumping on so many different bandwagons.

# 8

## Computers and Scientists

There are a good many people scattered around the world, from California, Israel and Japan to England, Switzerland and Germany, who are probably hoping that I will never get near their computers again. I shall now explain why they may be feeling this way, and I will begin with an independent eye-witness account of one of my recent encounters with a piece of modern technology.

In March 1985, I went to see my Swiss lawyer, Dr Ulrich Kohli. In addition to being an attorney-at-law and owner of the Zürich law firm Dr Kohli and Partners, he is a lieutenant-colonel in the Swiss Army, where he is second-in-command of a tank regiment. In his early forties, he takes professional care of a demanding and high-standing international clientele in corporate, financial, contract and private investment matters. He is married, and has three children.

In the middle of a general conversation, he said, 'I heard so much about how you can affect computer discs.'

'Oh, sure,' I replied casually, although it was not something I was in the habit of demonstrating. So Dr Kohli asked me to show him what I could do, and later he kindly wrote out his own version of what happened. He entitled it 'The day I got goose-pimples', and began with a summary of our ten-year business relationship:

I met Uri Geller unexpectedly in 1976, and it became clear at our first meeting that we would become good friends. I felt somehow that our minds were in a state of communication, and on several subsequent occasions we have simultaneously thought of the same project or course of action, even when we were miles apart.

One evening in 1976 we went to the Kronenhalle restaurant in Zürich for dinner. There were about seven of us around the nicely-decorated table. The management knew that Uri Geller was coming, and we had the full attention of all the waiters.

During dinner we casually discussed several subjects, and then I happened to ask Uri when he had first discovered that he could bend spoons and keys. He began to tell us about his childhood, explaining that he had found that he could bend metal when still a small boy. At that point, something incredible happened.

Uri was eating some salad, holding a massive silver fork in his left hand. I remember, as clearly as if it were yesterday, that while he was talking about his childhood the fork in his hand suddenly started to bend, very considerably. It was quite startling, and even Uri was baffled. We could not believe it. The evidence, however, was overwhelming. The Kronenhalle's strong silver fork was irreversibly distorted.

The waiters stared at it in utter disbelief, and said they would frame it and hang it on the wall beside the distinguished works of art there. They did so, and the fork is still there today.

Over the following years I had many opportunities to be with Uri, in Switzerland and in New York City. Whenever he came to see me in my office in Zürich and we had new staff in the law firm, he would put on a little private show for them. He would bend keys, coffee spoons or letter-openers, or have one of the girls draw something while he was out of the room. He would come back and ask her to look into his eyes and concentrate hard on the drawing she had just made. We were all thrilled when he managed to read her mind and put an almost identical drawing down on paper.

I knew Uri could do much more than this with his powers, but I did not ask him to put on shows for fun too often. We became involved in many successful enterprises, in which I could really appreciate the extraordinary power of his mind. Now and then, he had to cope with difficult situations or take important decisions for himself or for others. Sometimes there were very tough negotiations with hard-core business people. It was quite fantastic to see how, sooner or later, everything would fall into place the way we thought it should.

Concentrating his mind on something and sending messages – and getting results – is something at which I would say Uri Geller is an absolute master. Most people would not believe the results because their minds do not have an adequate dimension in which to process such phenomena properly.

One of the most exciting experiences I have had with my friend Uri was in March 1985, in my Zürich office. All of us who witnessed it, including myself, were completely taken aback. For my part, I freely admit that I got goose-pimples, and I would not be surprised if the flesh of some of my staff began to creep as well. This is what happened:

The day Uri and Shipi Shtrang came to see me, I happened to have had a short session at my personal computer. Uri asked me to give him a diskette, a floppy disc used for working and writing with personal computers. Due to a slight misunderstanding, I thought he wanted to read the contents of the diskette with his mind, so I gave him one with an important legal text which my secretary [Barbara] had just finished processing. I thought it was a good idea to let him work on a clear and coherent draft of a document.

Uri took the diskette and went next door into my private office, a large well-furnished room with a solid round antique conference table near an old Louis XIII wardrobe which serves as a filing cabinet. The rest of us followed. He sat down at the round table, and the others standing around and watching him were Matthias Meister, one of my associate lawyers, his secretary Beatriz, Barbara and myself.

He carefully slid the diskette into a light plastic folder in front of him on the table. We all held our breath in silence. Then Uri clenched his fists, held one above the other and brought them close to the diskette in its plastic folder.

He never touched the diskette, and there were no instruments or anything else around that might have been hazardous to floppy discs. The plastic folder was supplied by us.

He made some strange twisting movements with his fists directly above the diskette, and I could see him concentrating all his will-power on it. His eyes gleamed and flashed – it was as if lightning were about to strike the table in front of us.

Then he suddenly spoke the word 'Erase'. He repeated it, then leaned back and relaxed. I quickly took the diskette from inside its plastic folder.

'Now try it,' said Uri. 'Whatever was on it has gone.'

We went back into the other room where the computer was. Barbara took the diskette and inserted it in the disc drive of the IBM PC computer. Then she started the program to retrieve the contents of the diskette. The tension rose, and I expected something sensational to happen. We were all staring at the display screen when the message appeared: 'ERASED'!

Barbara was worried, because a full day's work had been saved on that diskette. She had naturally believed me when I told her that Uri just wanted to read its contents. In disbelief and anger, she tried to reload and retrieve the text, but to no avail. It had all gone. The diskette was empty, dead.

Matthias Meister, the computer enthusiast among my attorneys, also tried to retrieve the text and found that Uri had even erased the format on the diskette. A floppy disc must be formatted before it can be used on a personal computer, but the formatted part had been removed as well, making the diskette virgin and temporarily useless.

Uri was very quiet and in complete self-control. I felt that something big had happened, something that could not be explained rationally but that was made to happen in the act of total concentration that is part of Uri's incredible ability to create, to get things done, to make other people act, or to make things move with the powers of his mind.

All of us who witnessed Uri's amazing performance with the diskette had no doubts at all that there was no trickery involved. I have known Uri for several years and I am absolutely sure that what he does is real. Such was the impact on all of us of what he did to that computer diskette that my staff began to wonder what else he could do to computers. Somebody suggested locking up the diskettes every time he came to see us.

Poor Barbara had a hard time. She had to rewrite the whole document that Uri had erased. She, for one, will never forget what Uri Geller is capable of doing.

Another person who may be feeling the same way about my effect on a computer is Avraham Mardor, the general manager of Israel's state-owned telecommunications company. During a trip I made to Israel at the end of 1984, he assembled a large group in his Tel Aviv office, including at least a dozen reporters and one of the few female magicians I have ever met, a lady named Dalia Peled. He inserted a demonstration disc in his Columbia computer, and asked me to do my stuff. The picture that appeared on the screen was of a comic-looking elephant.

Once again, I will let somebody else describe what happened. The witness on this occasion was Yitzhak Oked, a reporter from the *Jerusalem Post*, who had this to say in the issue of the paper of 21 November 1984:

Geller took the disc and put it on a table, looked at it, concentrated on it for about two minutes, and then put it back on the machine.

'I couldn't believe my eyes when the words DISC FAILURE blinked at me,' Geller's challenger stated. 'I've never seen the program state that. Everything on the disc was garbled, not erased but garbled. The main operating filing of this program became non-operational.'

The international manager of the company that had made the computer, who was present, took the disc and announced that he was going to have it examined in an effort to find out what I had done to it. I never heard whether he succeeded or not.

A couple of months later, the *News of the World* arranged for me to visit the headquarters near London of the Wang company. This time, the technicians at the computer centre not only watched me scramble the floppy disc, but joined in themselves. This was how reporter Stuart White described what happened:

Geller waved his hand over the disc, stared intently at it, and got staff to shout 'Erase!' When the disc was put into the computer, the machine refused to display any information.

Mr Cliff Edwards, a computer expert who was present, testified that he had personally tested the disc before I set to work, and found it to be performing perfectly. 'This is absolutely amazing,' he was quoted as saying in the 17 February 1985 issue of the paper. He reckoned the odds against it going wrong when it did were 'astronomical'.

My association with computers of the inexplicably malfunctioning kind dates back to November 1972, and an incident that was to have far-reaching consequences. It was my first day at Stanford Research Institute in California, where I was to take part in the long series of laboratory experiments supervised by Harold Puthoff and Russell Targ. Over the previous weekend, I had already given them an idea of what I could do by bending a heavy copper ring that Hal had made especially for me, and also by breaking his own silver bracelet into three pieces.

SRI International, as it is now called, is quite an impressive place. More than 2,000 people work there on all kinds of top secret defence projects, and the security is tight by any standards. Russell and Hal showed me inside one or two of the buildings, but I saw nothing more exciting than some people making model aeroplanes and another group of technicians working on some costume jewellery. What that might have had to do with the US defence programme was not made clear. There was, of course, a lot more that my hosts could not show me, such as the bank of computers on the floor below theirs that belonged to the Advanced Research Projects Agency (D-ARPA) of the Department of Defense, one of the highest security agencies of its kind in the country.

After my weekend warm-up, I felt on fairly good form. The first thing I was asked to do was to deflect the needle of a chart recorder that was connected to a magnetometer, an instrument that measures very small changes in magnetic fields. I clenched my fist and shouted 'Move!' as I tried to send bursts of energy at the machine, whereupon the chart recorder began to behave very erratically. The needle jumped almost off the paper altogether.

While this was going on, it seemed that something else had begun to behave erratically: one of the D-ARPA computers down below. It had apparently shut down completely, and word began to spread around the building that it was all because of me, especially after I had given a spontaneous demonstration with an ultrasonic scanner, making the image on the screen move up or down on demand. Before long, it seemed that not only were Targ and Puthoff investigating me, but somebody was investigating them. A three-man team of psychologists, one of whom was also an amateur magician, turned up to have a look at me on the orders of the head of D-ARPA himself, US Air Force Colonel Austin Kibler.

The team was headed by George Lawrence, a D-ARPA staff psychologist who was in charge of research funding. The other two were Ray Hyman (a psychologist and amateur magician) and Robert Van de Castle, a respected member of the professional parapsychology community. (I did not know it then,. but he had just come back from the conference of the Parapsychological Association in Edinburgh, all his travel expenses having been paid by D-ARPA. This suggests that the US defence community had a fairly serious interest in psychic matters at that time.)

As you will see, there was a connection between the visit of the men from D-ARPA and my next encounter with a computer. It was certainly not my most successful one to date. In fact I should count it as a failure for two reasons. I did not do quite what I intended to do, and I had no witnesses. So you just have to take my word for it. This is what happened:

One result of my work at SRI was an invitation to the headquarters in New York of *Time* magazine. I already knew one of their reporters, John Wilhelm, quite well, as he had been following me around for some time and had witnessed me in action, as he described in his book *The Search for Superman*. He had told me in advance that everyone in his office had decided I was a fraud – the science writer Leon Jaroff had even made a bet on it before he ever saw me, so I expected a fairly hostile reception.

This was what I was given, and on 12 March 1973 the magazine printed a long story about Targ and Puthoff's research with me, which had not even been published. Hyman had written some notes on what he had observed during his brief visit to SRI (not all of it very well observed, for he described my dark brown eyes as blue). Somehow or other, a copy of these notes, made without Hyman's knowledge or permission, reached the *Time* office before my visit, for one of those present has since admitted in print that he had a copy in his pocket. So did a copy (also unauthorized) of a letter written by Targ and Puthoff to the publisher of *Scientific American*.

Based on this material, and ignoring the weeks of careful first-hand research of one of its own reporters, *Time* ran a story that was not only negative but full of incorrect statements. It alleged, for instance, that I had left Israel 'in disgrace', which I did not, as a reporter from the New York *Post* easily verified by checking with the Israeli Consulate. According to Benjamin Ron, vice-consul for scientific affairs, in a reply dated 19 December 1973, 'there is no official reason to claim that Mr Geller left Israel "in disgrace"'. He also denied the allegation that Israeli scientists had 'duplicated' all my feats.

Leon Jaroff may occasionally get something about me right. In 1984, he told a meeting of sceptics that his 'exposé', of me in 1973 helped 'rocket me to stardom'. I did not appreciate that at the time, as negative articles used to annoy me in those days, though they no longer do.

Early in 1974, I was tipped off by a friend who worked for Time-Life that a cover story on parapsychology was to come out in the issue of *Time* of 4 March. It was very negative, he told me, and included some more defamatory references to me. This time I decided to answer the magazine's charges – in my own way.

A few days before the magazine was due to appear, I went out on the balcony of my apartment on 57th Street, looking in the direction of the Time-Life building at the Rockefeller Center, and began to concentrate as hard as I could. I did not know anything about their printing schedule, or even where the plant was. I simply formed a strong 'blocking' thought in my mind, repeating the words 'Don't let it happen' and visualizing the pages of the magazine rolling off the press with just my name replacing all the copy – column after column of *Uri Geller Uri Geller Uri Geller* . . .

I stood out there for at least half an hour, until I felt I had done all I could. Whenever I put that amount of time and effort into a task, something usually happens even if it is not quite what was planned. What happened on this occasion was duly reported by the publisher of *Time* himself, Ralph P. Davidson, in his regular letter to his readers.

First, he said, there was the small matter of Leon Jaroff's clock-radio. Three mornings in a row over the past week, it had inexplicably failed to go off and wake him up, so that he was late for work. (I am not claiming any responsibility for that, although I do have something of a reputation for interfering with clockwork.)

'Even more bizarre', Mr Davidson went on, 'was the mysterious force that glitched *Time*'s complex, computerized copy-processing system on closing night – at almost the precise moment that our psychic-phenomena story was fed into it. Against astronomical odds, both of the machines that print out *Time*'s copy stopped working simultaneously. No sooner were the spirits exorcised and the machines back in operation than the IBM computer in effect swallowed the entire cover story.'

What had happened, the publisher explained, was that the ultramodern IBM 370/135 had developed a flaw in its programming. This in turn 'sent the copy circulating endlessly through memory loops from which it could not be retrieved'. It took a further thirteen hours and a second overhaul to get it back.

I am sorry about that. I always was synchronicity-prone.


In August 1973, on my second visit to Stanford, I was able to do some constructive work involving a computer, for a change. During the series of experiments that were described in *Nature* (18 October 1974), Puthoff and Targ wanted to see if I could read the 'mind' of a computer as well as a human mind, so they put me in an electrically shielded room about fifty yards down the corridor from their computer room. Targ then drew a picture of a kite on the display unit, while Puthoff stayed near me. I then drew a square with intersecting lines inside it that looked very much like the original, although I received no impressions of a kite, just a shape.

We did two more experiments using the computer. In

the first, the picture was stored in the machine's memory, and not displayed at all. In the second, it was displayed and the screen was then wiped. The targets were a church, and a heart with an arrow through it. I did not do very well with the church, though I reproduced part of its outline accurately, and for the second target I picked up the arrow but put it inside a square suitcase instead of a heart. Of course, all these pictures existed in the mind of the programmer, so I may well have been reading that.

I always do this kind of experiment in the same way, by looking at a screen in my mind and waiting for something to appear on it. If it stays for ten seconds or so, I am very confident that I have picked up the right image. Often, I am less sure, and pick up the right shapes but assemble them wrongly, maybe upside-down or back to front.

Sometimes, it seems that I miss the target for other reasons. In one experiment at Stanford, the drawing was of a figure supposed to represent the devil, holding a trident. I worked longer than usual on this one, and did three different sketches. The theme of all three was the same: the tablet on which Moses wrote the Ten Commandments dominating the globe, and some symbols from the Garden of Eden. I finally added a couple of pitch-forks, but no figure. The scientists guessed correctly that my inability to reproduce this target may have been 'culturally induced'. I had drawn a representation of the forces of light and good instead of those of darkness and evil.

The first time I was specifically asked to interfere with a computer in a major scientific laboratory was in 1974, when I visited the Lawrence Livermore National Laboratory in California, a huge place employing more than 7,000 people, where nine out of ten American nuclear weapons are designed. The quality of both their security and their researchers is very high. Ronald Hawke, the physicist who invited me there, had published several articles in his highly specialized fields.

He asked me to wipe out the pattern on a magnetic program card or at least to alter it, which I did on two out of four attempts, by holding the cards and rubbing them a little. They were then fed into a Hewlett Packard 65 calculator and both were rejected, although they had been accepted just before I had touched them. Dr Hawke wrote an account of this experiment, which is included in *The Geller Papers*.

A couple of years previously, I had been asked to repair an electronic machine by the distinguished space scientist Dr Wernher von Braun, when Edgar Mitchell and Andrija Puharich took me along to see him in his office. He was very sympathetic and open-minded, especially after I had bent his heavy gold ring for him while he held it in his closed fist. (I never touched it.) Then he found that his calculator was not working, so I offered to fix it for him on the spot.

I held it for a short while and gave it back to him. He switched the button to ON and the light came on at once, which it had not done a couple of minutes earlier. A whole lot of numbers came on as well, which did not look right, so I took it back and tried again, ordering the machine to 'work, work, work!' It then worked quite normally, much to Dr von Braun's delight and amazement.

These were not exactly controlled experiments, of course. To date, I have only taken part in one well-controlled encounter with a computer, and for reasons to be explained later I am not particularly interested in repeating it. It took place in Tokyo on 29 March 1983.

I had been engaged by Nippon TV to take part in an hour-long special, for which the producers wanted as much live action as possible in the studio. They asked Professor Toshibumi Sakata, head of the computer department at Tokai University, to help set up something involving a computer that could be filmed. He kindly agreed, but insisted, reasonably enough, that everything must be under his personal control. The experiment would have to be in his own laboratory, where he could monitor everything himself, instead of in the studio. We eventually agreed to do the filming before the live show.

Eldon Byrd, the US Navy scientist with whom I had done some of my first controlled metal-bending experiments back in 1973, was with me on this trip. We had been good friends for ten years, and I knew how keen he was to see me back in a laboratory setting. He came along when we began the filming on 28 March.

When we arrived at the laboratory, a special program had already been inserted in the Hewlett Packard computer and thoroughly tested. It consisted of a coloured pattern that passed continuously from top to bottom of the screen over another fixed pattern that remained in the centre. My specific task was to stop the moving pattern, which was a representation of a picture of Tokyo taken from a satellite. Before we started, I was checked with a large magnetometer probe – as I was every time I left the room and came back.

I went through my usual routine for trying to influence anything, clenching my fist, concentrating hard, and ordering the tape to stop. I had no luck, and tried again. Still the picture went on appearing at the top of the screen and drifting down and off it, only to reappear almost at once. I yelled at it to stop, but that had no effect. I tried passing my hands close to the tape, but that did not work either. I went on trying for hour after hour, until I felt I was not going to get anywhere. It was just not my day.

The patient Japanese agreed to set the whole experiment up again on the following day, and I went back to the hotel feeling very depressed. I had wasted a lot of people's time, and miles of film, and had nothing to show for it.

At first, it seemed that it was going to be the same story when we all started again on 29 March. Again and again, I balled up my fist and shook it at the screen, commanding the image to stop, erase, wipe, just go away . . . Yet it kept on coming back with infuriating regularity, as if mocking me. The session had begun in the early evening, and it must have been well after midnight when I finally slapped my thigh in exasperation and exclaimed, 'It's not going to work!'

As a last resort, I asked Professor Sakata if he could fetch some water – not for me to drink, but to place near the computer. I thought it might help, as I have often noticed that it is easier to produce effects when there is water, preferably running, or metal around. One of the five or six assistants immediately went out and fetched a large kettle of it, which the professor agreed to hold as he stood beside his computer. If he thought he must be looking rather silly, he never showed it.

Eldon was getting as tired as I was. He sat silently through both evenings of this infuriating experiment, in which he had taken no part at all except that of an observer – or so I thought at the time.

Later, however, he told me that when the kettle of water had been brought, he decided to see if he could send me a silent message:

*Uri, if you can do telepathy, get this. I'm getting tired.*

*Do it, get it over with, and let's get the heck out of here!*

Eldon has noticed that psi effects often seem to occur just after the person stops concentrating on making them occur. He calls this the 'disconnect' effect. 'They concentrate and concentrate,' he explained to me, 'and if nothing happens, they give up. And then it occurs.'

If I had thought of this at the time, I might have given up several hours earlier. For he was absolutely right.

The tape was run for yet another control test. I decided it was to be now or never, and sent a final burst of power at the computer screen, shaking my fist at it in defiance. The picture went on slithering down the screen. I turned my back in disgust.

Thank heavens for the patience of the Japanese, especially that of the cameraman. After all those hours of disappointment, he was as fresh as the moment he had started, and he captured the whole scene.

'Uri! You've done it!' somebody yelled. The cameraman pulled out his zoom with a lightning reflex action for a close-up. His film clearly showed the exact moment at which the moving image appeared at the top of the display screen and then froze.

For a moment, I just could not believe what had happened. I had already half-admitted defeat. Yet there was the image, or about 10 per cent of it, absolutely motionless at the top of the screen. Yes, I had done it.

Professor Sakata's face was also frozen. Then I rushed over to him and hugged him, rather to his embarrassment. I felt as if I had just won a top tennis championship.

I went back to my hotel and collapsed, exhausted but delighted at this unexpected turn of events. For Professor Sakata and his assistants, however, there was work to be done, and the next morning Eldon told me what had occurred after I had left the laboratory.

'They ran the tape back,' he said, 'and they kept trying to figure out what had happened. Eventually they analysed it – two bits on the tape had swopped, and the machine, not knowing this, thought there might be something terribly wrong, and if it continued to play this tape, damage might occur. So it shut down.' The technicians had played the tape several more times, but it had always stopped at exactly the same place. 'It was not a tremendous effect, such as erasing a part of the tape,' Eldon said, 'but it was still very effective – it stopped the tape from doing what it was supposed to do.'

Nobody could deny that, for there it was on film for millions of Japanese to see on the evening of 31 March. Whether or not I was really responsible for stopping the tape, the incident put me in good form for the live part of the show. I managed to make a radish seed germinate, and also to perform an unusual feat of metal-bending: with the help of two tiny little children, I rubbed the steel shaft of a golf-club for a while and then held it up in the air, whereupon the thing fell apart in the middle, right on camera. During the show, the host was surprised to find that one of his metal jacket buttons had fallen off, having parted company with the ring secured by the thread. So was I.

Professor Sakata did not have much to say to the reporter from the US Department of Defense newspaper *Pacific Stars and Stripes* (3 April 1983). He admitted that there had been a 'parity error' indicating that the data on the tape had changed. It could have been caused by any number of things, from dirt, static electricity or a magnet to the tape just wearing out, he added. The reporter, Frank Sugano, was rather more positive, describing how I had reproduced the drawing he did behind my back almost exactly, and how he himself had bent his own key

– a heavy steel one – after I had shown him what to do.

Later, Eldon made some interesting comments on the computer experiment in a filmed interview.

After six gruelling hours, it looked like it was not an easy thing to do. However, Uri does not practise how to do this sort of thing. Maybe he should give up sooner? Maybe there's something about starting the process, disconnecting, and it'll happen right then? This intense concentration he puts into things seems almost counter-productive until he gives up.

The fact that he was able to influence these two bits on a magnetic tape doesn't sound like a major event. But very small amounts of current flow through the chips in a computer, and most of the really good so-called PK effects occur at the levels of molecules and atoms. It's probably a quantum mechanical kind of effect.

With the ability to swap two small bits on a computer tape, you can start thinking of other things in that realm, such as making a chip malfunction. Whether or not you can get this long-distance still has to be demonstrated, but in the same room it certainly has been demonstrated.

As I have already described, it was demonstrated again a couple of years later both in Israel and in London, and not long after my demonstration for the technicians at the Wang office, I was given the chance to show an audience of several hundred highly specialized people what I could do to the latest model of IBM personal computer. The occasion was the annual meeting of the Young Presidents Organisation in San Diego, in October 1985.

The YPO is an élite group of business and community leaders from all over the world. It meets every year for a week-long seminar at which prominent members of their respective fields are invited to give 'keynote' addresses on all aspects of contemporary society from world politics to personal development. Keynote speakers for 1985 included former US President Gerald Ford, the West

German 'Green Party' politician Petra Kelly, oil magnate T. Boone Pickens, American Express board chairman James Robinson, well-known personalities such as Henry Kissinger and Alexander Haig, and me. It was my fourth appearance as keynote speaker – all speakers are evaluated by members of their audiences on a points basis, and ever since they gave me the honour of being highest-rated speaker on the course, they have kept inviting me back.

You can talk about anything you like, and the only condition is that you do not read from notes, which I never do anyway. After giving much the same presentation for several years, I decided to try something new in San Diego, and in fact I did three things I had not done before for this audience.

First, I made the needle of a ship's compass move by concentrating on it, with the help of a group of young women from the audience. Then I made a radish seed sprout by holding it in the palm of my hand and rubbing it for a few minutes. Both of these demonstrations were filmed on the closed-circuit television that I had specially requested, so that the whole audience could see what was happening on the large screen beside the stage. The seed was taken from a packet brought along by one of the YPO organizers and handed to me in full view of everybody, and there was enough of a sprout to be clearly visible on the screen.

Then I turned to the bank of computers that had been brought in from the IBM stand in another part of the building. There were several technicians from the company present, and they had all grabbed seats in the front row so that they could keep an eye on their precious hardware – and on me. I took one of the seven or eight floppy discs they had prepared for the occasion and began to work on it much as I had done on the previous occasions I have described. The men from IBM seemed to find the whole affair very amusing, especially when after five or six attempts I was unable to affect the disc. They refused to come on to the stage to insert the disc, so a member of the audience had to do this instead. Later, I learned that they had been ordered by a member of their legal department not to go near me while I was giving my presentation.

After about twenty minutes, I decided to try one more time, with the help of a group of women volunteers. I asked one of them to hold the disc, gave my usual order to 'erase', and then watched the screen as the written message began to appear as before. The audience cheered me on like a crowd at a baseball game, and they were all clearly on my side.

Lights began to blink on the computer, and the message stopped in its tracks, much as it had in Japan. There was loud applause and shouts of 'Hey, you did it!'

I walked over to the row of open-mouthed IBM men. 'Well, say something!' I said.

'It's not there,' was all any of them was prepared to say.

Afterwards, one of the conference organizers told me that the computers had been shipped back to company headquarters in Atlanta for a thorough examination.

Towards the end of the seminar, I was stepping out of the elevator in the hotel just as the YPO chairman, Douglas Glant, was about to escort two of his distinguished guests into it. They were David Kimche, director-general of the Israeli foreign ministry, and Henry Kissinger, who recognized me from our meeting in Mexico.

We were both in a bit of a hurry, and I just gave him a friendly 'Hi!'

When the doors had closed, Kissinger said to Glant,

'Wasn't that Uri Geller? I always believed in his powers.'

On 14 November 1986, I visited the offices of the West German magazine *Hör Zu*, which has a readership of twelve million. There, under the supervision of several computer experts, I was asked to affect a computer tape which I was unable to touch since it was behind a plastic cover. I went through my usual process of concentration, and results came much more quickly than they had in Japan, perhaps because I was not being filmed. On the screen there suddenly appeared the words MELMAGTAPE FAILURE.

A couple of months later, it was the turn of the Munich newspaper *Abendzeitung* to witness 'der Geller-Effekt' at work on its office computer. Again, there were technical experts present, but this time it was a floppy disc that I was asked to erase. As the paper reported in its 12 January 1987 edition, this is what I did.

'Everything in America is on a computer,' the astronaut Edgar Mitchell said to me, rather nervously, after he had seen one of my demonstrations at SRI in 1972. Today, just about everything everywhere is on discs or tapes, and if people like me can interfere with computers then scientists should be doing something about it. They will have to count me out as a guinea-pig, though, for a number of reasons.

Firstly, I reckon I have done my share. When Andrija Puharich came to Israel and helped arrange my first visit to the United States, the very first thing I did was offer my services to scientists. I spent a good deal of the period from 1972 to 1975 shuttling from one laboratory to another, usually for nothing except my expenses, and doing whatever I was asked to do. As a result, Charles Panati was able to compile a 300-page book on 'scientific observations on the paranormal powers of Uri Geller', as *The Geller Papers* was subtitled. There were twenty contributors, of whom four were magicians, and every one of them had something positive to report. (Many of them could have reported a good deal more than they did, but that is another story.)

None of these people won prizes for their work in psychic science. Most of them had to put up with a lot of general aggravation, often from people who had never met them. Hal Puthoff's work was attacked on the grounds that he had taken a course in Scientology several years previously. Russell Targ was written off because his father used to run a bookstore that sold works on astrology! Such was the level of criticism from some of the 'scientific' investigators of claims of the paranormal, who had no difficulty in 'exposing' me as a fraud without ever setting eyes on me.

Secondly, I am not particularly interested in being proved genuine or false. I am not an additive or a preservative or an ingredient. I am just a human being, and I do not need the scientific seal of approval. As a matter of fact I find all the controversy quite enjoyable, and I have never yet sued anybody for libel. I could have done so in the early days, if I had been able to afford it, and I could have won. Now that I can afford all the top libel lawyers I want, anywhere in the world, it seems I have nothing for them to do.

I am interested in people of all kinds, and I am fascinated by the different ways in which they react to what I do. For example, nearly all the pilots, policemen and military people that I have met tend to accept what I show them, as do top people in general. On the other hand, the most sceptical and hostile of all are the people

"*Never mind that. Can you bend the spoon?*"

3 *Omni Magazine*'s comment on the approach of some scientists towards parapsychological research.

you might think would be most interested in exploring the powers of the mind: medical doctors and psychologists. As for magicians, they can fall into one group or the other.

There are things I cannot do, and there are things I will not do, and it is because I have often been asked to do things I did not want to do that a barrier of suspicion has grown up between me and the scientific community. I will not go into much detail here, but I will give some idea of what I mean without mentioning any of the names of the people or the various countries involved.

I was once taken to a marine research institute in a certain coastal city, where I was asked to try experiments in telepathic communication with dolphins. I was given a two-week course on the sounds made by whales and dolphins, and then asked to try to emit these noises and signals in my mind in order to influence the behaviour of dolphins in a tank or in the netted-off area of the ocean nearby. I was quite successful at first, and I soon developed a strong rapport with these beautiful and intelligent animals. I found I could direct them towards certain shapes or colours, or away from the gap in the net. When they were let out of the nets, I could summon them back again. I did this by visualizing what I wanted them to do, rather as I had done in Mexico with the model aeroplane.

At first, I was told nothing about what was really going on at the institute, but gradually I found out. The project in which I had become involved was nicknamed Kamikaze Dolphin, and the animals were being trained to attack ships and submarines with bombs strapped to their heads. Some of the harnesses, I was told, could be adapted to take nuclear warheads, and I learned that some of the animals had even been operated on and devices implanted inside them. Naturally, the kamikaze dolphins would be blown to pieces together with the vessel they had rammed.

I learned later from an independent source (who knew nothing of my involvement) that earlier experiments had used limpet-bombs that the dolphins could attach by suction to the hulls of the target vessels before swimming to safety. This had been abandoned after one smart dolphin, having performed his task perfectly with a dummy bomb, was given a real one, which he promptly dumped on the sea-bed. Good for him.

There were many internal arguments at the institute about this project, and some of the civilian participants dropped out when they discovered what its real purpose was, which is what I also did as soon as I could.

Later, I became involved in some even more alarming experiments, again without having any idea at first of their real nature. These involved people, and their purpose was to study telepathically-induced change of behaviour. It was held at an army base, and the subjects were a mixed bag: some were prisoners, others were brought in from a mental institution, and there were also students earning some extra money. The experiments went on for about two months, during which I was asked to work with three types of subject: awake, asleep and under hypnosis. I never spoke to any of them, though I could observe them from my room next to theirs through a slit in the wall.

Among my tasks were to wake people from sleep, to induce dreams into their minds, to implant certain suggestions that would cause them to change their opinions about things, or make them reveal information. One of the experiments, I learned later, was designed to see if it was possible to interfere from a distance with critical stages in the nuclear-alert sequence. I was told nothing at all about my success rate, although I had the impression that I was much more successful with the sleepers and the hypnotized subjects than with those who were wide awake and alert, although I do not think my powers allow me to invade the privacy of others to a serious extent.

On one occasion at another place I was asked to try a really far-out experiment: to bend several keys at a time, and at a distance. I pointed out that I cannot even bend one key on demand, especially if I do not know where it is. I could not hope to do anything as ambitious as this unless I had some idea what it was all about. Eventually, after being kept in the dark for ten days, I gathered that it had to do with a certain stage in the nuclear-attack sequence, during which officials at missile silos would simply have to insert a key into a lock. I believe that this experiment, like some of the others I am mentioning here, was designed not to see what I could do, but what it might be possible for an enemy to do to the defences of the country concerned.

One very simple experiment that I carried out success-fully involved using me as a human polygraph, to see if a subject was telling the truth or a lie. I was asked to do this on the telephone and by listening to tape recordings, as well as in the presence of the subject. I found that I was only successful when listening to live conversations. This was essentially a defensive type of procedure and not an aggressive one, so I had no resistance to it.

That was not the case when I was taken to a laboratory where there was a stall full of large pigs and was asked to stop the heart of one of them from beating. Although this was before I became a vegetarian, I had no intention of doing anything of the kind, and I just spent four days there doing nothing. Then I left.

Could it be done? I think it could, given sufficient training and practice, though it could never be done by me. If my psychic powers rebelled on that silly gambling venture, I hate to think what would happen – to me, as much as to the victim – if I ever tried to use them for outright aggression.

\* \* \*

While I was being tested at the Lawrence Livermore National Laboratory, one of the security men there, Ron Robertson of the Atomic Energy Commission, wondered if somebody like me could trigger a nuclear explosion or, worse still, a malfunction. 'All it takes is the ability to move one-eighth of an ounce a quarter of an inch at a distance of one foot,' John Wilhelm quoted him as saying. The same writer mentioned reports of unexplained bomb explosions aboard American ships in the Vietnam area, and noted that I had already moved a one-twentieth-of-an-ounce weight on a pan balance at SRI.

Some time later, I was taken to a very high-security installation in another country where somebody with no connection with the Livermore scientists, as far as I know, asked me to do precisely what Mr Robertson had in mind. The nuclear warheads were real, though obviously they were not armed. During the experiment, which was continuously photographed, they were hidden from my view by a screen, so I could not see if I was affecting them or not, and I was never told.

Perhaps you now understand why I have not been 'serving the cause of science' recently. I still have many good friends who are scientists, and one day I would like to do some positive research with them in such areas as healing, or simply studying telepathy and spoon-bending in greater detail. Yet I cannot completely trust the scientific community as a whole. I cannot always be sure what an individual's real motives are, or for whom they are really working, although now and then I have found out from my own sources.

I am not ruling out any further scientific research involving me in the future, but one thing is certain: never again will I have anything to do with government-sponsored research in any country. In my experience, it has always been aggressive and negative in nature.

I have already generated a good deal of scientific research, in two areas. The first is the scientific community itself, where dozens of men and women now take a serious interest in psychic matters, which they never would have done if they had not worked with me or just seen me somewhere. This is not a boast, but what they have told me themselves.

The second is the group that science is supposed to serve: the general public. Millions of people in all six continents have had a little magic – real magic – brought into their lives as a result of something they have seen me do, or read about. Many have immediately found that they have powers just like mine, as I keep telling everybody, and that their lives have been enriched as a result. Again, this is what I have been told.

One way and another, I have done enough scientific research for the time being. As you will see, I have other priorities.

# 9

## *Big Business*

My first contact with the world of big business was in 1973, when I met Sir Val Duncan and was told by him that I could be making what he called 'real money' by applying my talents to the search for oil and precious minerals. Yet it was to be years before I did this, and what led to it was a letter from a Japanese businessman that arrived one morning at the end of 1982. The writer, whom I did not know, wanted me to fly to Tokyo as soon as possible, all expenses paid, for reasons not made very clear. This sounded like a good idea with a touch of mystery to it, so I accepted and off I went.

The Japanese have their own ways of doing business, and at first I was given little idea why I was wanted in Tokyo. My correspondent just wanted me to meet some of his friends, he said, and the first one he introduced me to was Mr Ryoichi Sasakawa.

He is a remarkable man. He made his first fortune out of boat-race betting, then he moved on to building boats and eventually became one of Japan's leading shipbuilders as well as one of its most generous philanthropists. In 1962, he set up the Japan Shipbuilding Industry Foundation, which is now the largest non-governmental contributor to the World Health Organisation, among other things. In the past ten years or so, it has raised more than $20 million for campaigns against leprosy, smallpox, blindness and tropical diseases.

Our meeting was a very formal affair in his office, where I was introduced to the delights of a traditional

Japanese tea ceremony at which no mention was made of anything that Mr Sasakawa or any of his friends might want me to do for them. Later I was invited to join another group for dinner in a restaurant.

Many of the guests were heads of leading corporations, and it soon became clear that this was not to be a purely social occasion. It began very formally, and as we all squatted around the low table and sampled the large variety of artistically prepared bowls and dishes, one of the guests remarked politely that I was not taking any meat. I explained that I was a vegetarian, which I had then been for several years. He seemed to find this very interesting, and later in the evening when the party had become less formal, he steered me into an adjoining room for a private chat.

Before I go into any details of it, I must explain that there is much that I cannot include in this book for the simple reason that I have signed agreements not to do so, and although the names of some of my major employers have been made public by others, they will not be mentioned by me.

Mr D., as I will call him is the head of a multinational company involved in everything from civil engineering to shipping and mining in twelve countries, with an annual turnover of more than one billion dollars.

'I understand that you have been working for mining companies,' he said. I guessed he had seen the article in *Newsweek* that had mentioned one of my early (and unpaid) associations with this field. Then he added, 'I would very much like to find gold in Brazil.'

He went on to give me a concise briefing on a country I already knew quite well, but adding much that was new to me. I was not surprised to learn that he already had interests there in many areas, for there has been a steady stream of immigrants from Japan since the early years of this century, and ties between the two countries are close. The largest Japanese colony in the world is now to be found in Brazil where almost every Japan-based company of any size has some local connection. His was no exception, and though not the largest, it had a considerable stake in one of the world's fastest-growing economies.

Many people wanted to find gold in Brazil, and many already had. In fact, the country's first capital city was named Ouro Prêto, or Black Gold. Yet the problems prospectors have to face there are enormous: Brazil is larger than the whole of Europe, east and west, and more than half of it is covered by the Amazon forest. Innumerable tributaries of that vast river wind their way into seven or eight other countries, and many South Americans have spent lonely and arduous lives roaming the region in search of a pan of gold of marketable quality. Some have found it, but it is still impossible to say what percentage of the country's mineral wealth has been tapped, or even located.

Mr D. was not interested in hacking his way through the forest or scratching around in river-beds here and there. He was thinking of a major exploration, but without a very substantial initial investment he could not decide even where to start looking. In the region he had in mind, everything had to be flown into Manaus and then moved on by river, or by light aircraft if there was a landing strip available. Somebody like me, he thought, could save him a lot of time and money by telling him exactly where to do his test drillings. He mentioned the kind of money he was prepared to put into his venture, and asked if I was interested, without quoting any precise figures. I said I might be, and we agreed to meet again the next time he was in New York, which would be soon.

* * *

He called me from the Hotel Plaza, as promised, and on our second meeting he lost no time in formalities, but got straight to business.

'Now, about our contract,' he said in his careful English. 'Do you have a figure in mind?'

'No, I really don't,' I replied. 'I'll have to think about it.'

'Well, why don't you just come over to Brazil, and I'll give you sixty thousand dollars?' he said. He had already prepared a letter of agreement to that effect. It was, I noticed, written on plain paper, as agreements of this kind almost invariably are in my experience.

I do not like discussing money, preferring to leave it to my lawyers. It was very nice to be offered a five-figure sum for a free trip to a country I already knew and liked, but I did not feel inclined to sell myself cheaply. I knew that I might be able to save the D. Corporation huge sums of money, perhaps many millions of dollars that could have been spent on years of digging or dredging in some very remote areas before enough of the right kind of gold was found to make the enterprise worth while.

'You must let me sleep on it,' I replied, 'and you must make me a higher offer than that.' I was not being greedy. Sixty thousand dollars was a fair sum, but I had earned a good deal more than that on my previous visit to Brazil.

I expected Mr D. to come back with a higher offer, but he took me completely by surprise with his next words. Spoken without the slightest change in his expression, these were: 'Would five hundred thousand dollars be all right?' The bidding had gone up more than eight times in a couple of seconds.

'I will really have to think about it,' I insisted. Mr D. told me he was leaving the next day, but I would not be rushed.

After our meeting, I called my lawyer, whose office was not far from the Plaza. 'Look,' I told him, when I had outlined the situation, 'I'd like to do the job, but over a long period and not just on one quick trip. I reckon I'm worth a million to Mr D., don't you?'

My lawyer knew the value of specialized services better than I did, and he had already signed deals for me in the past worth more than that. 'That's underestimating yourself, Uri,' he replied.

I asked him to get in touch with Mr D. right away, and later that evening he called me back.

'I did what you wanted,' he said. 'I asked for a million, and he agreed to a million, but for a six-year period instead of four, as you suggested. Oh, and there will be another million after that.'

The bidding had certainly risen fast, my fee being now more than thirty times the original offer made only a few hours previously. My lawyer thought it was the best deal I could get in this case. So contracts were exchanged, and a million dollars was punctually paid into my bank account.

We landed in Rio de Janeiro, where a private jet was waiting to take us on to Manaus, via Brasilia, a trip of nearly 2,000 miles. Then we transferred to a small propeller-driven aeroplane and headed for an airstrip that is probably not marked on any map except the one I was given to use in my work. To this day I do not know the name of the place, or even if it had one.

The Amazon forest is the most awe-inspiring sight on earth, especially when seen from a low altitude. You know what a cloud-bank looks like – a great mass of cotton wool filling the whole of the space as far as the horizon in all directions. From a few thousand feet,

Amazonia is one colossal green cloud, with little streams here and there for the tributaries that wind their way into the unexplored areas to either side of the river, which in parts is wider than the English Channel.

As you come in to land, the green cloud becomes a mass of individual trees of all shapes and sizes, each fighting for its share of the sunlight, and making its contribution to the world's oxygen supply. Once on the ground, you are in a strange new world. Your horizon is suddenly restricted to a few yards ahead, where the undergrowth can be so thick that you have to hack your way through it with a stout Brazilian machete, never being quite sure what exotic bird, animal or reptile you might be disturbing.

One day, perhaps, I will go back to look for lost cities and the treasures they are said to contain. On this occasion, however, I was not a tourist. The D. Corporation had not gone to all that trouble and expense just to show me the beauties of the jungle. I had work to do.

Remote sensing, as I practise it, involves very intense concentration over a long period, and it is very tiring, far more so than a lecture or a television show. Before I visit a prospecting area, I study maps I have been given for at least two hours a day, sometimes more. I memorize their main features, so that I will recognize them when I am flying over them later. I do regular spells of map-dowsing, much as Sir Val Duncan taught me to do, but using my bare hands instead of a pendulum and waiting to feel those magnetic sensations on my palms or fingertips. Sometimes these come quickly, sometimes not, but eventually I find myself zeroing in on certain regions which I mark in pencil. I check these over and over again for days or even weeks, to make sure that my impressions remain the same.

When they do, I feel very confident, and mark the areas to be flown over on site for some aerial hand-dowsing, and eventually to be tramped over inch by inch for the 'fine tuning' and the location of exact spots. When they do not, I simply keep going until either the impressions come or I feel that there is nothing to find. I have not yet discovered a way of locating great wealth on demand from the comfort of my sofa at home.

I would love to be able to claim that I am always 100 per cent correct, but I cannot. In fact, it is not possible to rate my success record on a percentage basis. In some of my early laboratory tests, it was very easy; when I was looking for objects concealed in film cans at Stanford, for instance, all the scientists had to do was open the lids of the cans I pointed to and check. In one experiment, I picked the right can out of ten fourteen times in a row, though once or twice I felt no reaction on my hand and did not make any choice. Overall, they reckoned the probability of the result being due to guesswork on my part was about one in a trillion.

Digging up hundreds of square miles of jungle, however, is not quite as easy as opening a row of film cans. It can take millions of man-hours, and tens or hundreds of millions of dollars. It is not surprising that people like Mr D. are prepared to pay me quite a lot of money for telling them where to start digging, or where not to dig.

The D. Corporation eventually examined several of the areas I marked on the maps they gave me, and a number of these are, I hope, now producing gold.

I also did something for this corporation that had nothing to do with prospecting. It had always wanted to get into business in a certain country, but had never succeeded. I happened to know the head of a major development company there, a man who was very interested in psychic matters and has said so publicly. Thanks solely to my efforts, he and Mr D. came together and went on to build a skyscraper in one of the world's leading business centres. A normal broker's fee for a deal of this magnitude would have been a considerable sum, yet I neither asked for nor received anything at all.

In 1985, I was contacted by Peter Sterling, a dynamic young Australian whose mining company, Zanex Ltd of Melbourne, became the first to secure a mining lease in one of the world's most promising areas of precious metal and mineral exploration: the Solomon Islands.

Gold was found there as long ago as 1568, within a year of the discovery of the islands by a Spaniard named Alvaro de Mendaña, who named them after King Solomon. However, it was more than four centuries before major gold production got under way on any of these remote islands, of which the best known is Guadalcanal, some 1,200 miles northeast of Australia. First off the mark was Zanex, which beat competition from several major international corporations to open its first mine on 9 November 1985. In a statement issued to shareholders in October, Sterling announced that 'The company is now combining both conventional prospecting and new exploration technologies in order to locate further mineral resources.'

He went on to report that as a result of advice given to Zanex by me (he mentioned one of my companies, but not my name), Zanex's exploration thrust was being expanded to include a search for diamonds on a previously unexplored island, where Kimberlitic rocks had already been found. One of these, extracted from a site which I indicated on the map, was analysed by scientists from Melbourne University, who reported, 'The sample indicates a high prospectivity of the rocks from that area for diamond-bearing host rocks.' Sterling confirmed this in an interview with the *Financial Times* (18 January 1986), in which it was reported that 'Sterling is well pleased with his investment in Geller' and that initial studies of the rocks were 'very encouraging'.

Immediately after my appearance in San Diego, which I described in the previous chapter, I flew to Guadalcanal to attend the opening ceremony, and also to put in a couple of weeks of very hard work. The island, I found, is not quite what it seems when you read the tourist brochures. It has plenty of beaches and palm trees, but it also has the hottest and stickiest climate I have ever come across and every kind of hostile wild life from poisonous coral snakes to malaria-carrying mosquitoes. I had to take two kinds of pills to protect me from the latter, and twice I nearly trod on what looked very like one of the former on the daily runs which I managed to go for in spite of the heat and the humidity.

The inauguration of the Mavu mine was rather unusual. The tape was cut by Sir Peter Kenilorea, who became the islands' first prime minister when they gained independence from Britain in 1978. He held the scissors in one hand, and a spoon I had just bent for him in the other!

Even doing that had been quite an ordeal for me. For a start, it took some time to find a spoon. It seems that the islanders are reluctant to part with their cutlery. Eventually, somebody produced a handsome heirloom at least a hundred years old, and very solid. I worked on it for at least ten minutes with the sweat running down my back like a waterfall and, mercifully for my reputation, it had begun to bend when I handed it to Sir Peter. By the end of the ceremony, throughout which he held it himself, it had reached one hundred degrees.

My on-site exploration was just as exhausting. We flew over several of the islands, and I indicated a number of areas that are now being closely examined by Zanex's geologists, who were encouraged by the accuracy of my initial long-distance predictions. Peter Sterling told me that I had managed to shorten the odds from about three hundred to one to more like three to one, which was enough reason to justify hiring me. He was also kind enough to give me an open testimonial letter, being the first of my employers to do so. He wrote:

I confirm that Zanex is about to commence exploration in areas identified by you in Solomon Islands. The most interesting area identified to date is on Malaita Island where upon your instructions we are about to commence a search for gold and diamonds. We have already confirmed the presence of Kimberlite which could be diamondiferous in this area. Other areas will be investigated in due course.

While I was there, a plane-load of international investment brokers came out to inspect the mine and assess its prospects. At first, Peter Sterling introduced me as just a friend who happened to be passing through, but by the end of their trip they had found out what I was really up to. We all flew back to Australia together, and during the flight I entertained them with some spoon-bending. I hope they were pleased as much by this as by the fact that Zanex shares had risen by more than 100 per cent in the few months since I had begun working for the company.

I had also provided some impromptu in-flight entertainment on my way to the islands, on the internal route from Sydney to Brisbane. It came about in this way.

One of the stewardesses brought me a note from a man named John Howard, asking if I could supply his three children with a signed photograph of me as a souvenir of one of my television shows they had seen and enjoyed. Peter Sterling told me he was a well-known Australian politician, so I had the girl ask if he would like to meet me. We duly met, and I bent a spoon for him in the usual way, allowing him to hold it himself for the last part of the process. Then he asked, 'What do you feel about me?'

'I have a feeling you will be prime minister of Australia one day,' I answered at once. Peter then told me that Mr Howard had just been elected Leader of the Opposition, and could very well be the next leader of his country.

Perhaps I should mention at this point that there is no need for people to get nervous, as they occasionally do, when I start bending things during flights. I have flown millions of miles all over the world for fifteen years, and have never done any damage to any of the aeroplanes. The only uncomfortable moment I have ever had on a commercial flight was when I flew to Budapest in 1979 to visit my Hungarian relatives. As we approached Ferihegy Airport, the pilot announced that pieces of rubber from the tyres of our undercarriage had been found on the runway at Munich from which we had taken off. So we returned to Munich, where the pilot made low passes over the control tower, while experts peered through binoculars and verified that parts of our tyres were indeed missing. The runway was then sprayed with foam and we were ordered to prepare for a crash-landing. This was a most alarming prospect, but mercifully our landing proved to be a perfectly normal one, and we later changed planes and arrived in Budapest. This kind of thing can be expected to happen to anybody who flies as much as I do, so there is no need to panic just because I am on board!

During my stay on Guadalcanal, I had a pleasant surprise. I went into the modest bookstore in Honiara, its capital, to look for a book about the island's role in the Second World War. (There are still a number of wrecks from this period off its coast, and several crashed warplanes on show where they came down, vivid reminders of the fierce battles fought in this now peaceful spot.)

'This is one bookstore where they won't have anything about me,' I said to Shipi as we went in. Like any author, I instinctively scan shelves for my own books.

The first book I picked up was called *Strange But True – The World's Weirdest Newspaper Stories*. That sounded interesting, so I bought it, only to find my picture on the frontispiece! The weird story that had earned my place in the book was the one about the Swedish woman whose intra-uterine device had bent while she had been watching me on television.

Another story that must have struck some Australians as fairly weird appeared a couple of weeks after the opening of the Zanex mine in several papers, including the *Sydney Morning Herald*, under the headline: MINING GROUP SIGNS GELLER IN BID TO BEND A LITTLE CASH THEIR WAY.

In fairness to Zanex, I should point out that as much of its initial success was due to its directors' conventional skills as to my less conventional ones. They went to far more trouble than their competitors to get to know the islands and their inhabitants, and to understand the deep-rooted landowning traditions that had prevented earlier exploration of natural resources in the region. By treating the villagers as partners, they won their confidence and beat at least eight other companies to the starting-line of the new Solomon Islands gold rush. Their use of my services was just one of several departures from traditional methods of mining companies, and I am glad to say that they paid off.

Just when I had decided to enter semi-retirement on my earnings from the oil and mineral businesses, I received a telephone call from Tony Hammond, a mining engineer who had followed my career since the early seventies and totally accepted my powers. He believed that my potential for locating oil and minerals had only just begun, and after introducing me to his colleague Dennis Thomas, who owns Hunter Personnel (an international placement and recruitment consultancy with thousands of geologists and engineers on its books and computers), the idea of Uri Geller Associates was born.

The concept was very simple: by combining my powers with the knowledge and experience of many of the world's leading geologists and engineers, a unique combination of conventional and unconventional talents would be harnessed to investigate, explore and locate oil fields and mineral deposits worldwide.

As the end of the twentieth century approaches, increasing global concern is being focused on the finite natural resources of our planet and on the ability to sustain life as we know it. Yet vast areas of the earth remain unexplored, as I mentioned in Chapter Seven, and countless oil and mineral deposits remain undiscovered.

There are many reasons why exploration programmes are limited – or non-existent – in our modern age. Exploration costs can be prohibitive in many parts of the world where there are considerable logistical problems to overcome and the probability of making a major discovery is very low. Our team, I believe, can significantly reduce these problems and can undertake projects anywhere in the world, whether under the sea or on land and including the most inhospitable deserts, mountains and jungles.

As soon as a project is commissioned, UGA professional staff undertake a preliminary review of the area, and all relevant historical, geological and mining information is researched, reviewed and discussed before my work programme is prepared. Assistance from the client is welcome throughout the programme, and is particularly appreciated in the initial stages. Our services are especially aimed at organizations which are responsible for large exploration areas, including national and provincial governments, ministers in charge of fuel or mineral development, organizations responsible for national resources and surveys, and public or private companies in exploration target areas.

I will end this chapter with an account of one of my most unusual assignments, which was carried out in 1984 and has not been made public until now. I was in Japan, where I had bought a small holiday house overlooking Mount Fuji and was enjoying a short rest in it when I received a cryptic telephone call from a certain Mr C. W. Lee. He was speaking from Seoul, the capital of South Korea.

He asked if I would like to take part in a live television show for the Korean Broadcasting System similar to the one I had done for Nippon TV in 1983. The fee on offer was, he said, the largest ever made by the government-controlled KBS.

I like to see as much of the world as I can, and Seoul is only a couple of hours' flight from Tokyo, so I accepted with pleasure. Mr Lee then added that I was wanted there for something other than a television show, but gave me no details. I had the impression that there were a couple of strings attached to what sounded like a very generous offer.

I duly turned up in Seoul, where Mr Lee came to meet me. He was not a television executive himself, I learned. According to his calling card, he was the founder and president of the World Religious Unification Mission, whose organization, I should explain, has no connection with the movement founded by his compatriot Sun Myung Moon. It soon became clear that he was well connected with the authorities of his country. There was something they would like me to do for them, he said. 'If you succeed, you will be given millions. The sky is the limit.'

I was intrigued, as I was when I received another of his brief telephone calls at my hotel. All this one consisted of was: 'Some men are coming to see you.'

It was not quite like the military invasion that had been sprung on me in Mexico back in 1975, but it was clearly a high-level delegation. Two of the men were in Korean Army uniform, and they all looked extremely business-like. One of them carried a large package, and when we had introduced ourselves he undid it and spread a number of maps on the table. Then he gave me a briefing on the state of affairs between South and North Korea.

For more than thirty years since the end of the Korean War in 1953, he began, relations between the two had been far from peaceful. North Korea's Moscow-trained premier Kim Il Sung had never made a secret of his intention to 'reunite' the two parts of the peninsula, and his regime had kept up a constant barrage of propaganda to that effect. Propaganda the Southerners could live with, but what was really worrying them was the knowl-edge that the North had made unmistakable preparations for a full-scale invasion.

I listened politely, wondering what on earth he expected me to do about that. He very soon told me.

It was known, my military guest went on, that a great many tunnels had been bored deep down beneath the DMZ – the demilitarized zone 150 miles long that sepa-rated the two countries. Three such tunnels had already been discovered, an American naval officer, Commander Robert M. Ballinger, having been killed in an explosion that followed the location of one of them in 1974. Presumably it had been booby-trapped.

The third tunnel had been found in 1978 after a tip-off from a defector. Yet despite massive and costly efforts over the past five years by special tunnel-detecting patrols, no more had been found. There were many difficulties: the tunnels were very deep and narrow, and their location was made especially hazardous because the ends had been sealed off, to be blasted open when the time came for the invading hordes from the North to rush out of the ground and attack the South.

'This matter is so important to us,' one of the officers told me, 'that if you can help us find even one of these tunnels, you will become a national hero. You will be awarded the highest honour of the Republic of Korea, and you will be given ten million dollars.'

Before I had time to recover from my surprise, and luckily before I had replied 'Keep the honours, just give me the money', as I thought of doing, the officer pulled out a sheet of paper and presented it to me. Headed 'Time Schedule', it read as follows:

|       |           |                    |
|-------|-----------|--------------------|
| 18 Sep. | 0900–1000 | Visiting at MND   |
|       | 1000–1100 | Arrival at (——)    |
|       | 1100–1300 | Detection Activity |
|       | 1300–1400 | Lunch              |
|       | 1400–1600 | Detection Activity |

Similar schedules had been prepared for the following two days, in which I was to visit three locations, the names of which I will not mention here. I was then to attend a final meeting at the Ministry of National Defence (MND).

What could I do? I had accepted the KBS television contract in the knowledge that there were strings attached, but I never expected these to lead me to one of the hottest spots in the Cold War, a zone that for all its 'demilitarized' status might well be the site of a major conflict at any time, either by mistake or on purpose.

It was too late to worry about that, however, for 'detection activity' had already been arranged, and my part in it was a high-level order rather than an offer. I would hardly be human if I failed to respond to the mention of $10 million, especially if I could be of some use to a country of which I had already become fond.

Before my trip to the DMZ, my military hosts had decided to test me. They drove me out of Seoul for an hour or so, and after bumping along a very rough road we drew up in front of a wretched-looking array of tin huts. They were nothing much to look at, but the smell was something else. It was a solid stench that nearly knocked me flat. As I was wondering what on earth was going on, one of the soldiers with me politely explained that we were at a chicken farm. Hence the smell. He then told me what we were there for.

The farm, he said, was located above a disused silver mine in which there were six tunnels, the exact locations of which were known. All I had to do was mark them on the ground, with a can of spray-paint which a man in civilian clothes handed to me. He was, I understand, from the Korean Agency for National Security Planning.

Under normal circumstances, I would not have accepted a challenge of this kind, since I do not feel obliged to prove to anybody what I can do. As I have said, I have done enough scientific experiments already. This was different, though. The Koreans had a real problem, and it was reasonable for them to make sure it was worth their while asking me to help solve it, especially with that eight-figure sum on offer. So I set to work, despite the appalling conditions. An overpowering smell of chicken droppings does not exactly enhance the psychic sensibilities, but I began to walk up and down in my usual way, palms outstretched and waiting for that magnetic push that tells me I am zeroing in on the target.

After two hours of very unpleasant work, I felt I could do no more. I sprayed paint where I believed the tunnels were, but I did not think I had been very successful. All I could think about was getting away and breathing fresh air again. The man from the ANSP, however, looked very pleased indeed. He showed me a map, on which six tunnels were marked, and told me that I had successfully indicated the positions of two of them. This is the only occasion outside a laboratory on which I have had immediate feedback in a test of this kind, and it was encouraging, especially in view of the opposition from the chickens.

I had evidently passed my test, for the following day I attended my formal briefing at the Ministry of National Defence and immediately began some 'detection activity' for real. We took off in a helicopter from a military base, accompanied by the US Army lieutenant-colonel in command of the EUSA Tunnel Neutralisation Team. He did not seem at all surprised to meet me on a mission of this kind; in fact he knew a good deal about me, especially the work I had done at Stanford.

We flew over the splendid stadium built for the 1988 Olympic Games and headed north. In a very short time we were in a different world, one I had hoped I would never see again after my military service in the Israeli Army: a war zone. Nobody was shooting at me this time, to be sure, but it was made clear to me that somebody might do just that at any moment. For this reason I had been ordered to wear combat uniform.

As we approached the border, there was a lively argument between the American and the Korean pilot, who was reluctant to fly so close to North Korean air space. It was the nearest he had ever been to it, he said, and he must have been aware of the many incidents in which the Northerners had opened fire on anything flying from the South, and had generally brought it down.

For three days we flew and drove all over the DMZ, frequently landing or stopping so that I could continue my prospecting on foot. I often went close enough to the border to see binoculars peering at me and mounted machine-guns pointing in my direction. After dark, the searchlights would blaze and the huge megaphones would constantly break out in torrents of angry propaganda. The atmosphere of tension and hatred began to depress me.

Each night, I was returned safely to my luxury hotel in Seoul, where there was everything available for guests' comfort. Yet I found it difficult to relax and to tear my mind away from that dreadful barrier just a short hop away. Why was this kind of thing still necessary in 1983, I wondered? Why do people still have to divide themselves into groups and spend so much effort in trying to annihilate each other?

It was as difficult to work in such an atmosphere as it had been tramping over the chicken droppings and the dead rats at my 'testing site'. All the same, I received some impressions, and marked the maps accordingly. At my final meeting a Korean major-general invited me to return after the winter to continue the search for tunnels. This was something I definitely did not feel like doing, for a number of reasons. The most practical of these was that from a security point of view there was not much point in locating one or two tunnels. To guarantee a solution to the threat they presented, you had to find them all.

I tactfully steered the discussion towards an idea of my own. The best way to locate those tunnels, I said, would be from a defector. Hundreds of people must have worked on them, and one person was enough to reveal the whereabouts of at least one tunnel.

This bright idea was greeted with typical Korean politeness, but I was soon told that very few defectors ever made it across that heavily guarded border. Not alive, anyway. In an attempt to get myself off the hook, I hinted that I might be able to use my powers to persuade somebody to come over. If they did not believe me, they did not show it. I hope I managed not to sound as if I did not really believe it either.

After the meeting, a two-star general took me aside and said, earnestly and conspiratorially, 'Uri, forget the tunnels for a moment . . . When am I going to get promoted to three stars?'

I heard nothing more from Korea until 30 July 1985, when an item in the *International Herald Tribune* caught my eye. There had, it seems, been a shooting incident near the 'truce village' of Panmunjom 'when a Russian defected while on a sight-seeing tour of the truce village'. Another press report a few days later described the Russian as a 'student' but gave few further details.

In due course, I learned from a source in Seoul that the 'student' was a foreign service trainee named Vasily Yakovlevich Matuzok, aged twenty-three, who was assigned to the Soviet Embassy in Pyongyang. He had been taking a look round the truce village and had suddenly made a dash across the demarcation line. The North Korean guards immediately opened fire on him, and in the ensuing crossfire three North Koreans and one South Korean were killed and there were four wounded, including an American. The incident took place on 23 November 1984, a couple of months after my visit.

What Mr Matuzok may have had to tell my friends in the Korean Ministry of National Defence I do not know. All I know for certain is that nobody has yet sent me a cheque for $10 million.

# 10

## *Gellermania and After*

On 10 September 1983, the West German newspaper *Bild* ran a headline on its front page in letters an inch high: NEUES URI-GELLER-FIEBER. 1000 GABELN KRUMM.

It went on to give details of the 'new Uri Geller fever' during which 'a thousand forks twisted'. The story began: 'Has your best dinner service become bent since Thursday evening? Uri Geller has been on German television again . . .'

The first outbreak of what the British press called Gellermania had been on my visit to West Germany early in 1972, before my arrival in the USA. Then, I had been given the credit for performing a number of unusual feats, such as bringing a department store escalator to a halt and stopping a cable car in mid-air. In January 1974 there had been another epidemic of Geller fever when I appeared on Wim Thoelke's *Drei Mal Neun* television show and caused all kinds of odd things to happen in viewers' homes, as I had done a couple of months earlier in London and was eventually to do in at least twenty other countries.

The epidemic was said to have been eradicated as early as 1978, when a writer in the *New Scientist* (6 April 1978), basing his claim on some evidence which will be mentioned later, announced that 'the Geller myth finally disintegrates'.

It seems to have put itself together again, however. Although my show business career was diverted in a number of directions from 1975 onwards, as I have already described, it flourishes intact to this day. I may have chosen to make fewer public appearances over the past five or six years, but to judge from my files of press cuttings, they have all proved as infectious as my early ones.

My 1983 appearance on the Thomas Gottschalk Show on West German TV was fairly typical. A student in Heilbronn held her mother's wrist-watch in front of her television screen while I was appearing on it, whereupon the watch began ticking after thirteen years of total paralysis. In Freiburg, an even older watch came back to life when held by its owner at my suggestion. He had been wearing it when he was wounded in a battle against Soviet troops during the Second World War, and he had kept it ever since as a lucky charm. Now it was ticking for the first time in forty years.

There was one German, however, who probably wished he had missed my show. This was the Berliner who went along to the police to complain that I had bent fifty-one of his knives and forks – and his birdcage. 'I want compensation,' he said.

There is no need for me to appear on television or on a stage to produce results like these. A public appeal through a newspaper has much the same effect, as I have shown more times than I can remember. For example, in its issue dated 14 April 1981, the New York *Star* invited its readers to 'Find out if you share the amazing powers of the most baffling man in the world'. It would have been slightly more accurate to have said 'Find out that your own powers are just the same as Uri Geller's'. For this is true. My powers are no more amazing than anybody else's. I simply use them more, and whenever I can I show others how to use them too.

Readers were invited to test their powers in three ways. First, they were to place any broken watches, clocks or battery-driven appliances on top of the picture of me in the newspapers, and concentrate on them for fifteen minutes beginning at 3 P.M. on the following Sunday. They could also put some keys or cutlery beside them if they liked. At the same time, they should hold a pencil and try to draw in the coupon provided by the paper the telepathic image I would be projecting to them.

'It will be your mind and your power of concentration that will create the energy to make things happen,' I told the *Star* readers. I also told them where I would be at the appointed time: in a commercial jet flying at 30,000 feet from coast to coast. Here is a typical response from a reader:

My family thought I was crazy, because they don't believe in psychic power. So I went upstairs to my bedroom to do the experiment. I put two wrist-watches that hadn't worked for some time and a spoon on Uri's picture. While I was watching, one watch started ticking and the hands of the other started moving after my 15-minute experiment had finished. I looked at the spoon and it had bent in the middle. Now my family doesn't know what to think.

A group in Pennsylvania put no less than fifteen broken watches on my picture, and managed to get four of them going, bending a couple of spoons and breaking a fork in half at the same time. A lady from Texas revived her cuckoo clock, while a California reader's electric grandfather clock started up although it was not plugged in. In North Carolina, a seventy-year-old lady restarted six watches out of eleven, one of which had been out of action for thirty-five years.

One or two readers did particularly well: a psychologist

4 As this 1975 cartoon shows, Uri Geller had become a
household name in the United States

from Florida reported that the hands of all eleven of her
old watches moved during the experiment, and a key bent
at the same time. One family psychically repaired a radio,
a tape recorder and a clock, all at once. Another fixed
four watches, an illuminated make-up mirror and a
toaster.

The newspaper followed up this nationwide experiment
by inviting three readers from the New York and New
Jersey areas to come along to their office to meet me and
try their skills on the spoons in front of witnesses. All
three managed to bend their spoons into near right angles,
and reporter Toni Reinhold testified that I had not
handled any of the cutlery, which was provided by the
newspaper. Two of the spoons went on bending by
themselves after they had been put down on the table.

Mrs Bonnie Harnden gave us an interesting description
of her impressions during the first experiment:

I felt a surge of energy and tingling that came from my head
down through my arms and body and then I just knew I would
do it. The bowl of the spoon I was holding actually folded up. I
just sat there looking at it – I couldn't believe that it had actually
happened.

The telepathy part of the experiment produced equally interesting results. The picture I drew up in the sky was of a simple sailing boat, with a mast and triangular sail. Out of 855 readers who sent their drawings in, sixty-four had drawn a boat, while a total of 195 drew parts of boats or something related to them. A sixteen-year-old girl from La Miranda, California, produced an almost exact replica of my drawing, and had this to say about how she did it:

I was in the kitchen alone and opened the paper to Geller's picture. I was just clearing my mind when the boat popped into it. I didn't believe it at first. It took a couple of days for me to send in the drawing. The image of a boat just kept coming back to me, so I sent it in.

My most recent mass experiment of this kind was carried out in England, with the help of readers of the *News of the World*. They were invited to 'tune in' at 3.30 P.M. on 3 February 1985 with their cutlery and broken possessions in front of them as they concentrated on my picture. On this occasion, instead of trying to transmit a drawing, I was to be at a well-known landmark and readers were asked to say where they thought this was.

The place I chose was Stonehenge, the ancient stone circle thought by many to have been built by Druids 3,000 years ago. It is probably the best-known landmark in England after Big Ben, so perhaps it was not so surprising that 1,500 readers guessed correctly. However, reporter Stuart White and I were in for a surprise of our own. Here is how he described it in his paper on 10 February:

The Geller Effect started at Stonehenge itself. As Geller began to concentrate at precisely 3.30, three girls walked along the perimeter fence.

One, 25-year-old Donna Smith . . . told me: 'I had a feeling Uri would be here.'

Holding out her *News of the World*, she showed me two broken watches placed on Geller's picture. Donna said: 'I thought I'd try this, but as you can see, it's not working.' A minute later she cried out: 'Oh my God, I don't believe it, it's not possible.'

Both her watches had started ticking. She assured us they had been out of order for 'ages'.

Similar repairs were being carried out all over Britain. One rather unusual one took place in a train, the passenger being the well-known disc jockey Anne Nightingale. In her version of events, given to Stuart White before my secret location was revealed, she began by saying, 'I feel sure Uri was at Stonehenge.' She went on:

I have an old watch which, even after being repaired, would only go if you wound it up fully and shook it a lot. But after a couple of hours it would stop.

I read the *News of the World* and decided to do the experiment. The watch was fully wound but wasn't going when I got on the train. I checked the time with the man sitting opposite in the buffet car and when he said it was exactly 3.30, I concentrated.

I thought about Uri's picture, holding the watch, and suddenly it started. I'm looking forward to telling my listeners this Sunday that the watch is still keeping perfect time. It's incredible.

Things do go wrong now and then during experiments of this kind. Mr and Mrs Holt, from Hyde, Cheshire, reported success with some knife-bending, but unfortunately at the same time their washing machine flooded and water poured out of it. It had been working perfectly until half-past three, but refused to work thereafter. Reporter Stuart White had some bad luck himself:

My tape recorder and that of another reporter both played inexplicable tricks. Mine switched itself off when its control buttons suddenly rose of their own accord. The tape in the other recorder burst out of its cassette.

He concluded, 'It seems anything is possible with Uri around.'

It is not always destructive, I am glad to say. During a BBC Radio Oxford interview in November 1986, my host David Freeman produced a small transistor radio which he said had not worked for almost twenty years. Although he had put a new battery in, it made no sound apart from a low crackle. I told him I would try to fix it for him, and as listeners to the programme clearly heard, I did.

That old Geller myth was still holding together, eight years after its final disintegration had been announced. I should mention that it has never depended entirely on the popular press, for a good many of the 'quality' publications of the world's press have made their contributions to it over the years. There have been cover stories on me in *Science News, Science Digest, Popular Photography, New Scientist* and *Der Spiegel*, and major features in *Business Week, Forbes, Esquire, Physics Today, Nature* and the American Medical Association's journal *Today's Health*. My activities have even been described in the defence technology journal *Combat Arms*, the Australian business journal *Rydges*, and *Computer World*, in addition to most of the world's leading newspapers from the *Wall Street Journal* to the *Financial Times*. At least ten books have been written about me, and I have been mentioned in more than 200 others.

I became controversial on my very first trip as an entertainer outside Israel, when I went to Italy in 1971. This was largely due to a widely-distributed photograph that apparently showed me in the company of Sophia Loren, although most people saw at once that it was a fake. I gave a full account of this episode in *My Story*, but it continued to be quoted by the witch-hunters as an example of my supposed dishonesty. Therefore I am grateful to the person who was really responsible for it for setting the record straight, which he did in this statement:

TO WHOM IT MAY CONCERN                    20 December 1985

I, Rany Hirsch, who once acted as Uri Geller's part-time nonexclusive promoter, was fully responsible for creating a photomontage of Uri Geller and Sophia Loren, and releasing it to the Israeli press.

Uri had absolutely no knowledge of this until seeing the photograph on the front page of a newspaper. I did this after Sophia Loren refused to be photographed at our meeting [with Uri], which indeed took place.

Knowing Uri, he would have certainly objected and disapproved of such a foolish promotional stunt.

I am fully aware of the damage I caused Uri in the early seventies, and I regret it very much.

(signed)
Rany Hirsch

Thank you, Rany, for scraping a little more of the mud off the Geller myth. I certainly did meet Sophia Loren, who received me very graciously in her home, but refused to be photographed by anybody except her personal photographer, who was not available at the time. Any actress of her standing would have done the same.

It was on that occasion that I realized for the first time that I had an entry to the world of the beautiful people, thanks to my unusual talents and background. Soon after my arrival in West Germany in 1972, I exploited that entry-permit to the full. You do not come across many jet-setters in Israel, and I only knew of their world from the glossy magazines and the James Bond films, all of which I had seen and loved.

Before I had been in Germany very long, I found that I was not only welcomed by the beautiful people set, but that I was enjoying an affair with a prominent member of it. It was one that was to teach me a lesson.

She had everything. She was extremely rich, very beautiful, and very well connected. She was fascinated by my strange powers, and I was fascinated by everything about her. I lost no time finding out how top people in Western Europe have fun: we cruised around in her vintage Ferrari from one glittering event to another where I met all kinds of famous people including two of my heroes, the footballers Müller and Beckenbauer. She took me to expensive restaurants, where she would order whole cans of caviar as casually as I would ask for a glass of water, and then she would slip me wads of banknotes under the table so that I could be seen to be paying the bill.

Lying in her swimming pool, with the sound of the Moody Blues to keep us company and the servants preparing another delicious meal, I felt like a new member of a very exclusive club. Yet I had hardly begun to enjoy its amenities and privileges when I resigned my membership. This is how it came about:

One day, she took me to the family castle, which was straight from a story book. I had no idea people actually lived in such places except in Disney films, but her family did, and had done for ages. It should have been the perfect setting for another scene in our romance. Instead, it led to the final curtain.

It was all because of my love of physical exercise. There was no pool at the castle, but there was a dusty old ping-pong table. I set it up with the help of one of the maids, but we could not find the bats. The maid said they were up in the attic, so I offered to go and fetch them while she gave the table a wipe.

Torch in hand, I clambered up the stairs to find what you would expect in the attic of a castle: piles of boxes all over the place, pitch darkness and a good deal of accumulated dust. I shone the torch in all directions, but saw no sign of any ping-pong bats.

One corner of the huge attic caught my attention. There were all kinds of military regalia: medals, uniforms, trophies, and a number of framed photographs. I found that I had stumbled across a miniature museum of the Third Reich. I took a closer look at one of the photographs, and saw two men with a little girl sitting in the lap of one of them. She looked about the right age for the present daughter of the house, and one of the men, I assume, was her father. There was no doubt as to who the other one was.

How does one describe the feelings of an Israeli *sabra* who finds himself living under the same roof as somebody with a connection like this? I could not blame her for anything, and I could not punish her for whatever her father had done to earn all those medals from his good friend, the Führer. She belonged to a new generation of a country that had welcomed me and helped me make a name for myself. I did not want to rake up the past, but it was time to move on.

I put through a transatlantic call to Edgar Mitchell, and told him I was ready to come to the United States. It was he and Andrija Puharich who were mainly responsible for my going there, but it was the discovery of the photograph that had much to do with the timing.

\* \* \*

This episode taught me that there are skeletons to be found in the attics of even the most respected members of society, however rich and famous they may be. It made me somewhat wary of the beautiful people. All the same, I have to confess that as soon as I began to amass a respectable fortune of my own, I wanted everybody to know it. For a time, I became as compulsive a spender as I had been an eater. For a start I had to have a custom-built Cadillac, of course, to show my friends that I had made it. I had to have a gold Rolex watch, Gucci wallets and suitcases, silk shirts costing £100 each, about 200 Hermès ties which I never wore, and so on all the way down to my handmade socks. I was cramming every corner of my apartment with expensive presents to myself and to Hanna, just as I was to gobble up bar after bar of Swiss chocolate during my period of bulimia. Fortunately, my overspending ended as abruptly as my overeating, although in this case the initiative did not come from me.

In 1979 I finally married Hanna, whom I had known for more than ten years since we first met while I was convalescing from the wounds I received during the Six Day War of 1967. I suppose we had been engaged ever since, in a subconscious kind of way, although neither of us had ever brought up the subject of marriage. It just seemed to happen naturally, and it happened at precisely the right time. I was getting worn out by all the rushing from airport to hotel to television studio or theatre, and then back to the hotel and then the airport to fly somewhere else and do it all again. I had begun to lose touch with ordinary life, and with the simple things that mattered to me. I was also losing touch with myself, and I needed a period of withdrawal and quiet.

It was a very simple ceremony, with no publicity and no guests, and I knew at once that I had the greatest wife in the world.

One day, when we were in the south of France, we walked past one of those fashionable boutiques full of 'name' items – Pierre Cardin this, Yves Saint-Laurent that, and so on. I suddenly decided we needed a suitcase, so in we went. I ordered a gorgeous Gucci creation, then another, then one more, until we had one of every single size in stock.

Hanna looked at me in her honest and down-to-earth way. 'Why are we buying all this, Uri?' she asked. 'Just so that everybody will see us carting Gucci bags around at airports? What are you trying to prove?'

I looked at her, and suddenly we both burst out laughing. There was no more to be said, and from then on there were no more buying sprees. We gave each other simple and inexpensive birthday presents. I wore my favourite T-shirts until they literally fell apart. There was no more need for me to prove anything. I still have my 1976 Cadillac today, ten years later, with only 26,000 miles on its clock. (I have run more than that over the same period.)

Ten years of performing to people had left me with an immense tiredness by the end of the seventies. I wanted to disconnect myself from the whole rat-race and disappear into my own world, where Hanna and I could settle down and start our family. I was well off enough to spend the rest of my life without working again, and I wanted to get back into my shell and experience some spiritual peace for once.

I had already acquired a number of home bases: a maisonette in Mexico City, an apartment in Tel Aviv, a country house (more of a log cabin than a stately home) in Japan, and a secret hideaway in Europe, in addition to the apartment and house I had bought for my mother in

New York and Connecticut. Hanna and I divided our time between them, living comfortably but very simply. My daily regime of running, swimming, and good home cooking worked wonders for both my body and my soul. I tried a strict vegetarian diet, and found that it made such a difference to my psychic powers that I vowed to stay with it. As Hanna soon showed herself to be the world's best vegetarian cook, this was an easy resolution to keep.

When Colin Wilson was with me in Spain, doing research for his book *The Geller Phenomenon*, which was published in 1976, he told me that the next stage of my career would be one of self-exploration. This was the last thing I had in mind at the time, but he proved to be absolutely right.

I did not become a total hermit. I did the occasional television show, newspaper promotion and business assignment, some of which I have already described. If they were fewer and farther between, that was the way I liked it. I cannot understand how some entertainers, such as the Rolling Stones, can go on for twenty years or more – after only five or six years as a celebrity I was more than ready for the quiet life.

I was certain that Hanna would give me a son and a daughter, in that order. The New York hospital technician who carried out a sonographic scan when Hanna was pregnant for the first time told us that the outline looked to him like that of a girl, but I knew he was wrong, and said so. When the time came to take Hanna to hospital, I drove her there and switched on the car radio and heard Elton John singing his song 'Daniel'. We took that as a good omen.

It was a difficult birth, however. As Shipi and I waited anxiously in the hospital corridor, a doctor came up to me and said he would have to perform a Caesarean section if Hanna did not begin to dilate soon. Later, I learned that the reason for the difficulty was that there was what is called a Rhesus factor problem, meaning that Hanna's blood was not compatible with Daniel's. This, I have been told, can lead to a baby's sickness and sometimes even death.

'If there's any chance that your powers can help,' the doctor said, 'now's the time to use them!'

I concentrated as hard as I could and shouted, 'Open! Open! Open!'

Heads peered round doors, wondering what on earth was going on. Just another anxious father-to-be, they must have thought. They can act rather strangely . . .

About five minutes later Dr Masood Khatamee, the gynaecologist who made the delivery, came up to me and said, 'My God, you did it.'

'Most babies would have been affected by the Rh-factor,' he told a reporter from the New York *Star* (31 March 1981), 'but Daniel was in fine shape. It really surprised me.' He was not prepared to say that my powers had influenced the course of events, but he did admit 'It was rather unusual', adding that 'we do see surprises in medicine'. He saw another one a couple of hours later, when Hanna walked out of the hospital carrying her baby, after signing a form releasing the hospital from any responsibility for her unusually early departure.

Later, Hanna recalled a curious incident that had taken place in Israel long before our marriage. She had been on her way to a party with some friends in her home town of Givataim. It was raining hard, and she had to jump over a large puddle that had grown around the grille of the drain. One of her friends caught sight of a black object that had become stuck in the grille and told Hanna to see what it was.

She fished it out. It was a copy of Elton John's 'Daniel'.

Coincidences will happen, of course. They seem to happen around me more often than could be expected by pure chance, however, and some of them have been fairly trivial. In 1985, for instance, I went on two separate occasions to take care of the sale of my mother's apartment and house. The buyer of the apartment was a lady of Korean descent named Hong, while the house was sold by a different agent to a gentleman of the same unusual name.

Other coincidences, or synchronicities as some people call them, are more meaningful. Take the case of Peter Sterling, the Australian businessman who flew to London in April 1985 to discuss the business deal I described in the previous chapter.

He told his secretary to make hotel reservations for him, his wife Merlene, and their three children. She had done this before many times, and telephoned the usual hotel. It was full up, so she tried another. Booked solid. Apparently, there was a big conference in London.

She kept trying, and had made more than twenty long-distance calls before she managed to find accommodation for the Sterling family, in a hotel where they had never stayed before. She did not have my address, incidentally.

A few days later, Peter rang to say he was in town and would be right over. I gave him the address of my apartment building, the entrance of which was in a side street that was unfamiliar to him. I assured him that London taxi-drivers knew their way around and would find it for him.

My doorbell rang about five minutes later. Peter had walked out of his hotel, gone to the corner of the block, hailed a cruising taxi and climbed in, giving the driver my address after he had driven off. The driver promptly made a U-turn and deposited Peter exactly opposite the spot at which he had picked him up.

There are more than 850 hotels listed in the London telephone directory, and it may have been pure chance that led Peter's secretary to find rooms for him in the one nearest to my apartment block, which not only has a different street address but is on a different telephone exchange.

One way and another, the Sterlings' visit was quite a memorable one. Here is Merlene Sterling's account of one incident which is rather hard to explain by pure chance:

Peter decided to ask Uri to bend a large coin so he could put it on his desk at work to show to the sceptics back home. So we shopped around, and came up with a magnificent silver sovereign dated 1890. The coin cost £25, and has a picture of Queen Victoria on one side and St George and the dragon on the other. It is about three millimetres thick and four centimetres wide. Eldon [Byrd], an ex-coin collector, said he thought it was too beautiful to bend. This did not deter Peter, who gave it to Uri, who said he would try it when he was in the right frame of mind, or something similar.

Merlene went on to describe how we all went out to an Indian restaurant, where we discussed psychic matters, and how she and Peter came along to my apartment to say goodbye the day before they were due to fly out.

As we were about to leave, Peter asked Uri if he had managed to bend the coin yet. Uri said, 'No. Where is it? I will do it now.' The three of us began searching for it . . .

Uri was looking concerned, and we gave up the search and returned to the hall. He picked up his jacket and looked in both pockets. He then remembered that he had left the coin in the restaurant the other night. We were all standing in the hallway discussing the loss of the coin when we were startled by a loud noise in the kitchen, like the sound of breaking glass.

We rushed in to see what it was. The room was empty and the hallway was the only entry, so we would have seen anyone coming or going . . . Peter and Uri ventured briefly into the room and did not see anything unusual, so they retreated, puzzled.

I felt guided by an unseen force and moved directly to the bench (that is, the worktop around the sink) and there was the coin in the sink – bent!

The other two rushed over, and we all jumped up and down with excitement at the sudden return of the coin. I can remember Uri looking at it and saying, 'Good, it is bent. Now I won't have to do it!'

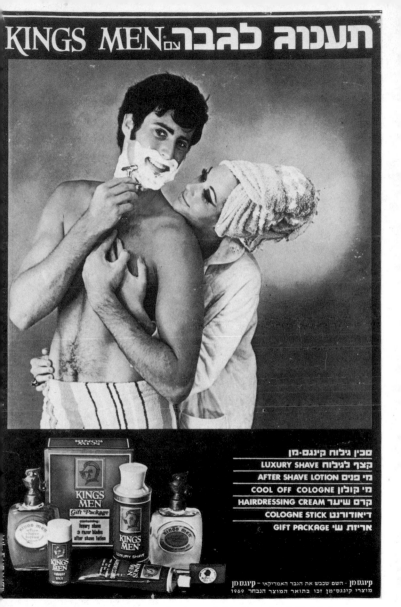

Early days as a photographer's model in Israel, 1969. Little did Uri know then that sixteen years later he would have his own cosmetics line.

THE 6th MARQUESS OF BATH
in October, 1975 invited to Longleat
**URI GELLER**
the world-famous Israeli psychic,
who bent the sword on the Lansdown Centre-piece
and broke the Georgian spoon

Geller's visit to Longleat, home of the Marquess of Bath, as
recorded for posterity. The sword directly below the horse's tail
was bent by him, and the silver spoon was bent to breaking point
while being filmed by BBC Television.

A showcase at Ripley's 'Believe It Or Not' Museum in San Francisco.

Keeping fit in an airport car park between engagements in 1981.

The spoon-bending sequence mentioned in Chapter One, photographed by co-author Guy Lyon Playfair. The angle of bend increases from the third to fourth picture although neither of Geller's hands has changed position. The spoon continued to bend a few degrees after being returned to its owner.

Korea, 1984. Locating tunnels below a chicken farm for the Korean military.

Geller's successful attempts to scramble the contents of a floppy disc at Wang UK's London headquarters, 1985, followed by a conference with mystified employees.

Influencing a computer tape in Japan by means similar to those shown on Geller's 1983 Japanese television programme.

A well-witnessed demonstration of computer-stopping at the
Young Presidents Organization seminar in San Diego, 1985.

Computer specialists look on as Geller erases the Axel Springer
publishing group's computer's memory, 1986, as featured in the
bestselling West German magazine, *Hor Zu*.

With Wernher von Braun *(centre)* and Edgar Mitchell *(right)*
photographed secretly in a NASA rocket laboratory examining a
computer tape just erased by Geller.

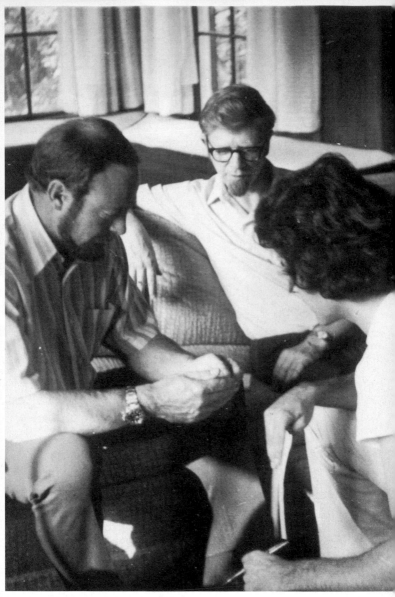

With astronaut Edgar Mitchell *(left)* and Kent State University metallurgist Dr Wilbur Franklin. Captain Mitchell is teaching Geller how to sprout a seed using only the power of his mind.

Sprouting a red radish seed in front of seventeen million West Germans on the Thomas Gottschalk TV show.

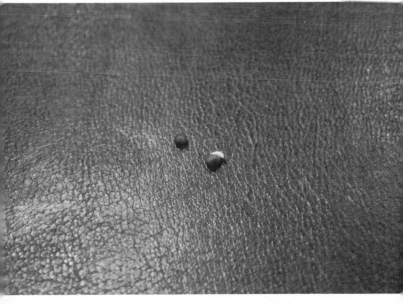

The same seed, before and after sprouting.

One of Geller's first experiences of precious mineral location underground.

Aerial prospecting over the Solomon Islands with Zanex director
Peter Stirling *(right)*.

Prime Minister Sir Peter Kenilorea witnesses the deformation of an
islander's heirloom at the inauguration of the gold mine.

Geller's aerial dowsing technique during a flight over one of the Solomon Islands in 1985.

The first gold is mined on Guadalcanal near one of the sites indicated by Geller.

Searching for gold in the Amazon region of Brazil. *Above:* an inspection of a selected site. *Below:* studying the maps.

*(left to right)* Barry Thompson, Geller, Tony Hammond and Dennis Thomas at the offices of Uri Geller Associates, studying a map before flying out to the location to find gold.

Geller lecturing at the Small Mines Symposium held at Imperial College, London, sponsored by International Mining and The Royal School of Mines, with session Chairman Barry Smale-Adams of RTZ looking on.

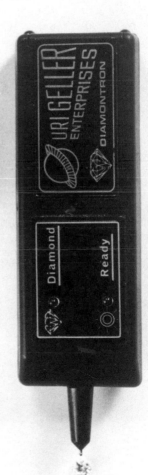

Two of Geller's successful inventions – the Diamontron and the bestselling Moneytron.

'Uri Geller's Strike!' – his first board game for Matchbox Toys.

Lecturing to the United Nations Parapsychology Society.

Entertaining front-line officers and troops in Lebanon *(above)* and civilians *(below)* during Geller's 1984-5 tour of Israel, the most intensive of his career.

Mexican and American
Presidents. Jose López
Portillo and Jimmy Carter in
the White House, 1979.

Geller in Aeromexico T-
shirt.

The gun presented to him by López Portillo.

Sightseeing with Mexico's First Lady.

Reading Henry Kissinger's mind. Rosalynn Carter (next to Geller) holds a recently bent spoon, which continued to bend in her hand. On her left is Señora Carmen Romano de López Portillo. On the far right is Jośe López Portillo ('Pepito').

Two influential figures in Uri's career: Sir Val Duncan *(above)*, Chairman and Chief Executive of the Rio Tinto-Zinc Corporation; and lawyer Dr Ammon Rubinstein *(below)*, later a minister in the Israeli cabinet.

With Israeli politician Ezer Weissman *(centre)* and fellow inventor Meir Gitlis *(left)*.

More seed sprouting during Geller's significant visit to the US Mission at the Geneva Arms talks. With *(left to right)* Senator Claiborne Pell, Chairman of the US Senate Foreign Relations Committee, Yuli M. Vorontsov, First Deputy Foreign Minister of the Soviet Union and Chief Soviet arms negotiator, and Ambassador Max M. Kampelman, Head of United States Delegation Negotiations on Nuclear and Space Arms.

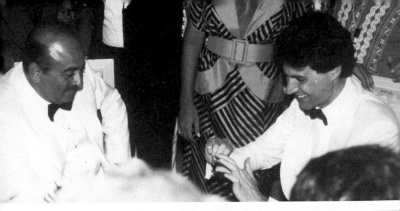

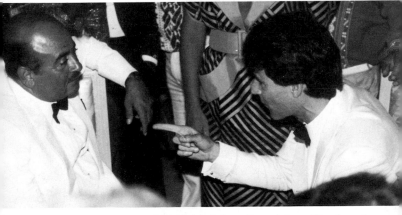

After breaking a spoon as a fiftieth-birthday gift to Adnan Khashoggi *(left)*, Geller sets about cementing Middle East relations.

Dr David Owen, leader of the Social Democrats, forms a spoon-bending alliance with Geller *(above)* at a 1985 garden party at the home of Clement Freud, MP, while *(below)* Geller socializes with Liberal leader David Steel in 1986.

With Nazi-hunter Simon Wiesenthal – a confidential meeting in
London.

Uri and his family in relaxed mood in front of their home in Berkshire.

Flying off on a business trip from the private Geller helipad.

On board Uri's boat *Paranormal* at his private mooring on the Thames.

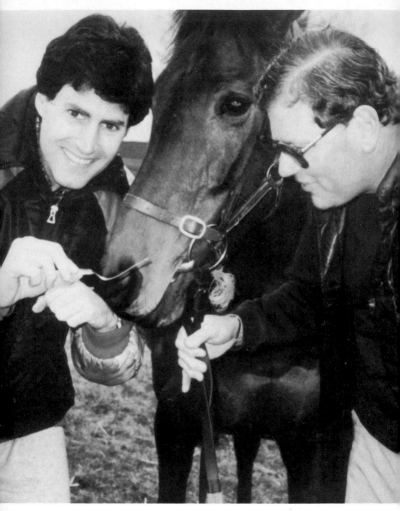

Uri with his horse Spoonbender (owned jointly with MP Clement Freud) and trainer Toby Baldwin *(right)*.

With son Daniel in one of Uri's American homes; behind them a
Dali statue which he subsequently gave away.

The Geller Effect has regularly made headlines and cover stories for the world's leading magazines since Uri's debut in 1969.

# 11

## *Straightening the Record*

In 1984, I received an offer from Danny Shalem, one of
Israel's leading impresarios, for four stage performances.
I had to think it over for some time before deciding to
accept. My five years of semi-retirement from the public
scene had invigorated me psychically as well as physically
and spiritually, and I felt ready to face my home public
for the first time in twelve years. It would be a good
opportunity for Hanna to spend some time with her
parents, and I wanted to show Israel to Daniel and his
little sister Natalie, who had been born in 1983.

However, I knew there might be problems. As it says
in the Bible, 'No prophet is accepted in his own country'
(St Luke 4, verse 23), and there is a mean streak in the
Israeli character that leads to jealousy of anyone who
becomes successful abroad. I would not say that people
such as the violinists Itzhak Perlman and Pinchas Zuker-
man, the actor Topol or film-maker Menachem Golan are
not accepted back home, but I had already had a taste of
the resentment that tends to be felt towards Israelis who
achieve fame and fortune elsewhere. Then again, I might
have been the most sought-after entertainer in the country
for a time in the early seventies, but how would the new
generation react to me? And what would the older
generation think of what was essentially the same act?

These were some of the doubts in my mind as we hit
the runway of Tel Aviv airport with a reassuring bump.
Yet within minutes I found I need not have worried.
Although my press conference was not until the following

# Dry Bones

5 By 1974 Geller's reputation in Israel was well established, as this *Jerusalem Post* cartoon shows.

day, the entire Israeli press corps had turned out just to come along and greet me.

'How does it feel to come back as a hero?' one reporter asked me. I was quite taken aback, and cannot remember my reply.

He set the tone for the press conference, another full-scale media turn-out, at which Danny Shalem announced that both my shows in the 3,000-seat Mann Auditorium in Tel Aviv were sold out, as were the others in Jerusalem and Haifa. The reporters, to my surprise gave me the full conquering-hero treatment, and there was not a single hostile question. What, I wondered, had become of all those 'witch-hunters' who had set out to get me fourteen years ago?

According to the press, no less than ten magicians stationed themselves in the front row for the first of my shows in Tel Aviv. No doubt they were hoping to catch me using the tricks of their trade. If so, they must have been surprised when I walked onto the stage to see that there could not be anything up my sleeves, for the simple reason that I was not wearing any. For the first time in my career I did what I am sure has never been done in the history of the Mann Auditorium and appeared in a T-shirt and tennis shorts!

After the show, which went very well, I received a most unexpected visitor in my dressing room. He was Ronai Schachnaey, Grand President of Israel's Society for Promoting the Art of Magic, who had been knocking me on television a short time previously. Evidently, he had changed his mind, for his first words to me were, 'Uri, I take off my hat to you. You are fantastic.' He then gave me a medallion inscribed with his society's coat of arms. Why did he give it to me? Did he think I was the greatest illusionist or a true psychic?

Danny Shalem had booked me for four shows, but demand was so tremendous that I ended up doing thirty. By the time I left to fly to London in February 1985 I had collected a total of 113 press clippings about me from every one of Israel's leading newspapers and magazines, and 99 per cent of them were positive. I had to take it all back – Israelis can honour their returning celebrities and artists.

One whose tribute I particularly appreciated was Uri Avneri, owner and publisher of the popular weekly magazine *Haolam Hazeh*. This was the magazine that had printed a long cover story on me in its issue of 20 February 1974 that, as one of my critics put it, was 'designed to put Mr Gellèr out of business for good'. It was based on false information, including 'interviews' with my parents which neither of them gave, a lengthy statement attributed to Hanna of which she never spoke a single word, and the revelation that Shipi was 'signalling' to me from the audience.

Since this story had been translated in full by one of my witch-hunters, and is frequently mentioned as if it were a scientifically-produced exposure of my fraudulence rather than an assortment of second-hand gossip and purely imaginary testimony, I am glad to be able to include here some extracts from Mr Avneri's 'Personal Diary' column for the issue of 21 November 1984. This was based on his own observation and that of his wife Rachel.

'Do you believe in telepathy? What do you mean, believe? I live with it,' he began. His wife, he explained, was able to 'steal' thoughts from his head before he could express them in words. 'This is why I wanted to meet Uri Geller. What happens when two telepathists meet?'

He goes on to describe how we did meet, in his own apartment, noting that I had come to see him and his wife alone. Shipi, my famous 'accomplice', was not even in the country at the time, having some business to see to in Europe, and did not arrive until shortly before the end of my tour. Mr Avneri also mentioned that I was not wearing a watch. (A local computer expert named Yosef Allon had been insisting for years that I used a watch to reflect drawings made behind my back.)

Suddenly, he [Uri] asked for a spoon. He took it and started stroking it gently. After a few seconds the handle began to bend upwards. Uri put the spoon on the table and let go of it, and it went on bending in front of our eyes until it reached an angle of ninety degrees.

Next, Uri asked me to draw something. He closed his eyes, and I took care to hold the paper so that he could not see it. I drew a ship, with three funnels, keeping the paper covered. Finally he drew something himself, then seemed to give up. 'I don't know exactly what it is,' he said, 'I'm not sure.'

He showed it to me. It was definitely a ship, except that my three funnels had turned into three portholes.

Next, Mr Avneri wrote, he asked me to do an experiment with his wife, so I asked her to think of the name of a capital city. He decided to join in as well.

I had no pen, so I went into the next room, found a pen, and wrote the word Tokyo in my notebook. Uri then asked Rachel what city she had chosen, and she said 'Moscow.'

'No,' said Geller. 'I got it wrong.'

So I thought, for what I had written while Mr Avneri was out of the room was – Tokyo. He gave quite a start when he saw this, and he had another surprise to come:

Then I interrogated my wife and she admitted that she had also 'received' Tokyo, but had decided to write Moscow despite her impression.

So I don't believe in telepathy. But then I also do not believe in electricity. I don't believe that somebody can sit in London and I can sit here in Tel Aviv and hear him, with no cable connecting us. Absurd, isn't it?

One way and another, *Haolam Hazeh* had tried to do my reputation a good deal of damage in the past, so I was surprised to receive a telephone call from its former editor Eli Tavor soon after my meeting with its publisher. He came to see me in my hotel, and it seemed that he wanted to make amends for all those attacks on me he had published in the early seventies. He also had some remarkable confessions to make about the way the magazine had been run in his time.

He could not remember who had written the article in the 20 February 1974 issue, though he admitted that it was quite possible that the writer had made it all up and had never met Hanna. They were quite capable of writing articles that were pure fiction.

He himself had genuinely believed all the nonsense he published about me. His scepticism, he added, had been forced upon him by others. Now, however, this scepticism was directed towards his own former attitude, which he admitted to have been 'biased'. He later confirmed all this in a letter dated 20 January 1986.

'I have changed my mind about you,' he said. 'I am convinced today that you are endowed with abilities that allow you to perform feats which I cannot explain.'

Early in my tour there was one of those crazy coincidences that often seem to happen when I travel somewhere. This one began at Zürich airport, where I had been standing in line waiting to check in at the El Al counter. I chatted for a few moments with the man next to me, but saw no more of him after I had checked in. A week or so later, I found myself with a free morning, so I decided to take a sentimental jog around some of the places in Tel Aviv that I remembered from my childhood. One of these was the small apartment block that contained one of my first homes.

I felt a sudden longing to visit it, so I went up the stairs and knocked on the door. The man who opened it was as surprised to see me as I was to see him. It was my fellow traveller from Zürich airport.

He invited me in, and I took him out to the balcony to show him where I had written my name in the cement more than twenty years earlier. It was still there.

One way and another, I made my mark on Israel in some unusual ways. A woman who had seen me performing one of my regular feats on television, in which I would order broken watches to tick by repeating the order 'Work!', had a broken hair-dryer. She took this to be repaired the following day, and as she was on her way out of the shop she heard somebody shouting from the back room, 'Work! Work! Work!' I hope it did.

On another occasion, I was going for one of my regular runs along a street in Tel Aviv when I literally stopped the traffic. A passing motorist recognized me and screeched to a halt to ask for my autograph. He forgot his highway code as he did so, and the car behind ran straight into him, leading to a fair amount of bumper-bending and general commotion.

The well-known cartoonist Gidon paid his respects to me in the newspaper *Ma'ariv* (12 November 1984) with a drawing of a scroll that looked something like a bent tablet, and was inscribed with the words 'Now I believe in Geller'.

The mayor of Rishon Letzion in the wine-growing region asked me to come and look for oil in his area. I was not very optimistic, and after exploring the land he had in mind I told him I did not think there was any oil there, as unfortunately seems to be the case in the rest of Israel.

I was also asked to help in one of those sad incidents of child abduction by a parent after a dispute over guardianship rights. I told the worried mother that her son was not in Israel, but either in Canada or in Florida, and was glad to hear shortly afterwards that he had been located in the latter.

As in Korea a few months earlier, I suddenly found myself back in a war zone when I was asked by the Israeli Army to entertain the troops serving in Lebanon. I was flown in by helicopter for a single show, which went down well enough for the authorities to invite me back, and to put my picture on the cover of the military magazine *Bamakhaneh*. My visit to the front line brought back memories of the good times I had enjoyed during my own military service, but it brought back the bad memories as well – of the violence, the hatred and the sudden death. After a spate of guerrilla attacks on Israeli helicopters shortly after my visit, the authorities decided that a return trip was not advisable.

I was able to make a modest contribution to peace in the Middle East, when Ezer Weissman introduced me to the Egyptian diplomatic envoy in Israel. I bent a spoon for him, much to his delight, and he told me I would be welcome to visit Egypt. He even suggested I should do a show at one of the pyramids!

Meanwhile, my exhausting tour went on and on, and one of my shows was in the town of Beersheba. Although it was sold out in advance and was a great success, it brought back a memory of the less agreeable kind, of an incident which has been inflated beyond all reasonable proportions by the witch-hunters. The true facts are these:

In December 1970, I gave my first show in Beersheba. I cannot remember anything special about the performance, having now given thousands of almost identical ones, but a short time after it a student named Uri Goldstein decided that he had been deceived by the poster used to advertise the show. It had promised a demonstration of psychic powers, but in his opinion it was just another display of stage magic. So he went along to the local civil court and made a complaint against my promoters, a firm called Solan, and me.

The court heard and upheld his complaint, and he was awarded the price of his ticket plus costs, all of which came to the equivalent of a few American dollars. The summons, if there ever was one, was sent to Solan and not to me. The first I ever heard of the case was when I read in a newspaper that a member of the public had paid the fine and enclosed an ironic little fable in a letter he sent to the court. A translation of this letter can be found in John Wilhelm's *The Search for Superman*, in which he wrongly states that it was sent by me.

I went to some trouble to look into the facts of this case in 1984 and 1985, and I did so rather more thoroughly than any of my critics have bothered to do. Eventually, I was able to obtain documentary evidence from the Hashalom Civil Court that the complaint was heard *in my absence*. The case file number, for those who would like to check for themselves, is 3772/70.

It is therefore rather exaggerated, to say the least, to refer to me as having been 'convicted in a court of law for pretending to have paranormal powers', as Bernard Dixon, a former editor of the *New Scientist*, did in the issue of 22 October 1975 of a journal called *World Medicine*.

Just to make quite sure that I had never committed any

crimes that might have slipped my memory, I have now obtained a statement from the National Department for Investigation of the Israeli Police. Dated 2 December 1984, it reads: 'At your request, please find enclosed the conviction sheet of the above' (i.e. – me). The attached sheet contains my name and date of birth, and the single line: *No criminal record found*.

I have never replied in the past to any of my individual critics. I have, however, been doing a good deal of research of my own into some of the more persistent of them, with the help of news clipping services, reporters and journalists, teams of private investigators and lawyers in North, Central and South America, Japan, Europe and Israel, all of whose thorough and tedious inquiries, some involving the Freedom of Information Act, have resulted in a staggering amount of information and have been carried out entirely within the law.

The same cannot be said of all of my attackers. One of them resorted to illegal activity in his efforts to incriminate me in 1985, when he filed a false record of payment ('1099') form to the US Internal Revenue Service, using a false name but having somehow or other learned the correct sum I had received for an engagement overseas. To his disappointment, no doubt, I was not subject to taxation on this in the US, since I was never resident there.

One way and another, I have amassed an enormous pile of documentation, from newspapers, magazines, radio and television shows, lectures, press conferences and private conversations. I keep receiving more from unexpected sources, and I am grateful to all those well-wishers, some of them unknown to me, who have been helping me compile such a valuable archive. When I recently had it moved out of my home, I weighed it and found it came to more than 100 kilograms.

I am sorry for some of the more extreme witch-hunters and I pity them, though I also have to thank them for making their priceless contribution to the Geller myth over the past fifteen years or so.

While I am in this record-straightening mood, let me now give you the facts concerning my very brief career as a stage 'magician', which I described in more detail in *My Story*.

In 1970, less than a year after my first public performance, I was booked to appear at the Beit Hachaial (Soldiers' Home) auditorium in Tel Aviv. The promoter of this particular event felt that my act was becoming a little repetitive, which was quite true, and he thought it would be a good idea to add some trickery to the genuine displays of psychic power. A friend of his whom he particularly wanted to impress was coming to see the show, so he told me the number of the man's car licence-plate and asked me to produce it 'clairvoyantly' during the performance.

I thought this was a stupid idea, and I told him so, but he insisted and I finally agreed to keep him quiet. He was so pleased with the result that he persuaded me to include it in my repertoire. At the age of twenty-four, and a beginner in show business, I was in no position to argue with a man far more experienced than I, who was, after all, helping me earn my living. I gave in, though not for more than four or five performances.

Then I confessed what I had done against my better judgment to a trusted and respected friend – Dr Amnon Rubinstein, who was then the dean of the Law School at the Hebrew University and went on to become a member of the Israeli cabinet. Amnon was horrified, and made me promise never to cheapen my talents again.

At the same time, he told me I should be co-operating with scientists and trying to find out more about the workings of the human mind. I obeyed both his orders. I never did the licence-plate trick, or any other kind of deliberate deception again, and as soon as the opportunity arose I offered my services to the scientists I have already mentioned, whose findings you can read in *The Geller Papers*.

A curious thing I have noticed again and again over the years is that when somebody like me is denounced as a cheat, the allegation is accepted without question, however dubious the original sources may be. The denunciation is repeated again and again, even by people who would check their facts carefully if they were holding forth in public about their own professional specialities. It is then regarded as established fact.

Here is a very recent example of how this process gets under way. In January 1986, a friend called me from the USA to let me know that Russell Targ had apparently just denounced me in public as a fake, a cheat and even a thief. At least, he had been quoted as having done so.

This did not sound like the behaviour of the Russell I knew, so I called him up at once to check exactly what he had said at the meeting mentioned.

'It's a complete fabrication,' he told me. All he had said was that he had never personally done a successful experiment in metal-bending with me, which was quite true and which he had already said several times in print. The rest was pure invention, and I am sure that will not stop the debunkers from writing one more lie into their versions of history.

On the other hand, when I go from one scientific laboratory to another, submit to all kinds of controlled experiments directed by professional scientists, most of them physicists, who then publish their findings in respectable science journals, it is a very different story. I find it quite amusing that those same critics who reject what they read in *Nature* will accept the second-hand libels they read in the popular press.

Even more curious, to me, is the fact that some people will not even accept the evidence of their own eyes. Or they may accept it at first, but then allow others to change their minds for them. Professor John Taylor, for example, asked me to do several experiments in his own laboratory, such as bending a piece of metal that was fixed to a letter-scale. I did this, and various other things, but later he concluded that I must be a fraud simply because I would not agree to do them all again after some magician or other had told him how to tighten up his controls. Even if I had done this, another magician would have come along and said the first one's controls were no good, and so it would have gone on.

The writer Arthur C. Clarke saw his own key bend in front of his eyes during one of the visits I made to Professor John Hasted's laboratory in London in 1974. 'My God!' he said at the time, 'it's all coming true. This is what I wrote about in *Childhood's End*. I can't believe it!'

Ten years later, however, his mind had been changed for him by somebody who was not even present, and in *Arthur C. Clarke's World of Strange Powers* (1984) he quoted my account of the episode and accused me of faulty memory. 'He *did* take the door-key out of my hand,' he wrote, 'and he placed it on a *firm metal surface while stroking it*. Interesting, to say the least . . .'

Interesting indeed. He forgets to mention that his own thumb was on top of his key as it bent, according to Professor Arthur Ellison, head of the electrical engineering department at City University, who witnessed the incident at point-blank range, and gave an accurate description of it in a lecture in London in 1985, which he repeated in print in *The Times Higher Education Supplement* for 22 August 1986.

Mr Clarke has some strange views on scientific research. He describes *The Geller Papers* as an 'astounding farrago', many of whose contributors 'must now wish that the entire edition had dematerialized'. Why? Because they published positive results?

According to Professor Ellison, writing in the article mentioned above, the reason why people tend to change their minds after witnessing something unusual is quite simple. 'Such occurrences are "impossible",' they say, 'therefore they cannot happen. It is not necessary to look further into these matters: it would merely be a waste of time. All the claims, confirmed by so many distinguished scientists and others, must be false. They must all have been deceived by a conjuror . . . And nobody likes to be thought naïve: better to keep quiet.'

Several people mentioned in this book have later suffered attacks of what Brian Inglis calls retrocognitive dissonance – that is, they say one thing to me when I meet them and something quite different to some reporter or other several years later. Among those who suffered recently from this complaint, when the *Mail on Sunday* contacted them in 1986, were President Carter, Henry Kissinger, Clive Menell, Jorge Luiz Serrano and a spokesman for the Korean defence ministry. I can only say that I have discovered that I have a new talent: for inducing loss of memory in others.

Fortunately, however, retrocognitive dissonance works both ways, and sometimes it can help straighten the record rather than distort it. I referred earlier to the *New Scientist* article (6 April 1978) in which the 'final disintegration' of the Geller myth was announced. The man who allegedly provided the evidence for this was a former manager of mine named Yasha Katz, with whom I parted company in 1974 after a disagreement over his share of my takings – a problem with which many entertainers are familiar.

Yasha was quoted as having made a number of allegations, some of which were printed in a journal called the *Skeptical Inquirer* (Spring/Summer 1978). One of my most persistent detractors credited him with 'the single greatest indictment of Uri Geller I have ever heard'. Among Yasha's allegations were that Shipi and I had 'taken refuge' in Mexico, which had no extradition treaty with Israel, and were 'wanted for questioning' in Israel in connection with Shipi's military service.

If I was indeed wanted for questioning in Israel, now was the time for the authorities to catch up with me. My arrival in November 1984 was plastered all over the newspapers, and my daily appearances in every major town in the country were well advertised. I gave enough press conferences for everybody in the whole of Israel to question me as much as they liked. Shipi, who arrived later in my tour, was also freely available for questioning by all and sundry.

Soon after my arrival, I was surprised to read in the newspaper *Ma'ariv* (9 November 1984) that Yasha was now stating: 'Never did I say that he is not real', referring to me. I was even more surprised to hear that he had wanted to help promote my tour and have his name on the posters along with that of Danny Shalem.

I got in touch with Yasha and explained that although I forgave him for having done me a good deal of harm in the past, I wanted him to set the record straight. Here is part of the affidavit he signed on 10 December 1984 in the presence of lawyer Moshe Ben-Haim:

I have known Uri Geller since 1971. I confirm that all the information I gave [in 1977] about him and his relatives, and Mr Shtrang, was lacking any real basis and was false. I confirm that everything I said was a consequence of the fact that there had been a disagreement between myself and Mr Geller, whom [sic] I thought owed me certain payments.

I specify that people who wanted to damage Uri Geller approached me at that time [1977] and pressed me to make statements aimed at harming him. I agreed under pressure, and gave information that was completely untrue.

It is not true that Uri Geller fled to 'exile' in Mexico because of an inquiry into him by Israeli authorities. As far as I know, there was no such inquiry or any reason for one.

It is not true that I said Uri Geller was a fake, or was cheating while performing either on or off stage. It is also of course untrue that I helped him cheat in any way.

I specify that people who wanted to harm Uri Geller used me for the purpose of damaging Uri Geller in an unjustifiable way.

Another person whose reported statements surprised me in the past was my former girl-friend Iris Davidesco, with whom I had a somewhat public but nevertheless satisfying reconciliation.

'You were the love of my life, Uri,' she told me when we met. 'I was hurt because you left me, and I went along with what the others were saying because I wanted to hurt you back, and it was the only way I could.'

In February 1985, I left Israel totally exhausted both physically and mentally after so many performances and interviews. It had been my most gruelling tour since Brazil in 1976, and I vowed I would never do another like it. All the same, it was very good to have been welcomed home so warmly, and to have made my peace with so many detractors of the past.

Life is full of synchronicities, and I seem to receive much of my share of them at airports or in aeroplanes. As I waited in the lounge of Tel Aviv airport for my London flight, I noticed a man of about my age looking at me and smiling. I assumed he had recognized me from one of my shows, and nodded politely to him. Then it was time to embark, and soon after we had taken off and the 'fasten seat belts' sign had been switched off. I felt a tap on my shoulder. It was the man from the lounge, now sitting right behind me.

'Uri, look at my face,' he said. 'Do you remember?'

'Well,' I replied, 'yes, I saw you in the airport.'

'Look again,' he went on. 'Don't you remember me?'

His face looked vaguely familiar, but I could not put a name to it.

'If it wasn't for me,' he said, 'you wouldn't be on this aeroplane.'

'What do you mean?'

'Don't you remember the day you nearly drowned when you were ten years old?'

'Avi!' I exclaimed. Of course I remembered now. During my brief stay at the kibbutz at Hatzor, near Ashdod, in 1955 and 1956, I had gone swimming in the sea one day with some of the other boys. I was a terrible swimmer then, and had no idea how strong the undercurrent was or what to do if I got myself caught in it, which is just what had happened. What I had done was clutch in terror at the only person within reach, which was Avi. I had nearly drowned the pair of us in my panic, but mercifully he was stronger than I and a good swimmer,

6  A Marc cartoon from *The Times*, 1973.

7  A Heath cartoon from the *Sunday Times*, 1986.

and he managed to drag me to the beach. He was right – but for him I would not have been on that aeroplane, or anywhere else.

We had a good chat about old times and promised to keep in touch when we said goodbye to each other at Heathrow Airport. Avi was flying on to Canada, where he now lives, and since I had already begun to plan this book I asked him to write to me with his account of an unusual episode from the same period as my near-drowning, which he also remembered clearly. For the benefit of those who still believe the witch-hunters' claim that I learned all my tricks from Shipi Shtrang (who was only a few months old when the incident in question took place), here is part of the long letter Avi sent me, dated 10 June 1985:

The first and only time I remember you demonstrating your powers was on a warm summer afternoon. We were walking on a footpath across from the main dining-hall, just past the steps leading to the new swimming-pool. To our left was a good-sized grassed area and to our right a hill with young pine trees.

You took your watch off your wrist and gave it to me so that I could admire it. I think it was a gift from your Dad. I thought it was a great watch, and you said, 'See what I can do with it.'

I watched you take it in your hand and hold it tightly. Then the hands started to move forward on their own, and later backwards. I thought you were playing tricks, so I said, 'I think you're playing with the knob on the watch.'

Then I took a closer look. At this point we stopped among some larger trees covering the footpath, and I said, 'Do it again, without touching the knob.'

You laughed, and did it again. I was sure that you *did not* touch the knob, but I thought just the same that you were playing some trick on me. I must admit that I did dismiss it as just some crazy thing you were doing, but as a kid twelve years old I put the thought away as 'So what?' We kept on walking to our class-house, and that was it.

I really do not think you even knew what it all meant. It was very natural to you, and you liked the idea of 'Look what I can do' . . .

> (signed)
> Abraham Setton
> Victoria, BC, Canada

My arrival in London in February 1985 was the direct result of yet another of those airline coincidences. This one came about like this:

When Daniel was three, in 1984, it was time for some serious discussion between Hanna and me about where we wanted him to grow up and go to school. We could not go on carting him and Natalie around the world indefinitely from one of our home bases to another, as we had done throughout their lives to date. We needed a more permanent home base somewhere. At about that time, the British businessman Richard Branson invited me to come along on the inaugural flight of his Virgin Airlines, from London to New York.

As you would expect from the owner of a successful record company, he put on quite a show, and the send-off at Heathrow left me fairly exhausted even before we got off the ground. I made my way to my seat in the first-class section of the Boeing 747 and collapsed into it, hardly noticing who was already seated beside me.

He was a comic-looking and amiable fellow with a beard and a lively glint in his eyes, and before long we began to make polite conversation. He introduced himself, and although I knew nothing about him I commented on the fact that we both had the same family name: Freud – my mother's maiden name.

My mother's family comes from Vienna, although she was born in Berlin and brought up in Budapest. She has always been told that her father and Sigmund Freud were second or third cousins, although I have not been able to trace the exact connection. My fellow passenger had never had any such difficulty, however, for he was the grandson of the founder of psychoanalysis.

We had a pleasant flight chatting about food, music, horses and women, about all of which he seemed to know a good deal. I invited him to come and spend a couple of days at my mother's house in Connecticut, and it was only there that I found out who he was: Clement Freud, Liberal Member of Parliament, veteran radio and television personality and author of several books. When I happened to mention that I was looking for a new home base, he immediately suggested England. 'It's a civilized country,' he assured me.

It sounded like the right choice to me. I had been given an English education, in Cyprus, and I could not wish for a better one for my own children. I already had many friends and contacts in London, and on the whole I had always been well treated by the British media, which did more than any other to help me make an international name for myself back in the early seventies. Another advantage was that my secret hideaway in Europe was only a short flight away. Finally, after watching one more television item about increasing crime and drug addiction among New York school children, I decided that all roads seemed to lead to London.

Clement Freud told me how to go about satisfying the British authorities that I qualified for residential status, while making it quite clear that he was in no position to obtain any special favours for me, for which I never asked him. So, after going through the normal channels, I and the rest of the Geller family took up residence in a whole floor of an apartment building overlooking the treetops of Hyde Park.

Clement and I became good friends. Soon after I arrived in England we bought a racehorse together, naming her *Spoonbender* and entrusting her to the care of the well-known trainer Toby Balding. She came in sixth in her first race, and third in her second. On 26 November 1986 I went along to see her in action for the first time, in the 3.30 race at Huntingdon, having told the press the day before that I was going to give her a little telepathic help from my seat in the grandstand.

One racing expert who was not too impressed was Templegate of *The Sun*, who announced in the race-day issue of his paper that he preferred to concentrate his energies on the form book, reckoning that the favourite, *Preacher's Gem* 'is more than good enough to thwart Uri's psychic powers'. He went on:

Uri, who does not gamble, is anxious to point out that should another horse be leading *Spoonbender* by a healthy margin at the last flight, he would not try to will it to fail.
'There is evidence that it can be achieved,' he said. 'But I would never use my powers in a negative sense. I will be quite happy if the horse comes second or third providing I believe I have heightened her performance.'

My horse got off to a slow start, and was lying in eighth position out of nineteen as the field leaped over the hurdles. On the final straight, she showed what she could do and moved steadily ahead, finishing with her nose a couple of feet behind that of the winner. The favourite was nowhere in sight.

I was relieved, in a way, that *Spoonbender* had not quite made it. If she had come in first, I am sure there would have been allegations that I had been doping her or poisoning the other horses, or maybe putting a curse on them. I was satisfied with second place, and from what

I saw I reckoned that my horse did not really need any extra-sensory help to win one day.

On another occasion in 1985, I gave Clement Freud and a number of his friends a spontaneous demonstration of my own winning methods. The occasion was a garden party at his country home, where I made use of my magic number: eleven. When it was time to buy tickets for the raffle, I asked for the numbers 111 and 121 (eleven times eleven). The first won me a handsome Wedgwood plate decorated with the portraits of distinguished Liberal Politicians of the past, and the second won the top prize, a huge hamper of luxurious food and drink. I gave this back, in order not to appear to be overdoing things.

At Clement's party, I met a man who, like John Howard in Australia, gave me the impression that he could become prime minister of his country one day. This was Dr David Owen, leader of the Social Democratic Party. I bent a spoon for him while he was holding it, and learned that he had been interested in parapsychology for some time.

My lucky number kept turning up all over the place in 1985. When Andrija Puharich stopped off in London on his way to a conference, I booked a room for him at the Royal Garden Hotel, near my apartment. I went round to see him there.

'That's funny,' I said when I arrived. 'You're in the same room that Byron and Maria Janis were in last week.' The number was 1105.

Shortly afterwards, another friend of mine called from the USA and asked me to make a reservation at a hotel near me. I called the Royal Garden, and once again my friend ended up in room 1105. Then it happened yet again – four times in a row.

I began to feel slightly paranoid. Were all my friends

being put there on purpose so that their conversations could be bugged? I had a word with the manager, who assured me that it was pure coincidence.

In December, I was watching BBC breakfast television without paying too much attention. An auction was being held for the Leukaemia Research Fund, and I had a sudden impulse to put in a bid for a gold bracelet studded with rubies that was being shown on the screen. I phoned in with my bid, and heard later that I had won it. I was also told that it had been donated by the well-known British medium Doris Stokes, and that it was – you've guessed it – Lot Eleven.

One recent coincidence that I particularly enjoyed involved both my lucky number and my name, which is one you might think it difficult to spell incorrectly. In fact, I had never seen it misspelt in any of the thousands of press items about me that have appeared over the years, until January 1986, when the journal of the Society for Psychical Research printed a letter from my old friend Brian Inglis containing the phrase:

'. . . in circumstances which preclude the kind of deception Gelller was supposed to have practised . . .'

# 12
## *Waging Peace*

On a warm evening in July 1985, a fleet of buses wound its way along a hillside road in southern Spain. Its destination was a secluded luxury villa standing in grounds five times the size of Monaco, and its passengers were some of the 400 guests who had been invited to a birthday party. Meanwhile, a helicopter shuttled back and forth from the 285-foot yacht anchored off Marbella to fetch some of the more distinguished guests.

This was no ordinary party. One of the world's wealthiest and most influential men was jointly celebrating his son's fifth and his own fiftieth birthdays, and his guest list must have read like a draft for *Who's Who in the Middle East*. Most of them were Arabs, and many had flown over specially for the event from the Middle East. There was also a handful of eminent local residents, and some family friends from other parts of the world.

The buses turned into the driveway, cruised along between rows of guards dressed in medieval uniforms and holding large pikes, and drew up outside the huge villa, where the host was waiting to greet his guests. For three of them, at least, it was their first meeting with him.

They knew a good deal about him, however. As the Saudi Arabian chairman of the vast Triad group of companies, he was said to be personally worth about £2 billion, and to have an income of around a million pounds a day. He certainly knew how to spend it: he had eleven other homes around the world in addition to this Spanish country palace, and his parties tended to leave the gossip columnists at a loss for superlatives. His yacht *Nabila* was the one you may have seen in the James Bond film *Never Say Never Again*.

Among the guests who stepped out of their buses and lined up to shake hands with Mr Adnan Khashoggi were a Jewish-American musician named Byron Janis and two Israelis, Shipi and myself. What, you may want to know, were we doing at this glittering gathering of the élite of the Arab world? Let me explain.

About a year previously, Byron and I had been talking about ways in which people like ourselves – musicians and entertainers – could use our talents to bring people together and turn their minds towards peace instead of conflict. We both felt we could do more than merely provide audiences with an evening of pleasure in our respective ways. But where to start? Starting a war was fairly easy, we agreed, but how do you go about starting a peace?

I had an idea. 'Whether we like it or not, Byron,' I said, 'many parts of this world are dominated by very powerful individuals. I don't see any chance of real peace until they can be brought together and made to sort out the obstacles that keep them apart.'

We drew up a list of those we reckoned to be capable of influencing the hearts and minds of large numbers of people in various ways, and the first name we came up with was that of Mr Khashoggi. We decided to get in touch with him somehow or other, and began asking around.

He was not an easy man to meet, as he was constantly on the move. Anyway, we wrote him a letter asking if it would be possible for us to see him. Nothing happened for six weeks, then Byron received a telephone call from a man who identified himself as one of Mr Khashoggi's personal aides. What, he asked, would we like to see him about?

'We just want to come as human beings,' said Byron. 'We have something very important to convey to him.'

'I understand that,' said the aide. He must have heard it before. 'But what is it about?'

Byron went straight to the point. 'The world has a lot of problems, and we think that together we might be able to identify some of them, and maybe do something about them. Who knows?'

The aide's tone of voice changed at once. 'We're always ready for that,' he replied, and immediately announced that he would like to invite us both to Mr Khashoggi's birthday party. It was as simple as that.

The formal invitations duly arrived, and I telephoned the aide to ask if he would like some background information about me. I was a little concerned that he might not know I was an Israeli. 'Shall I send you a press kit?' I asked.

'Oh, that won't be necessary, Mr Geller,' was the reply. 'We know all about you.'


I shook the mothballs out of my dinner jacket, which I had not worn since I had been one of the judges at the Miss Universe pageant several years earlier, and here I was, one of the few Israelis outside the diplomatic corps ever to meet a Saudi Arabian, let alone shake hands with one in his own home. As our line moved forward, I remembered the day I had queued up in the White House to send my message to President Carter. Now, I had another message to deliver.

My turn came. The aide muttered something into Mr Khashoggi's ear, and after eyeing each other hesitantly for a moment, we shook hands. I immediately had the feeling that here was no villain, but a man of great warmth and goodness. This was not the time for a discussion about world peace, though, and I was ushered into the enormous glass pavilion that had been built especially for the occasion.

It was like a Hollywood set. A band was playing on the stage, and tables had been laid out for a sit-down dinner that was already well under way. Every beautiful woman in the world seemed to be there, each of them wearing a new creation from a top fashion house, and there was more priceless jewellery on display than you would find in the whole of Bond Street or Fifth Avenue. I saw emeralds the size of golf balls, clusters of sixty- or seventy-carat diamonds, and examples of just about every other precious mineral that ever came out of this earth. Balloons were floating up to the domed ceiling, the champagne was flowing like the river Jordan, and the din was tremendous. Despite my experience of high life in Mexico, West Germany, and the homes of a number of presidents, dictators and ministers, I have never seen anything like it.

Although Byron and I had been asked previously by the aide if we would demonstrate our 'powers' – his on the piano and mine on the cutlery – it was obvious that this was no occasion for a formal show of any kind. It was a great big noisy family party, not a show business event. The only celebrities I recognized throughout the evening were Brooke Shields, a friend of the family, Shirley Bassey, whose performance was limited to a rendering of 'Happy Birthday to You', and the original 007 himself – Sean Connery. Although he was there as a neighbour and was not on business as a secret agent, his presence only added to the illusion that I had wandered on to the set of the next Bond picture.

For the first hour or so there was no further sign of our host, and we decided to relax and enjoy ourselves. Eventually, the aide appeared at our table, took my arm and said he would like me to meet Mr Khashoggi's wife. This, I thought, was a step in the right direction.

Whatever I had been expecting the wife of a Saudi Arabian businessman to look like, it was not what I saw: a ravishingly beautiful Italian lady of about my own age, who greeted me with a smile that only Sophia Loren could match.

'Oh, Uri Geller!' she cried. 'I've heard so much about you. Come and sit down.'

I was too dazzled by her beauty to make much in the way of conversation. Before long, she handed me an expensive-looking spoon and asked me to show her what I could do with it. I let her hold it herself and watch as it began to curl upwards at my command, in the usual way. Then, all too soon, the aide whisked me away to meet a member of King Faisal's family and numerous other pillars of Arab society – Sheikh this and Prince that – all of them clearly men of considerable power. Like our host, they gave me an impression of great human warmth, and they greeted me as a fellow creature.

I managed to bend a couple more spoons in my spontaneous strolling cabaret act, and was getting fairly tired when at last the hard-working aide found his way to me again and led me into a private room. I prayed for all available strength, both to bend another spoon if necessary and to do what I was really there for: deliver my message.

To my disappointment, there was still no sign of Mr Khashoggi. His son was there, however, and we made some polite conversation. He was intrigued to hear that I was from Israel, and I was tempted to ask if I was the first

Israeli he had ever met, also to tell him that I actually had a Saudi relative. My wife's mother was at one time married to a Palestinian who had gone to Riyadh after their divorce, taking their daughter with him, and still lived there. Thus I have an Arab half-sister-in-law, with whom we are still in touch.

Before I had time to embark on that rather complicated story, Mr Khashoggi at last came into the room and greeted me for the second time that evening. The atmosphere was relaxed and very private and, as I had expected, the first thing he wanted me to do was another spoon-bending job. I had already done more than I can usually manage in one evening, but this was one request I could certainly not refuse, and mercifully all went well. As I had also expected, he immediately wanted to know if I could teach him how to do it!

A few minutes later I was quite exhausted after all the concentration I had needed, not so much to bend the spoons but to push my silent message into his mind. Luckily, it was a short one, consisting of the single word: peace.

Although we said little to each other, I know he received the message. When we parted, he did what I am sure no Saudi has ever done to an Israeli: he came up to me and planted a kiss firmly on each of my cheeks.

I felt that I had accomplished my mission, and it was clearly time to leave. On my way out, before I had fully realized what had just taken place, I ran into somebody I already knew personally for the first time that evening. It was NBC television producer Robin Leach, whom I might have expected to be there, although he looked surprised to see me. He had filmed an interview with me a couple of years previously for his series *Lifestyles of the Rich and*

*Famous*, and now he was recording an example of the lifestyle of somebody a great deal richer than I was. The next thing I knew was that there was a television camera pointing at me, a microphone under my nose, and Robin was asking me, 'What do you think of the party?'

I cannot remember my exact words. This is what I was thinking, and what I hope I said, though I expect most of it was cut:

'How can you ask me such a banal question? What do you want me to say? It's a great party, the food and the champagne are fine? Look at the people around me – don't you realize that I'm an Israeli? And I'm among what some people think are my enemies: Egyptians, Jordanians, Palestinians, Saudi Arabians, even members of the King's family? Do you realize that Adnan Khashoggi got up and kissed me on both cheeks? All barriers were demolished when he gave me that sign. Here I am among my so-called enemies, and all I am getting from them is feelings of peace, love and unity. That's what I think of this party. Anybody can celebrate a birthday, but to celebrate the coming together of "enemies" is not so easy.'

I was not over-reacting. Nor was I overestimating what had happened. It is possible to break down barriers by a simple gesture. When that great man, President Sadat of Egypt, flew to Israel and stepped on the soil of the country he had fought a few years before, he made a tremendous and lasting impact without saying a word. Hatred between Egyptians and Israelis began to dissolve at once, not because of anything he said, but because of what he did.

It is possible to reshape the world for better or worse by simple gestures and simple intentions, provided those concerned have the power and the influence to get them across. Remember how pop singer Bob Geldof got off his backside and raised over £50 million for starving Africans! It was not just the money, but a change in attitudes that was his real achievement. That was mind-power in action, and if he can use it then so can anybody else. All you need to begin with is imagination.

More than a year after Mr Khashoggi's party, I learned of a curious sequel to my meeting with him and my delivery of my silent message. In the autumn of 1986, the NBC team came to film me at home for their programme, bringing with them a copy of the material they had shot at the party. After I had left, they had interviewed the host and asked him if he had any message for the world on his fiftieth birthday. He had, and it was a short one: 'Peace'.

I was interested to read recently that scientists are making a study of people who are what they call 'fantasy-prone', and finding that these people are more likely to have experiences of telepathy, clairvoyance or precognition than those who do not make much use of their imagination. It has also been found that such fantasy-prone people are very good hypnotic subjects, although they are just as normal and well-balanced in their personal and professional lives as people who do not go in for much in the way of fantasy or imagination.

I have been very highly fantasy-prone for as long as I can remember. Perhaps being an only child without too many toys to play with helped. I have already mentioned my first experiments in space travel, when I used to launch my little rockets made from old bullets towards the moon and the stars. Long before the first Sputnik went into earth orbit (in 1957) I was designing special suits for space travellers with all the necessary fittings for oxygen and heat supplies, pockets for their proteins and liquids, and so on down to the smallest detail.

When I was at Terra Santa College in Cyprus, I often used to entertain my class with my imagination: at the end of term, after the exams, our teachers would ask some of us to come to the front of the class and make up a story, and I soon became the most successful of the spontaneous storytellers. One of my classmates, Joseph Charles, remembered my space-fantasies clearly more than twenty years later.

'They were all about men going up in rockets and meeting people from other worlds,' he told me when we met in London in 1985. 'You would describe flying saucers and little spacemen, and your stories sometimes went on for two or three hours. If you hadn't finished when the bell went, you would go on from where you left off the next day, or the next week. I wish I could have written them all down.' (Later, I did manage to write one of them down myself in my novel *Pampini*.)

This may explain some of the confusion that was caused by Andrija Puharich's book *Uri* (1974), in which he included a lot of material about extraterrestrial forces that were supposed to be controlling me. Although much of his book was accurate factual reporting, many people were put off by the space-fantasy passages, and I admit that they caused me some embarrassment. You must remember that all of this fantasy material was obtained while I was under hypnosis, and I cannot be held responsible for what my imagination produced under such conditions. One reason I wrote *My Story* was to give my own version of events, though I must emphasize that there is a slight possibility that some of my energies do have some kind of extraterrestrial connection. Andrija and I are still the closest of friends and I have never forgotten how much of my success is due to him.

I have made good use of my imagination in the past, and I shall continue to do so in the future, whatever the areas into which it may lead me. If it should lead me astray, as it has once or twice, I know that my internal alarm system will sound as it did that morning after my visit to that London casino.

I am glad that more interest is now being shown in the areas of imagination and fantasy, but it may surprise you to hear that I really do not want to know what theories or conclusions the scientists might come up with. When I was very young, soon after I discovered that I could do things that other people thought unusual, I accepted my natural gifts without question and made use of them without worrying at all how I was able to make the hands of watches move, or how I could tell what other people were thinking of doing.

There were times when I was curious to know how these things were done. Yet when I began to work with scientists, in 1972, I found that I had built a protective barrier around myself between wanting to know how my powers worked and just using them. The barrier was put up to keep the explanations out, and every time somebody drilled a little hole in it and pushed through some scientific theory or other, I felt threatened. I was afraid that the hole would explode, like a dam bursting, and that I would be flooded with information that would destroy me. If Hal Puthoff, Russell Targ or Wilbur Franklin had come up to me one day and said, 'Hey, Uri, we finally figured out how you do it!', I know I would not have wanted to listen to them. My protective barrier would have been demolished. I was glad to demonstrate my powers for scientists, for a time, because I was asked to by people I admired and respected, as I still do. However, I did not and still do not want to know what any of them discovered.

I do not want to clutter up my mind with theories or conclusions. In any case, these will probably be disproved in a few years' time, and then proved again, and so on. People often ask me what I think about Edgar Cayce, or some other famous psychic of the past, and I tell them I know nothing about them because I have never read a book about anything to do with psychical research or parapsychology in my life. I have never even read right through any of the books or scientific papers about myself. Some of my friends think I should, so that I can be better at what I do, but I would rather go out for a run in a park and enjoy nature than break my head over theories of the mysteries of life by reading books about them. I prefer to live the mysteries.

Fantasy has played an important part in the evolution of the human race ever since our remotest ancestor crawled out of the mud. Our species is unlike the rest in the way that it has evolved, and especially in the speed with which it still evolves, both physically and mentally. Much of this rapid evolution depends on the way we use something probably no other species can equal: our minds.

There are people alive today who were born before the first aeroplane left the ground. They might even remember being told that heavier-than-air flight was scientifically impossible, and reading all the technical explanations that proved this. We have forgotten the names of the scientists who provided the explanations, but we remember the names of Langley, Santos-Dumont and the Wright brothers. They were the ones who used their imagination and made their fantasies come true. It was the same with space travel – learned professors went on assuring us that it was out of the question right up to a year or so before Sputnik went into orbit.

The first modern Olympic Games were held in 1896, shortly before the first aeroplanes flew. In that year, an American named Robert Garrett threw the discus just over ninety-five feet to pick up the gold medal. In 1960, the year before Yuri Gagarin went into space, another American named Alfred Oerter flung the thing more than twice that distance. If we can evolve both physically and imaginatively to this extent in a mere seventy years – roughly a human lifespan – what is still to come?

I can visualize two scenarios: the good one and the bad one. I will describe them in that order.

As the next thousands and millions of years go by, our bodies gradually change. We have less and less hair on them. Our hands, feet and legs grow less powerful because we no longer use them as we once did. Our heads, however, are much larger, especially our foreheads. As we make increasing use of our intelligence, we evolve to the point where our brains are more important for our survival than our limbs and our primitive sensory organs.

Moving ahead still further, I can see a species without anything we would recognize today as a body. We will have found new ways of seeing that do not require eyes, new ways of transportation or teleportation that do not involve the use of limbs, and new ways of pleasure-seeking and reproduction that do not depend on the archaic sexual organs we use at present.

Finally, we will no longer have physical bodies of any kind. We will no longer be men or women, but masses or fields of consciousness that will be able to travel through the universes and the cosmoses towards the infinite.

The second scenario is very different. According to this, in a matter of two or three hundred years we will be forced to abandon our planet, after making it uninhabitable, and start all over again elsewhere. Only a privileged few will be able to escape, for the rest will have polluted themselves to death or simply exterminated each other. Those lucky survivors will adapt to new environments and their seeds will create new civilizations, and for all of them there will always be the choice of futures: evolution towards the Creator, or self-destruction and starting again from the beginning.

I wish I knew which of these scenarios is going to come true. If we make full use of our minds and our fantasies, it will be the first. If we do not, it will be the second. The choice is ours.

Real psychic power is not about reading tea-leaves or tarot cards and telling people what they should already know. It is something to use to help us evolve. Somerset Maugham once wrote that money is 'the sixth sense which enables you to enjoy the other five'. He was wrong, it is not money which enables you to enjoy them, but the sixth sense itself.

You may be using your sixth sense already without realizing it, or dismissing it as mere intuition or coincidence. If you are a religious person, you use it every time you pray. Prayer is an energy of the soul used for a specific purpose, and if it never produced any results people would not still be using it.

I have never had to learn how to use psychic power, and I have never taught anybody to use theirs. All I have done is show them they have it. Thousands of people all over the world know this, and they have something to prove it: a drawing, a bent piece of cutlery, or a watch that has started working again.

There is not much I can say about how I do what I do. To bend a spoon, I simply hold it and order it to bend, without visualizing anything at all. I just say silently, 'Bend, bend, bend!' Some scientists, such as Eldon Byrd, Thelma Moss and Jack Houck, have developed a way of teaching anybody to do the same, although their methods are different from mine and involve intense visualization exercises in which you 'see' a force flowing out of your body into the spoon, which then becomes warm and flexible.

When I am transmitting a word or a picture by telepathy, I hold it on my mental television screen and will it into the mind of the receiver. When the image starts to fade, I usually know I have been successful. When I am receiving something, the procedure is similar: I visualize my blank TV screen and wait for something to appear on it. If it stays there for ten or fifteen seconds, I know I have picked up the right message, and I write it down. In the case of a drawing, it is nearly always exactly the same shape and size as the original, although all the details may not be right.

You can practise doing this at home, just by looking at a picture and trying to send its contents to your partner across the room or in the room next door. Or you can do 'remote viewing' experiments like the ones Puthoff and Targ did at SRI, where one of you goes out to a certain spot at a certain time, and the other describes whatever impressions come in about the place. Once you have learned to concentrate and keep your mind under control, it is really very simple. The difficulty for many people is believing that they can do it.

I have used my psychic powers to entertain people, to

show them that they too have the same powers, and with them I have diversified into several professional fields. What you do with yours is up to you. In a thousand years, if we are still around on this planet, we will look back at the twentieth century much as we now look back on our cavemen ancestors. They rubbed sticks together to make fire for cooking and keeping themselves warm. In a thousand years, the psychic and paranormal activities of today will seem as primitive as those cavemen's fire-lighting methods seem to us.

What will be possible once we have learned to control psychic power and make full use of it? In this book, I have told you what I have been able to do with my own powers over the past fifteen years, and whether I have made full use of all of them time alone will tell. Maybe in ten years' time I will be able to write a completely different kind of book.

A good example of what can happen when psychic powers are not controlled was described in detail by the writer Dotson Rader, in an article entitled 'A Charming Evening with Uri Geller' which appeared in the March 1976 issue of the magazine *Esquire*.

It was quite an evening, for both of us. It began with a meal at the brasserie in the Seagram Building on Park Avenue, during which Mr Rader noticed the salt-shaker 'moving determinedly by itself across the white tablecloth toward the edge of the perfectly level surface' while I was looking the other way. Then we went back to my apartment to continue our conversation, and things really got moving.

First, a wooden carving shot off the table right beside him and 'flew across the room, hitting the opposite wall and falling on the floor'. Then a spoon appeared from somewhere or other and did the same thing. Next, a lump of rock landed on the floor behind him, having apparently fallen from the ceiling. This was followed by a steel tape measure whizzing around the room on its own. By the end of the evening, my guest was in quite a state. I drove him back to his apartment, and as he was getting out of the car his front door key bent in his hand, so that he had to borrow one from the porter in order to get home.

He came to see me again a couple of days later. While I was in the bathroom, he took the wooden carving, put it under a cushion and sat on it, hoping this would stop it flying around. Apparently it did, but when we went out to the lobby we found it standing in front of the door of the elevator. I told him I was used to this kind of thing, which was true, though there had been more of it than usual in his presence. None of it was caused by me – I cannot imagine why I would want to throw my belongings around my own home, even subconsciously, and almost nothing like this happens when I am on my own. The unusual activity must have been caused, at least in part, by *his* psychic powers. That Brazilian journalist was right. We are all Uri Gellers.

One day, we will be able to teleport objects, and people, much as we transmit words and pictures today by telex. Space and time are not what we have been taught to believe, and once we have learned full control of the mind and all its powers, there will be no more physical barriers. Even today, some of those barriers are not as impenetrable as they might seem. Anything is possible. Everything is possible.

What is very probable is that in the future I shall continue to be attacked and debunked by all kinds of individuals and committees who have appointed themselves to save mankind from the paranormal, and indeed from any kind of religious expression or belief.

According to one of my most persistent detractors, Martin Gardner, 'people who no longer believe in religion are searching for some sort of substitute', and 'the paranormal provides a way of believing in the supernatural without having to adopt a traditional religious point of view'. He laments the fact that the media exploit this public interest and stimulate it further, thereby 'keeping the ball rolling'.

He and his colleagues do not seem to appreciate that they are doing more than anybody to keep the ball rolling. They have made a religion – a very profitable one – out of their anti-religious crusade, and by attacking the whole area of human psychic experience they have only added to popular interest in it. As far as I am concerned, every time they think they have finished me off for good all they are doing is oiling the wheels of my publicity machine. In fact, now and then they actually do me a major favour.

One recent example: on 30 July 1985 the *Sunday Times* published a letter from a British member of the 'Committee for the Scientific Investigation of Claims of the Paranormal' which was, to say the least, unflattering. However, it was read by the chief of a major mining company who promptly flew several thousand miles to London in order to sign a deal with me, which I am happy to say he did.

I hope my critics will keep up their good work. In spite of their efforts, or perhaps because of them, the magic and the mystery of Uri Geller will continue to survive, as they have already survived for fifteen years. This is because the believers outweigh the non-believers.

*   *   *

I cannot of course omit to mention my chief publicist, James Randi, who has contributed so much over the years to the boosting of my career that I am often asked if he is on my payroll! (In fact in 1986 he won a $272,000 award for his services to the anti-psi cause.) He has been announcing my professional demise for as long as I can remember, and life is not long enough to answer all the allegations he has written, spoken and circulated about me, although I have already dealt with some of the more blatant ones.

He admitted to reporter Connie Woodcock of the *Sunday Sun* (26 December 1976) that he wrote a book about me to 'destroy' me. 'With great pleasure', the reporter wrote, 'he waves his book and claims smugly he has "put him [Geller] out of business".' He claimed on the Long John Nebel WMCA radio programme (22 March 1977) that 'You don't hear anything about Geller. He's not heard of at all now. He's pretty well out of business.' Three years later, he was still at it, assuring an interviewer (*Omni*, April 1980) that I was 'generally discredited'.

Randi has in fact come very close to going out of business himself, according to the *Toronto Sun* (5 November 1974):

The Amazing Randi, magician by trade, almost died of embarrassment yesterday, not to mention lack of oxygen – while bound and locked in the *Sun*'s office safe.

The world famous magician was pulled unconscious from the safe nine minutes and 35 seconds after he entered it while horrified staffers looked on . . . It had started out as a demonstration of how to crack a safe from the inside. It turned out to be a brush with death for Randi.

He described himself to the reporter as 'a professional fraud', and took the opportunity to refer to me as 'a very good magician'.

He must have been somewhat surprised when I turned up on the NBC television special *Magic or Miracle*? (8 February 1983) and was given virtually equal time on what had originally been planned as a show entitled *The Miracle Seeker* and featuring him. (Our contributions were filmed separately, and we did not meet.) At one point on the programme, I was asked to give an example of what I considered to be a miracle. My answer was 'The birth of a child', to which Randi, a bachelor and self-confessed agnostic, commented 'Messy!' To me, this epitomized the fundamental differences between his attitude to life and humanity and mine. A well-known sceptic later told a friend of mine that 'Uri made Randi look terrible'.

'We could have been good friends, you and I,' he says in one of his books. No, Randi, we could never have been good friends. Not even friends. You have told a newspaper reporter that you admired me as you admired Adolf Hitler. You have seen fit to mention my name in the same breath as that of a mass-murderer, and also with that of Jim Jones, who brought about the suicide of hundreds of religious fanatics in Guyana. You have circulated a statement, dated May 1986, alleging that I have blackmailed and defamed you, which is absurd because I would not resort to such activities. You have alleged that one of the scientists who investigated me 'died not long afterward under conditions described as not natural'.

I will merely repeat the self-analysis Randi gave on the *PM Magazine* television programme on 1 July 1982: 'I'm a charlatan, a liar, a thief and a fake altogether. There's no question of it.'

I do not have to challenge, confront, argue with or even defend myself against anybody. Individual opinions, however extreme, cannot outweigh those of the hundreds of thousands, perhaps millions of people who have experienced a little real magic in their lives after seeing what I – and they – can do, or those of countless millions who have been experiencing the same thing in many forms throughout recorded history.

I am now able to afford the luxury of being able to tell any of my witch-hunters exactly where they can go and what they can do there. As I have indicated throughout this book, there are more important challenges to be confronted: those that can lead to new possibilities and new realities.

It is for those challenges that I will save my energies.

I have made a good living, by making the best use I can of my natural abilities. This has brought me comfort, and something much more important to me: the 'quality time' I can spend with my wife and children and with my close friends, or in pursuing my other interests of painting, writing and enjoying nature.

I only regret one thing in my life, and that is that my father did not live to see his grandchildren.

I thank God every day for having given me and my family health, love and peace. I pray every day for the sick in body or mind to be healed, and for a better world to come for us all.

I also give thanks for my share of some mysterious human abilities which neither science nor I can explain, but the reality of which can no longer be denied.

Almost exactly ten years ago, I ended my first book with the words: 'Either the people accept *My Story* or they don't. There is no in between.' So it is with *The Geller Effect*. You are free to accept or to reject this effect, as you please. I do not think you can deny its existence.

# Part Three

*by*
Guy Lyon Playfair

# 13

## *The Bolívar Syndrome*

### Uri Geller a cheat
Magicians Disclose the Secrets of the Telepathic Impostor

This announcement was made on the cover of the 20 October 1970 issue of the sensationalist weekly magazine *Haolam Hazeh*, and within a few months of Uri's first public appearance in Israel the anti-Geller campaign was under way. It was based on the assumption: magicians can do all kinds of clever things; Geller can do all kinds of clever things; therefore Geller is a magician.

What else could he be, it was thought by many at the time and has continued to be thought by some? Geller began his career on the stage, and he has never objected to being called an entertainer. His public performances were to follow a routine that was to be repeated almost unchanged for fifteen years, during which professional conjurors showed that they too could bend spoons, make watches tick and reproduce drawings made by members of their audiences. They found no difficulty in accepting Geller as an unusually skilled manipulator of both crowds and individuals who had developed a highly polished and original performance. Marcello Truzzi, one of the more good-natured of his early critics, suggested that the Society of American Magicians should name him Conjuror of the Year and leave the criticism of him at that.

Others were not so generous. To them, Geller's claim that he was demonstrating real magic brought the art of conjuring into disrepute. Their sense of outrage was well expressed by magician James 'The Amazing' Randi in his polemical book *The Magic of Uri Geller* (1975): '. . . I am proud of my profession. I am even jealous of it and resent any prostitution of the art. In my view, Geller brings disgrace to the craft I practise. Worse than that, he warps the thinking of a young generation of forming minds. And that is unforgivable.' Randi's book was hailed by popular astronomer Carl Sagan as 'a witty and fascinating dissection of Uri Geller's humbuggery'. Leon Jaroff of *Time* saw it as 'a devastating blow to the pseudo-science of parapsychology'. Martin Gardner of *Scientific American* declared that 'all who respect truth should take off their hats and cheer'.

On the other side of the fence, some of the most sympathetic members of the scientific community began to have their doubts about the young Israeli who, for a time, had apparently performed his feats as successfully in the laboratory as on the stage or in the television studio. He did not fit into the pattern to which for more than a century they and their predecessors had become accustomed. The star psychic performers of the past had generally placed themselves at the service of science ever since the 1870s, when the spectacular medium Daniel D. Home submitted himself willingly to more than three years of scrutiny by one of the leading scientists of the time, William Crookes. Later, the Neapolitan Eusapia Palladino was tested by more than fifty scientists, including four Nobel Prize winners, for nearly thirty years. Leonore Piper of Boston offered her services on a full-time basis to members of the Society for Psychical Research, who published volume after volume of reports on the information she produced while in a state of trance. Then there was Rudi Schneider, a modest Austrian garage mechanic who spent much of his spare time throughout his life doing whatever scientists asked him to do with his psychokinetic powers, and then doing it all over again for another team of investigators. The Irish-American clairvoyant Eileen Garrett even went to the lengths of commissioning and financing scientific investigations of herself.

Geller was different. Although he spent a good deal of time from 1972 to 1974 in laboratories, he soon became tired of serving as a human guinea-pig. Sitting down wired to machines and being told what to do did not suit his temperament at all. He was an entertainer, who only felt at home when performing in front of an audience, and he could not wait to get back to where he felt he belonged: the public stage.

Some of his supporters began to have second thoughts. Professor John G. Taylor of London University stated in 1975 that 'the existence of the Geller Effect alone shows that the scientifically impossible can sometimes occur' after describing (in *The Geller Papers*) a number of incidents in his own laboratory involving his own equipment. However, he added, 'I could always try taking the safe line that Geller *must* have been cheating . . .' This was the line he did take five years later in his book *Science and the Supernatural*, after setting up what he considered to be a fraud-proof experiment with the help of a magician, and failing to observe any Geller Effects during it. He concluded, 'As far as I am concerned, there endeth the saga of Uri Geller; if he is not prepared to be tested under such conditions, his powers cannot be authentic.'

Let us return to the beginning of the anti-Geller saga, and the three-page cover story in the Israeli magazine already mentioned that launched it in 1970. The article was unsigned, but most of it consisted of statements by a magician named Eitan Ayalon who announced that 'all of

Israel's magicians have assembled for a witch-hunt against Uri Geller' and went on to explain why.

There were three reasons. First, Geller was overdoing his claims to be a genuine psychic. He was not the first 'magician' to do this, Ayalon recalled. The performances of David Berglas, a well-known master of mental magic and illusionism, had been billed in Israel as making use of telepathy and 'parapsychology', as were Geller's. Berglas could be forgiven since he had never made such a claim himself, but Geller could not. He had gone too far.

The second reason for the 'witch-hunt' was more serious: he was interfering with Israeli politics. Prime Minister Golda Meir's off-the-cuff reply to a question on the country's future – 'I don't know, ask Uri Geller' – had been widely reported. Geller had recently met the minister of transport (later to be the country's prime minister) and had bent some cutlery for him. 'He even broke Shimon Peres's pen without touching it,' the magazine revealed, adding, 'We also have a report that Uri Geller was called this week to demonstrate his powers to Minister of Defence Moshe Dayan.' The 'telepathic impostor' was, in short, becoming 'a national menace'.

It was the third reason, however, that had been chiefly responsible for Ayalon and his colleagues' decision to embark upon the witch-hunt. 'He started to hurt our earnings,' said Ayalon. 'That is why we decided to hit back.' They did so initially not by revealing his secrets, but by training a couple of youngsters named Eddie Moore and Nurit Pai to perform as phoney psychics. Ayalon even grew a 'mystic' beard and had a go himself, claiming to have fooled several audiences with performances based on Geller's routine.

'Uri Geller will disappear,' he prophesied. 'We give him an ultimatum: if he does not stop his imposture in two weeks, we will reveal all.' He was reluctant to do this, he said, but it was a question of 'saving the Israeli people'.

Geller confirms he met Shimon Peres. 'His pen bent and broke in his pocket,' he told me. He also had this to say about his meeting with General Dayan, to which he never referred publicly in any detail while the hero of the Six Day War was still alive:

He telephoned me and said he would like to meet me, and invited me to have a meal with him at the White Elephant steakhouse near the town of Zahala, where he lived. This was an honour for me, because Dayan was everybody's idol at that time.

I demonstrated my powers to him. First, he did a drawing, and I received it. Then I did one for him to receive, which he did. Then I bent a key for him, and we discussed the potentials of these powers. He was very intrigued. I remember his one eye flickering and gleaming. Then he said he would like to meet me again in a less public place. I paid the bill, by the way.

Two or three weeks later he telephoned me again and invited me to his home. It would be very private, he said, just the two of us.

I went to his house, and when he had shown me some of his collection of archaeological antiques, he said, 'Look, Uri, I have hidden a photograph somewhere in this room. I would like you to do two things: find it, and describe it to me before you look at it.'

I used to do this kind of thing at parties, but with rings or bracelets, not photographs. I told him it might not work, because I was nervous, which I was. Anyway, I started to walk around with my hands out in my usual way, and I ended up at a row of about forty books on a shelf. I pointed at one of them.

'It's in there,' I said. 'In this book.'

'You're right,' he said at once, with a laugh. 'Now, what is on the photograph?'

I asked him to project the photograph to me, which he did, and I picked up all kinds of impressions. Then I asked him for a pen and paper.

'Oh no,' he said. 'I don't want you to leave my sight. Don't write it, describe it.' I will never forget that – it depressed me because I thought he was being negative and cautious.

Anyway, after about five minutes I said, 'It's a photograph of the flag of Israel.'

He really collapsed, and just sat in his armchair laughing his head off.

'Are you laughing because I was right, or because I was wrong?' I asked him. He told me to open the book and see for myself. I did, but could not find any photograph. Then he took the book, and turned to page 201, where there was a small photo of the main tower of Lod Airport showing part of the roof, a flag-pole, and the flag of Israel.

'You've proved yourself, Uri,' he said to me. 'I don't want to see any more. There's no need for you to bend anything. Now, what can you do for Israel?'

Geller was not prepared to describe the two-hour-long conversation that followed, except to indicate that Dayan was interested in 'very major things' and clearly saw more potential uses for psychic powers in military contexts than he did.

'He seemed resigned to the fact that I was more interested in becoming rich and famous than in being a psychic superspy,' Uri told me. He was equally unforth-coming about his alleged meetings with Golda Meir and the head of Israeli military intelligence, General Aharon Yariv. However, from what is known of the methods of Israeli's intelligence services, it is most unlikely that Geller would not have been checked out very thoroughly, and without his knowledge, by at least one of them. It is also very unlikely that those findings would have been passed on to anybody except on a need-to-know basis. Who needed to know what when Targ and Puthoff were briefed by the Mossad in 1973 has not been revealed.

\* \* \*

Geller did not disappear in 1970, as forecast by Eitan Ayalon, and the people of Israel showed no sign of wanting to be saved from him. Yet the witch-hunters refused to give up. *Haolam Hazeh* returned to the fray in its issue of 14 March 1973, in which editor Eli Tavor dismissed Uri as 'a proven crook', largely on the evidence of the forged photograph of him and Sophia Loren, for which Uri's former publicist Rany Hirsch has now admitted that he was solely responsible. Two weeks later, the magazine published its long-promised revelation of how it thought Uri was doing his metal-bending, introducing the 'hidden chemical' theory which was popular for a time in witch-hunting circles until James Randi, no less, pointed out that any substance capable of softening metal is far too dangerous to use and should be withdrawn from sale in magic shops.

On 20 February 1974, *Haolam Hazeh* published its most determined effort to date to save Israel from the menace of Uri Geller. This was the article reprinted in full in Randi's book, in an English translation, and it has been widely cited as if it were an official report from Israel's Academy of Sciences. In fact it is a string of inaccuracies from start to finish. A good deal of it is based on statements attributed to Hanna Shtrang, who has assured me that she never said a word of any of them and never even met the writer of the article. Eli Tavor himself has now admitted that the whole article may have been pure invention.

Even the British press, which on the whole covered Geller's early career objectively and fairly, contributed its share of confusion. On 15 January 1974, Richard Herd reported in the *Daily Mail* that he had been to Israel 'seeking to track down the legend which Uri Geller has woven around himself'. He got off to a shaky start, revealing that Geller was born in Hungary and taken to Israel at the age of ten by his father, who died in 1957, whereupon his mother 'married again and had a son by Uri's stepfather'. (Uri was in fact born in Tel Aviv and taken to Cyprus by his mother. His father died in 1979, and although his mother did remarry she had no further children). Stumbling further along the trail, Mr Herd complains that 'no one remembers him doing anything at all until he was serving as a paratrooper'. This is not surprising, since he was not in Israel, but in Cyprus, where his teacher Mrs Jenny Agrotis remembered him very well. As she wrote to the *News of the World* in December 1973:

Uri Geller was a pupil of mine for five years in Cyprus. Even while so young he astonished his friends at the [Terra Santa] College with his amazing feats, i.e. bent forks, etc. The stories he told them of the wonderful scientific things that could, and would, be done by him, seem to be coming true. I for one do believe in him, he was outstanding in every way, with a brilliant mind, certainly one does not meet a pupil like him very often.

Had Mr Herd stayed at home, he might have been able to locate a couple of Geller's old schoolmates in England, as I did without much difficulty more than ten years later, when they still remembered a good deal. I will return to them in due course.

I have given a brief sample of Geller's early press coverage to show that the witch-hunt against him was based on some very insecure foundations. These consisted of assumptions, rumours and outright lies, and very little actual evidence at all. It is indeed strange, as Uri has already pointed out, that sources such as the popular *Haolam Hazeh* were accepted without question, whereas the scientific papers in refereed journals, such as *Nature*, were rejected without hesitation or reflection on the professional reputations of their authors.

When it came to complicating the Geller legend, a major contribution was made, ironically, by the man who discovered him and brought him to the West: Dr Andrija Puharich.

By the time he met Geller, Puharich had a long record of imaginative research in both straight science and parapsychology. He had patented more than fifty of his inventions in the field of biotechnology and written two fine books, *The Sacred Mushroom* and *Beyond Telepathy*. His research with unusually gifted subjects made him the ideal person to explain the mystery of Uri Geller.

His 1974 book *Uri* contained some excellent passages of straight reporting, based on abundant tape-recorded first-hand evidence, in addition to some shrewd observations and reasonable speculations. Interspersed with these, however, were passages that seemed to have strayed from a science fantasy novel by A. E. Van Vogt, in which we were asked to believe that Geller was no ordinary kid from the Middle East, but the emissary of a group of extraterrestrials called The Nine, whose duties included controlling the universe from a space-org called Spectra. They communicated with us, through Uri, by means of messages on tapes that, once played back, would dematerialize. Colin Wilson, the most open-minded and sympathetic of Geller's commentators, found all this 'astonishing and unbelievable', and 'a bit too much'. So did most people. Even Uri, as he has already said, was considerably embarrassed.

The simplest explanation for some was that Puharich had gone off his head. However, as is the case with the 'explanations' put forward by the witch-hunters to account for Uri's feats, it does not stand up to close examination. Puharich, whom I have met several times, is a man with an unusual mind. In a long career in scientific research, his thoughts have found their ways into distant orbits, where they have captured some practical and successful inventions, such as the series of miniature deaf-aids that have earned him a good deal in royalties over the years. If his thoughts have occasionally led him where the rest of us are unable to follow, the same can be said of many inventors. Edison, for example, firmly believed that communication with the dead was possible, and he designed a machine for the purpose. Tesla, on whose genius much of our electrical industry is based, believed that power could be plucked from space and driven through the core of the earth to any point on its surface. An element of apparent craziness is an essential component of the mind of a successful inventor.

All the information from The Nine was provided while Geller was in a hypnotic trance state. Puharich is a skilful hypnotist, who has long made use of hypnosis to enhance the abilities of his research subjects, and Geller admits to being an excellent hypnotic subject. As he has told us, his earliest childhood fantasies were of space travel, rockets and distant civilizations, and by his early teens he had woven these into stories that fascinated both his classmates and his teacher. Neither he nor I can say how those fantasies came into his mind, or where they originated. The fact is that they were there, and under hypnosis, as we would expect, they came out.

As long ago as 1844, an English mesmerist, Rev. C. Hare Townshend, discovered that a good subject was able to blend his thoughts with those of the mesmerist or hypnotist:

. . . my patient's ideas shifted so visibly with my own, and were so plainly the echo of my own thoughts, that not to have perceived the source whence they came would have been pertinacious blindness indeed. I was but taking back my own, and receiving coin issued from my own treasury.

Puharich had received much material of supposedly extraterrestrial origin before, through subjects other than Geller, and it is surprising that he does not seem to have allowed for his own role in the utterances of The Nine. These would have made an interesting book in themselves, but their inclusion in what was otherwise a straightforward and factual account of Geller's early career did neither the author's nor Uri's reputation any good at all. It took Geller some time to live them down, although he promptly did his best to set the record straight with his own account of his (terrestrial) life, *My Story*.

Puharich's book added greatly to the scepticism of those who were already feeling in 1974 that Geller was too good to be true. I was one of them.

I first became aware of the existence of somebody called Uri Geller in 1973, when I read the article on him in *Time* magazine's 12 March issue. I was living in Brazil at that time and researching the local psychic scene for my books *The Flying Cow* and *The Indefinite Boundary*. I was finding much material that struck me as genuine, as it still does, and had little interest in this exotic spoon-bender who, according to *Time*, was just a smart conjuror. Then the June 1973 issue of the magazine *Psychic* arrived through my letter-box. It contained a long interview with Geller and an article by Alan Vaughan, who had clearly studied his subject far more thoroughly than *Time* science writer Leon Jaroff had done. According to Vaughan, Geller was able to accomplish practically everything of a paranormal nature ever reported, with the exception of the Indian rope trick. I was intrigued. However, one of the many incidents in Uri's eventful life stuck in my mind. This is how he described it:

One experiment I did with Andrija [Puharich] was when he asked me to go to Brazil out of the body. I got to this city and asked a person where I was, and he told me it was Rio de Janeiro. Then someone came up and pressed a brand-new one-thousand cruzeiro note in my hand, and it appeared in my hand on the couch by Andrija – to prove I was there.

This took place in Puharich's home in Ossining, NY, on 24 March 1973, and it struck me as very odd for a number of reasons, in addition to the inherent improbability of simultaneous teleportation from Brazil to the United States. I wrote to *Psychic* mentioning some of them, beginning with the fact that the 1,000 cruzeiro note had been out of circulation following the introduction of the 'new cruzeiro' in 1967. I went on:

For an old 1,000 note to have remained brand new for something like five years in Rio de Janeiro is very unlikely. Usually they fall apart in a few months and have to be held together with tape. Moreover, the people of Rio do not usually hand money to foreigners in the street. Sometimes they do just the opposite.

I ended by expressing the hope that Puharich would help solve the mystery of this apparent teleportation through both space and time. He promptly obliged, in the same issue in which my letter appeared (December 1973), providing the serial number of the banknote and adding that he liked my approach to the case. I had little difficulty in establishing that the note had been printed and circulated in April 1963. A Bank of Brazil official confirmed that its expected life before being withdrawn for pulping would have been nine months at the most.

I also discovered that Puharich had visited Brazil in the same year, and I wondered if somehow or other this note had been issued to him and kept, later finding its way between the cushions on his sofa. I duly wrote up my findings – my first published contribution to psychical research – which appeared in print no less than three times: in *New Scientist* (14 November 1974), the *Journal of the Society for Psychical Research* (June 1975) and, with my permission, in Randi's book *The Magic of Uri Geller* (1975). Doing my best to impress my fellow members of the SPR with my impeccable scepticism, I concluded:

[This episode] does suggest to me that further examination of Geller's paranormal abilities can lead to totally normal hypotheses as to how he performs his feats.

Randi commented, 'Thank you, Mr Playfair, for an excellent piece of work', and for a time I was quite popular in the SPR, until my colleague Maurice Grosse and I upset many of its members with our uncompromisingly positive reports of all kinds of paranormality from the Enfield poltergeist case of 1977–8.

Uri's own version of the Brazil event, in a letter to me dated 21 March 1978, was as follows:

I will now tell you exactly what happened. The money . . . did appear in my hand when I woke up from the trance. As far as I can remember when I was in this strange hypnotic state Puharich put me in, I remember very clearly walking on a sort of main street. I was lost and scared. I stopped a passing couple and asked for money. It is not clear to me exactly who gave me the note, but as it was put in my hand I woke up on the bed in Ossining. And that is the honest truth. To this day I wonder if maybe Andrija could have . . . hypnotized me so deeply that this event looked so real to me, and then stuck the money in my hand. As far as I'm concerned I tend to believe that this was a real happening, and I don't think Andrija had any interest in faking such an incident. I really can't tell you anything else. Strange things do happen and this was one of them.

I have mentioned this episode at some length to establish my credentials as the first person anywhere, as far as I have been able to discover, to have published a critical piece on Geller that was based on both original research and hard evidence. I hope this will be borne in mind when I describe my own further examinations and reach new conclusions.

Proving conclusively that strange things happen can be very difficult. How do you go about it? In most areas of science, you form a hypothesis and test it, and if enough people test it independently and get the same results as you, it can be considered proven. However, in the psychic sciences this method does not work. Numerous eminent scientists from William Crookes onwards have testified to the occurrence in their presence of some very strange things, but although their word was not questioned on other matters, their findings in the psychic realm were rejected out of hand. Why?

'Ah,' say the magicians, 'because they were deceived. It takes one magician to spot another. We know how he or she tilted the table, bent the spoon or read the mind, but we won't tell you because you don't give away trade secrets.' We are asked to take the words of the magicians on trust, although this is hardly reasonable since magicians are professional deceivers who are frequently deceived themselves by their colleagues and even, as I will describe, by laymen.

All the same, when a magician spends several days closely observing Uri Geller, and concludes that his psychic powers are real, his findings should be of special interest. He might have been deceived, of course, but this argument is balanced by the equally valid one that the witch-hunters might also have been deceived. Furthermore, it is harder to fool somebody who knows what to look for.

The first magician to make a careful first-hand study of Geller was a Dane named Leo Leslie, whose book *Uri Geller: Fup eller Fakta*? (Fraud or Fact?) was published in 1974. It has received less attention than it deserves, partly because no English translation has yet appeared and partly, I suspect, because of the author's uncompromising conclusion.

Leslie, adviser on magic to Denmark's National Museum, was called in by the state television company to supervise arrangements for a performance Geller gave in Copenhagen in January 1974. He was able to introduce a number of controls, without Geller's knowledge, thus eliminating the more obvious methods of cheating. Some of these were quite ingenious. He arranged, for instance, for Geller to be continuously monitored by cameras from the moment he entered the studio before the programme went on the air. 'Experience shows', he noted, 'that it is always in the last hectic moments before a live transmission that a magician checks out his equipment.'

One cameraman was ordered to keep Geller's hands in view all the time. Leslie and three accomplices watched him both live and on monitors throughout the .evening and reported no suspicious movements either before or during the show. Leslie also managed to ensure that none of Geller's entourage entered the studio at any time.

Before the show began, Geller learned to his annoyance that he was expected to try to bend or break the metal clip of the brassiere worn by a large-bosomed photographer's model, in the hope that she would reveal all on camera. He refused to do this, considering it to be in bad taste. Leslie sprang another surprise on him by presenting him with an array of clocks and watches that he had rigged beforehand so that it was impossible for any of them to start ticking. Geller told Leslie afterwards that he would have tried harder if he had known in advance that they were jammed. On a recent Australian television programme, he had managed to start a clock that had been doctored by a professional clockmaker, who had inserted some pieces of plastic in its works.

He was more successful with his drawing-reproduction routine. A drawing of the front view of an elephant had been sealed in an envelope and handed to the photographer's model, who slipped it under her bra, then apparently forgot what the drawing was. All the same, Geller managed to draw what Leslie described as 'a rendition of an elephant seen from behind'. It was, he noted, exactly the same size as the original, which was opened on camera.

Geller also bent and broke a fork during the programme, but Leslie admitted he had not had an uninterrupted view of the whole proceedings. After the show, however, things improved considerably. Although Leslie confessed that he was a magician, Geller offered him a personal demonstration.

First, he did a telepathy test while he and Leslie were sitting with their backs to each other and a colleague of Leslie's was observing the two of them. Leslie thought of a flower and began to draw it, taking care to make distracting noises as he did so. The colleague noticed that

Geller also began to draw a flower. Moreover, it was Geller who began to draw first. That was good enough for Leslie.

'I had to admit defeat,' he wrote. 'Uri had apparently read my thoughts.'

Leslie then produced a key which he had prepared in advance by coating it with enamel and nickel plating, making it impervious to acid. He had experimented beforehand with some mercury bichloride, finding that he was unable to reproduce 'phenomena that resembled Geller's even slightly'. Geller began to rub the key and immediately noticed there was something unusual about it.

'You have done something to it,' he said. 'I can't get in touch with the metal.'

'I licked my lips,' Leslie wrote. 'Now he was caught! It was chemicals after all, I thought.' Leslie took the key and studied it closely. 'While I sat looking at the key, the enamel started to crack, and a second later strips of the nickel plating curled up like small strips of banana peel as the key started to bend in my fingers.' While all this was going on, 'The telephones started ringing. The populace had apparently run wild. The sick were healed, watches started, silverware and cutlery bent. The Geller landslide had begun.'

The judgment of Leslie and his accomplices amounted to total vindication.

'We found his metal-bending and his ability to receive telepathic signals reasonably documented.' After a lengthy discussion of several possible methods, he concluded, 'There was no possibility of trickery.'

Just to make sure, Leslie obtained the names and addresses of some of the callers to the television studio and spent some days checking up on them. After visiting several of them, he was satisfied that some were able to bend metal and receive telepathic messages in much the same way as Geller had done. Then came the final straw that caused the last traces of his scepticism to disappear.

'Of course, it had to happen that my own son came and told me that he could bend teaspoons!' When the boy had 'convinced his sceptical father', Leslie immediately called a fellow magician who had a Geiger counter and asked him to bring it over. He did, and although Leslie junior was unable to do another spoon-bending job in the presence of this stranger, he did manage to produce readings on the counter while he was rubbing away at the spoon. Neither of the two magicians was able to do the same.

Leo Leslie's final verdict, after a total of sixteen meetings with Geller and a good deal of discussion of all aspects of his performances: 'I must emphasize that nothing I have seen or heard in my investigation of Uri Geller has changed my initial conviction that he is in possession of certain psychic powers.'

If Leslie had reached a negative verdict, it would no doubt have been widely quoted. In the event, he was generally ignored. Four years later, *The Times* published a letter from a certain Dr John Worrall claiming that no professional magician had yet been involved in tests of Geller's abilities. By then, the findings of at least four magicians – Leslie, William E. Cox, Abb Dickson and Artur Zorka – were already in print.

Cox, an associate member of the Society of American Magicians with forty years of experience in conjuring, described an experiment for which he had prepared his own double-backed pocket watch by jamming the works with a piece of aluminium foil. It began to tick shortly after Geller touched it, and on opening it up Cox found that both the foil and the regulator arm had moved. There was no conceivable way in which Geller could have touched them.

Zorka, chairman of the Occult Investigation Committee of the Atlanta Society of Magicians, sent an official report to his society's executive committee stating that he and Dickson had tested Geller under conditions of their own design, nobody else being present. A fork with a rein-forced nylon handle literally exploded in Geller's hand while Zorka was staring straight at it, and Geller repro-duced a picture of a dog of which Zorka had merely been thinking, matching it in size as well as in general outline. (Geller was delighted to hear later that Zorka had named one of his Dalmatian puppies Uri, in memory of this event. The dog went on to win several prizes.)

'There is no known way, based on our present collective knowledge, that any method of trickery could have been used to produce these effects under the conditions to which Uri Geller was subjected,' Zorka stated in his report. Dickson wrote a polite letter to Geller on 3 June 1975, the day after they met, offering to co-operate with him on future controlled tests.

'You proved to me that what you are doing is for real,' he wrote. 'I am convinced that those who wish to call you a fake are no more than fakes themselves, and out for the publicity they would gain by it.'

The reaction of his and Zorka's fellow magicians was interesting. James Randi, then on a tour promoting his recently published anti-Geller book, wrote a statement that, according to Zorka, contained no less than nine errors of fact in nineteen lines of typewriting. Randi even alleged that Geller himself had written out the magicians' report and persuaded them to sign it.

Zorka replied with an open letter (6 January 1976) in which he vigorously rejected all of Randi's allegations. His conclusion is worth quoting at some length, since it can be applied to a good deal of the activities of the witch-hunters:

Randi has come to realize that controversy is very lucrative. He also realizes that the more controversy which surrounds 'Randi versus Geller', the more copies of Randi's book will sell . . .

I have discussed Randi's statement, along with his attempt to discredit me. I have done so with little effort. His statement lacks substance, not because Randi did not dig to find it, but because none exists.

I do not appreciate Randi's apparent *commercial* attacks on serious scientists and investigators, such as myself, who are genuinely seeking answers within the realm of parapsychology . . .

His past performance as a deceptionist regarding the Geller affair is apparently void of respect for honest investigations into the paranormal. This applies especially to the well-earned reputations of the scientists who have tested Uri Geller. Randi also has mocked scientists in general who have delved into parapsychology at all.

Whether Randi is the crusader for the 'poor misinformed public' that he wants to be regarded as being is questionable. If he were interested in informing the public, he would be interested in both sides of the coin.

Randi's brand of commercialism is extremely distasteful to me. I am one of many who wish to set the record straight. Randi, through his own contradictions, has brought himself into a pseudo-exposé which is so weak that it is in effect groundless. More and more, Randi is being realized as an unreliable source.

To add insult to injury, six members of Zorka's own society wrote to Geller dissociating themselves from their colleague's report, considering it to be 'merely opinions of relatively inexperienced investigators'. (They had not been present during the investigation described in it.) The same society, incidentally, had only just named Zorka as its Magician of the Year.

'I sincerely believe that had Mr Dickson and I discovered Mr Geller at some sort of trickery, and released that information, there would have been no concern,' Zorka retorted. 'If that is so, then I'm afraid we have a contradiction here.'

He and Dickson must have felt what most honest investigators of Geller were to feel sooner or later. The feeling was well summed up, albeit in a somewhat different context, by the nineteenth-century Latin American reformer Simón Bolívar:

'Those who have served the cause of revolution have ploughed the sea.'

# 14
## *The Witch-Hunters*

In the United States, as in Israel, the anti-Geller witch-hunt began almost as soon as he arrived on the scene, and its stated purpose was identical: not to submit Geller to any kind of serious scientific study, but to save society from him.

Its early days were well witnessed at close quarters by John L. Wilhelm, a *Time* reporter and the author of *The Search for Superman* (1976). He named the chief hunters as Martin Gardner, a columnist for the *Scientific American*, amateur magician, and outspoken critic of anything he considered to be bogus or deviant science; the magician James Randi; and Wilhelm's (then) colleague Leon Jaroff, the magazine's science editor who later became editor of the Time-Life publication *Discover*.

'For Martin Gardner and the others in his magic circle, the issue of Uri Geller is a deeply moral one,' Wilhelm wrote in his book, quoting Gardner as declaring: 'Belief in occultism provides a climate for the rise of a demagogue. I think this is precisely what happened in Nazi Germany before the rise of Hitler.' He gave Wilhelm the impression that he thought it was about to happen again.

Stefan Kanfer, author of *Time*'s March 1974 cover story on 'The Psychics' was even more candid. According to Wilhelm, he believed that 'SRI should be destroyed' for having carried out research of any kind into paranormal matters. 'That's the way fascism began.'

Wilhelm soon discovered that separating legitimate criticism of Geller from 'the barrage of debunkers' moral outrage' was just as hard as evaluating the claims of his supporters. 'Regrettably,' he wrote, 'both sides argue on the basis of strong personal bias.' Randi, for example, rejected the evidence of Puthoff and Targ at SRI out of hand although he had not observed any of their experiments himself, 'I don't believe this kind of thing can happen if there are strict conditions,' he said.

The bugle-call that heralded the official start of the American witch-hunt was the *Time* article of 12 March 1973 by Leon Jaroff, and the circumstances under which it came to be written give some idea of the lengths to which the hunters were prepared to resort. On completing their research with Geller at SRI, Puthoff and Targ wrote on 28 December 1972 to Gerard Piel, publisher of the *Scientific American*, to ask if he was interested in printing their findings. A copy of this letter found its way somehow or other to Jaroff, as did a copy of the informal report to the Department of Defense by Ray Hyman, which he had written after his visit to SRI and also sent to his old friend Martin Gardner at the *Scientific American*. (I have been reliably informed that Gardner was not personally responsible for the report reaching Jaroff.)

At this time, according to Wilhelm, the 'circuit' consisting of Gardner, Randi, Jaroff and others 'rings continuously with the latest Geller goings-on, trading news clippings on Geller as kids trade baseball cards'.

Wilhelm provides further insights into the origins of the American witch-hunt. On 18 January 1973, he told Geller that Jaroff had already decided that he was a fraud, and had even made a bet on it. This was before Jaroff had ever seen Geller. The two met for the first time on 6 February, in the Time-Life building in New York.

Randi also met Geller for the first time on that day, and his published comments on the event are confusing, to say the least. On the one hand, he found Geller's telepathy demonstration 'the saddest, most transparent act I've ever seen', yet according to Wilhelm he found Uri 'extremely clever' and 'a good magician' with 'a beautiful routine'. Randi later admitted, in his book on Geller, that he had a copy of Hyman's letter to Gardner in his pocket at the time.

The crusade to save America from the menace of the occult took on new impetus with the founding in 1975 of the Committee for the Scientific Investigation of Claims of the Paranormal (CSICOP) by psychologist Paul Kurtz and sociologist Marcello Truzzi. Founder Fellows included Gardner, Hyman, Jaroff and Randi, in addition to those enthusiastic reviewers of Randi's anti-Geller book, Isaac Asimov and Carl Sagan. CSICOP's promotional literature for its journal included this:

Are you curious about claims of paranormal phenomena such as the Bermuda Triangle, precognition, UFOs, ancient astronauts, astrology, Bigfoot, astral projection, psychokinesis, cold reading, pyramid power, water witching and the like? . . . these and other similar interests are waiting for you to explore in the *Skeptical Inquirer*. This dynamic magazine . . . is bold enough to investigate *carefully* the extraordinary claims of true believers and charlatans of the paranormal world. Its findings are sometimes humorous, often sobering, always fascinating.

Of themselves, the Committee had this to say:

The more serious-minded among us are starting to ask what is going on. Why the sudden explosion of interest, even among some otherwise sensible people, in all sorts of paranormal 'happenings'? Are we in retreat from the scientific ideas of rationality, dispassionate examination of evidence and sober experiment that have made modern civilization what it is? In the past, the raising and answering of such questions has been left to commentators and journalists. This time around, however, some scientists are beginning to fight back.

CSICOP's first major attempt at careful investigation of an extraordinary claim was a total disaster. The claim was that of the French psychologist and professional statistician Michel Gauquelin, according to whom there was a statistically significant correlation between success-ful people in various walks of life and the position of the planets at the time of their birth. The extraordinary story of how CSICOP carried out a follow-up study, came up with results similar to Gauquelin's, initially failed to report them and eventually pretended that this had never been an official CSICOP project was spelled out in full detail by one of its own members, astronomer Dennis Rawlins, in the October 1981 issue of *Fate*. His skilful debunking of the debunkers led, not surprisingly, to his resignation from CSICOP, and also to the defections of some of its more active and influential members, such as the late Richard Kammann and the veteran British psych-ical researcher Eric J. Dingwall.

Long before then, co-founder Marcello Truzzi had left to found his own journal, the *Zetetic Scholar*. (Its first issue in 1978 included a most valuable 'basic bibliography' of Geller, listing 192 items.) Later, he founded his own research group, the Center for Scientific Anomaly Research (CSAR), and soon won the respect of many of those whose claims he investigated. Although he has assured me personally that he is a sincere non-believer in psychic powers of any kind, he has shown that civilized co-operation between sceptic and believer is possible.

CSICOP, on the other hand, soon resorted to methods of a kind hitherto unknown in any kind of scientific research, reaching some remarkable standards of 'dispassionate examination' in the process. Randi, for whom the pursuit of Geller became something of a personal crusade, invaded scientific laboratories, newspaper offices and parapsychology conferences wearing a variety of disguises, claiming to be a spoon-bender and mind-reader and attempting to deceive a number of individuals who were wholly unprepared for such behaviour. He toured the United States giving lecture-demonstrations, a regular feature of which was his 'I can do what Geller does' routine. In 1981, he launched the annual 'Uri Awards for Parapsychology' for what he considered 'the silliest and most irrational claims in relation to the paranormal'. Originally sponsored by *Omni*, they were taken over by *Discover* but have now been discontinued, no doubt as a result of the 1983 fiasco associated with them to be described shortly.

Randi even managed to sabotage a research programme by infiltrating a pair of young magicians, Steve Shaw and Mike Edwards, into the parapsychology laboratory funded by the late James S. McDonnell, a pioneer of the aerospace industry. There, as described in the *Skeptical Inquirer* (Summer 1983), they tried for nearly two years to trick the researchers into proclaiming them genuine Geller-type psychics. Randi revealed his hoax, dubbed 'Project Alpha', at a news conference in January 1983 sponsored by *Discover*, and in 1985 the laboratory was closed.

The public was encouraged to believe that since parapsychologists were so easily hoaxed, none of their claimed findings should be taken seriously. Then the inevitable happened: Randi and Jaroff were themselves taken for a ride. Shortly after Project Alpha's termination, the newsletter of a small Minneapolis research group, The

Archaeus Project, announced that a fund of $217,000 had been set up for a metal-bending research programme under Archaeus director Dennis Stillings, to whom gifted subjects should apply.

The newsletter was a fake, as Stillings made clear in his own news release. No such award had been made. Stillings printed just two copies and sent them to Shaw and Edwards, confident that they would promptly reach Randi. They did.

On 1 April 1983, a *Discover* news release signed by Randi had this to say about one of his Uri Awards:

Funding Category. To the Metronics Corporation of Minneapolis, who gave $250,000 to a Mr Stillings of that city to fund the Archaeus Project, devoted to observing people who bend spoons at parties. Mr Stillings then offered financial assistance to a prominent young spoon-bender who turned out to be one of the masquerading magicians of Project Alpha – a confessed fake.

Stillings could not believe it. Not only had Randi fallen for his bait – hook, line and sinker – but he had even managed to make a total of four mistakes in his brief news release: the non-fund had been increased from $217,000 to $250,000, the Medtronic Corporation had nothing to do with it at all, and was misspelled into the bargain, and Stillings had not 'offered financial assistance' to Shaw, Edwards, or anybody else.

To drive home the point that magicians can be fooled as easily as any other group, Stillings promptly did it again. An investment broker named Reid Becker wrote to Randi implying that some of his clients were somewhat concerned to hear of Medtronic's involvement with psychical research, and requested further information. Randi replied with the extraordinary allegation that the naming of Medtronic had orginated from Stillings, and suggested that Becker should contact him for clarification.

He had no need to do this, for it was Stillings himself who wrote the 'Becker' letter, on clumsily faked notepaper. He concluded, in his report on 'Project ROTSUC' ('Randi Ought To Sell Used Cars'):

Project ROTSUC was designed as a simple, inexpensive two-hour exercise in replicating the original experiment of James Randi (i.e. Project Alpha). We find the implicit conclusion of Project Alpha confirmed, namely: that some, perhaps all, people can be fooled for shorter or longer periods . . . Now that we know this, what are we going to do with it? I suggest that we all start behaving like civilized human beings . . .

What, many will be asking, has all this kind of thing to do with 'scientific investigation of claims of the paranormal'? Proving that people can be fooled is hardly necessary, since everybody who pays to attend a magic show already knows this. Proving that people other than Uri Geller can bend spoons by sleight-of-hand does not constitute proof in itself that he uses sleight-of-hand. As William James wrote, in the *American Magazine* (October 1909):

If we look at imposture as a historic phenomenon, we find it always imitative. One swindler imitates a previous swindler, but the first swindler of that kind imitated someone who was honest. You can no more create an absolutely new trick than you can create a new word without any previous basis. You do not know how to go about it.

James was referring to the physical phenomena of the Victorian seance room, such as table-tilting, but his words apply equally well to individuals such as Geller. Many conjurors have imitated him, but whom was he imitating the first time he bent a spoon? I will return to this question later. First, I must pursue my inquiry into the possible motivations of some of the more prominent members of CSICOP.

These become somewhat easier to understand if we regard the organization as a political rather than a scientific one, linked to the American Humanist Association by way of psychologist Paul Kurtz, a member of its board of directors and editor of its journal, *The Humanist*.

Humanism is a perfectly respectable philosophical movement dating back to the Renaissance, in which attention is focused on man and his potential abilities and away from theological or spiritual matters. In the United States, it has its roots in the writings of such social reformers and critics of the American way of life as Felix Adler and Irving Babbitt. The first humanist manifesto was published in 1933, and reissued forty years later, with a preface by Kurtz. Affirmation Fourteen reads as follows:

The humanists are firmly convinced that existing acquisitive and profit-motivated society has shown itself to be inadequate and that a radical change . . . must be instituted. A socialized and co-operative economic order must be established to the end that equitable distribution of the means of life is possible.

Neither Marx nor Engels could have put it more plainly, though while the American Humanist Association stands for much that the ideological fathers of communism stood for, it must be stressed that it does so quite legitimately, and there is no suggestion that it has ever behaved in an undemocratic or subversive way. The fact that it survived much attention from Senator McCarthy's infamous Committee on Unamerican Activities is, in my view, to its credit.

All the same, the most cursory of glances through the

pages of *The Humanist* shows that it has consistently attacked anything that can be seen as a deviation from classical Marxist materialism, sometimes using the kind of language employed by *Pravda* when referring to capitalism. Targets have included religions of all kinds, from traditional Jewish cognitive wisdom (Vol. 22 No. 1, 1962) to Zen Buddhism (Vol. 19 No. 6, 1959). The magazine has even managed to lay down a humanist party line on quantum mechanics (Vol. 19 No. 1, 1959), insisting that it does not lead to any change in materialist concepts of nature. As for parapsychology, in an article on the late Professor J. B. Rhine (Vol. 15 No. 4, 1955), it referred to his department at Duke University as a 'Super-Scientific Institute of Raciology' and gave the clear impression that the pioneer of academic parapsychology was mentally deranged. (*Time* went even further in its anti-psi diatribe of March 1974, printing Rhine's picture under the heading 'A Long History of Hoaxes' and alongside a photograph of the Cottingley Fairies.)

Suspicions that CSICOP no longer had any real interest in the scientific investigation of anything at all were raised at its 1983 conference, held in Buffalo, New York. As reported by a friend of mine who was present, there was an interesting exchange at question time between Kurtz and Dennis Rawlins. Rawlins wanted to know where all the money flowing into CSICOP from its journal's 18,000 subscribers (at $16.50 each) was going, now that its original research activities seemed to have ceased altogether. After some delay, Rawlins was told that all of it (nearly $300,000) went on producing the journal and organizing conferences. 'This', my friend commented, 'was patently absurd.'

It is a minor absurdity, however, compared with the principle that seems to underlie the actions of CSICOP and its parent body, the American Humanist Association: that widespread interest in the occult leads to fascism. It is true that the Nazis made clever and successful use of traditional magical ritual, symbolism, and propaganda with mystic overtones, but they came to power mainly by efficient organization and brute force. Interest in occult matters is widespread in West Germany today, yet there are no signs of any serious fascist threat in that country. It is also widespread in the rest of Western Europe, notably in Iceland, where would-be dictators will have a hard time seizing power since the country has no armed forces at all, other than its celebrated gunboats.

On the other hand, it may be no coincidence that the longest-serving dictator of this century, Enver Hoxha of Albania, banned all forms of religion altogether. One cannot escape the suspicion that CSICOP and the humanists would like to do the same, to judge from some of the published material I have mentioned. Serious occultists, at least those of my acquaintance, devote their energies to an exploration of any path that might lead them to a better understanding of the mysteries of nature, life and creation. The fact that many such paths lead to dead-ends is no excuse for not exploring them. However, if the humanists had their way, all such paths would be off limits.

The professional sceptic is for ever assuring us of his open-mindedness. Martin Gardner has written, 'Modern science should indeed arouse in all of us a humility before the immensity of the unexplored and a tolerance for crazy hypotheses.' He has shown no sign of either, indeed he has written a popular book, *Fads and Fallacies in the Name of Science* (1957), in which he tramples on every alternative hypothesis, crazy or not. Stefan Kanfer, author of the *Time* cover story of March 1974 already

mentioned, ended his six-page diatribe against parapsychology with a ringing call for a 'thorough examination of
the phenomena by those who do not express an a priori
belief'. One wonders why he did not attempt this himself.

It is ironic that while the humanists and CSICOP do their
best to wipe the paranormal from the face of American
society, the state of affairs in many communist countries
is quite different. There is considerable interest in para-
psychological matters in the Soviet Union and the Slavic
countries of Poland, Czechoslovakia and Bulgaria, and to
a lesser extent in Hungary and Romania. There has
recently been a major explosion of interest in China as
well. (Marcello Truzzi, who visited China and reported
on its psychic scene quite fairly, was told off in public at a
recent CSICOP meeting for even going there to look at
what was happening!)

Soviet researchers have developed an entirely new
scientific discipline, that of heliobiology, or the study of
the influence of solar and cosmic radiation on biological
systems. Its widespread acceptance and official approval
has led to an interest in subtle interactions of all kinds,
whether they be electric, magnetic or psychic. They have
changed the terminology, preferring 'bioinformation
transfer' to telepathy and clairvoyance, 'biophysical
effect' to psychokinesis and 'extrasensor' to medium or
psychic. They reject any suggestion of a spiritualistic
interpretation of any of these, but they accept the facts
and study them as enthusiastically as do their colleagues
in the West, as I can testify from first-hand experience.

Bulgaria is the only country in the world known to have
a state-run parapsychology research institute. It also had
a state-run clairvoyant, a blind lady named Vanga Dimi-
trova, who died in 1985. A special hotel was built in her

home town of Petrich, near the Greek border, to accommodate visitors. On arrival there they were presented with a sugar lump, which they were told to put under their pillows at night. When their turn came for a 'reading' from Vanga, they would hand it to her, and she would press it against her forehead for a moment, then embarking upon a detailed account of her client's past, present and future. She was studied for several years by Dr Georgi Lozanov, director of the Research Institute for Suggestology in Sofia, who unfortunately has not made his findings public. He gave little away when I met him for an hour's polite chat, except to make it clear that he regarded her clairvoyance as genuine, an opinion confirmed by every Bulgarian I met during a visit to that intriguing country.

Poland's Psychotronic Society, with 4,000 members, is the largest of its kind in the world. During the lecture I gave at its 1983 conference in Warsaw I counted more than 800 heads in the audience, the largest number I have ever seen at an event of this kind. During one of the breaks a young Polish medical doctor startled a group of us by diagnosing the past and present physical conditions of everybody at the table without any kind of examination or even any questioning.

Czechoslovakia has a long tradition of interest in non-material matters, which continues to this day. At a conference held in the smart new Trades Union Congress headquarters in Bratislava, also in 1983, I gave a talk on Victorian table-tilting, after which I was besieged by delegates from several Eastern bloc countries for more information – and immediate practical instruction. They wanted to go back to our hotel and get a table off the ground there and then. A young Soviet scientist told us that he had already attended table-tilting sessions back home, where such things seemed to be regarded as a normal weekend pastime.

In the Soviet Union, at least two individuals have made public careers out of their psychic abilities in much the same way as Uri Geller has done in the West. The late Wolf Messing brought telepathy and clairvoyance to every corner of the country with his stage performances, and his role was taken over after his death by one of his admirers, Tofik Dadashev, of whom Western visitors to a 1973 conference in Prague were allowed a brief and tantalizing glimpse.

In the course of many meetings with Soviet and East Europeans, most of them professional research scientists, I have never come across doubts as to the existence of psi phenomena. Their attitude can be summed up as: 'There's something interesting going on. Let's find out what it is.' On the other hand, a widespread attitude in the supposedly free Western world is: 'There's something dangerous going on. Stamp it out.'

Mud sticks. After fifteen years of the kind of debunking of which I have given several examples, it has become widely accepted that Uri Geller has been unmasked as a fraud. I have been assured of this personally by many who should know better, most of whom could not recall the source of this information. They seemed to remember reading it somewhere . . .

Geller has never been proved fraudulent. Nor has he ever been proved to have genuine psychic abilities beyond any reasonable doubt. It is possible that it never will be proved either way, and I suspect this is the way he likes it.

There was a time when scientific proof of a new hypothesis was a fairly straightforward procedure. You set up a controlled experiment, published your results, and waited for somebody else to repeat them. In recent years, some important new discoveries have been accepted very quickly, such as the structure of the DNA 'double helix' molecule, and the 'Josephson Effect' that contributed to the fastest technological revolution in history. Nobel Prizes were handed out to their discoverers in a very short time, once it was clear that nobody was going to disprove their claims.

Why was no prize awarded to Puthoff, Targ, or anybody else for the discovery of the Geller Effect? There are many reasons, the most important being that nobody can be sure exactly what this effect is. All that can be said with near certainty is that when Geller enters a laboratory, strange things are likely to happen. Nobody can expect a prize for announcing this. As Targ put it in his and Harold Puthoff's book *Mind-Reach* (1977), 'in the world of science no one at all cares what we think possibly may have happened. "Possibly" is not good enough.'

We cannot expect the human mind, the most complex thing in the universe, to behave as predictably in the laboratory as a microchip or a strand of DNA. Any experiment involving supposed psychic ability of any kind involves at least two minds: those of the subject and the researcher. If there is such a thing as psychic power, we can reasonably expect that it will be influenced by very subtle stimuli, and will only operate when conditions are exactly right. We can also expect that the researcher will be making use of it during the experiment, whether consciously or not. Moreover, it is almost inevitable that no psychic experiment can be repeated, since neither subject nor experimenter will ever be in precisely the same state of mind on more than one occasion.

One persistent critic of parapsychology, Professor C.

E. M. Hansel, declared in a 1983 television interview, 'If anybody was telepathic, they should be able to quite easily demonstrate the effect to anybody. I would be completely satisfied by just talking to the person for a few minutes and asking him to say what I was thinking of.' Such an argument (from a professor of psychology, moreover) is nonsensical. Suppose that we applied it to, say, falling in love at first sight? What would happen if we took a man and a woman off the street, placed them in front of each other and ordered them to develop an immediate and lasting passion for each other? In many cases, this would not happen. Yet there is no lack of testimony, from those who should know, that people have fallen in love at first sight and remained together until parted by death. The fact that many people have had no such luck is irrelevant.

Likewise, there is no lack of evidence for the existence of what are called psi phenomena: telepathy, clairvoyance, precognition and psychokinesis. As William James remarked in the essay already quoted, written the year before he died after a lifetime of first-hand observation of a vast amount of well-documented phenomena of this kind:

The first difference between the psychical researcher and the inexpert person is that the former realizes the commonness and typicality of the phenomenon, while the latter, less informed, thinks it so rare as to be unworthy of attention.

There are other reasons, as I have indicated, why inexpert persons choose to reject the positive evidence for the existence of psi phenomena. The anti-psi community can be divided into honest doubters and 'inexpert' doubters. The former quite reasonably consider the phenomena to be inherently so improbable that they require exceptional evidence before they will consider them. The 'inexpert' doubters are not prepared to concede that the phenomena *could* exist, since there is no place for them in the model of reality they have chosen to adopt. Therefore, any evidence that they do exist must not be considered even theoretically possible, it must be destroyed.

As Artur Zorka put it, there is a contradiction here, and Uri Geller brought it into sharp focus. On the one hand, we have a long list of well-qualified professional scientists who study him in their laboratories and conclude that, at the very least, he is worth further study. On the other hand, we have the dishonest doubters who have not examined him at all, and have decided that even attempting to study people like him is out of order.

Three centuries ago, Johannes Kepler warned his fellow astronomers not to 'throw out the baby with the bathwater' when dealing with astrology, 'the step-daughter of astronomy'. 'The belief in the effect of the constellations derives in the first place from experience,' he wrote, 'which is so convincing that it can be denied only by people who have not examined it . . . That the sky does something to man is obvious, but what it does specifically remains hidden.' However, the truth could be found if one looked for it, just as 'the persistent hen will find the golden corn in the dung-heap'.

This is the attitude shared by the great majority of today's professional parapsychologists. I have met most of them, and I have yet to meet one who is unaware of the vast amount of dung that has been strewn over the field ever since research into it began more than a century ago, not only by the fraudulent mediums and psychics but by some equally fraudulent researchers. These have at last been debunked in their turn by the historian Brian

Inglis, whose well-documented book *The Hidden Power* (1986) reveals that almost every 'unmasking' in the history of psychical research, from Daniel Home to Uri Geller, has been carried out not by persistent hens, but by ruthless baby-killers.

It is worth mentioning here that both of the two major scandals of psychical research of recent years were revealed by members of the community without any help from the professional sceptics and debunkers. A member of the late Dr J. B. Rhine's staff was caught fiddling a computer in order to produce spurious data and was promptly thrown out by Rhine himself, who equally promptly made the facts public. It was Betty Markwick, a member of the Society for Psychical Research, who produced the evidence that finished off the reputation of the late Dr S. G. Soal, author of some telepathy research once considered to be classic. Her findings were immediately published – by the SPR. One cannot help wondering if organizations such as CSICOP serve any useful purpose other than the satisfaction of its members' lust for blood. The psychical research community has shown that it can handle its black sheep without any help from them.

Several examples of fraudulent debunking of Uri Geller have been given in this book, both by me and by him. The rest of them would fill another book, and the fact that he has survived them is strong evidence for both the genuineness of his abilities and the falsity of the charges made against him. I will give one final example of the depths to which his attackers have sunk in their efforts to finish him off.

As I have already described, attempts were made to debunk the first serious research involving him, that of Harold Puthoff and Russell Targ at Stanford in 1972, even before it was published. As I have shown, they were made on a basis of hearsay, unfounded assumptions, and unauthorized use of private correspondence. The research was first made public on 9 March 1973 in the form of a film entitled *Experiments with Uri Geller*, shown at a public meeting at Columbia University. By then, the issue of *Time* dated 12 March and containing the offensive and inaccurate diatribe entitled 'The Magician and the Think-Tank' was already at the printers.

Once the research was out in the open, James Randi set about attacking it in his book, *The Magic of Uri Geller*. Not content with denigrating the characters of Puthoff and Targ and dismissing *in toto* their research – none of which he had witnessed himself – he turned, in a later book, *Flim-Flam*, to the professional photographer who had made the film, a Stanford employee named Zev Pressman, with an extraordinary series of unfounded allegations.

Pressman's name, said Randi, had been added to the film 'without his knowledge or permission'. Part of the film was of a 'reenactment', and one whole segment 'is now known to be a restaged and specially created one'. Pressman 'knew nothing about most of what appeared under his name, and he disagreed with the part that he did know about'. The objects of unnamed Stanford staff members were based on 'Pressman's revelations about his part in it' (i.e. the film). These quotations are from *Flim-Flam*, the subtitle of which – 'Psychics, ESP, Unicorns and other Delusions' – suggests a difficulty in distinguishing between babies and bathwater.

If true, this would be a very serious matter and Pressman would be guilty of complicity in deliberate fraud. But it was not true. Pressman flatly denied all of Randi's allegations in two public statements, neither of which was even mentioned in the 1982 reissue of the book. 'I made the film,' said Pressman, 'and my name appeared with my full knowledge and permission . . . Nothing was restaged or specially created . . . I have never met nor spoken to nor corresponded with Randi. The "revelations" he attributes to me are pure fiction.'

'Are we in retreat from the scientific ideas of rationality, dispassionate examination of evidence and sober experiment that have made modern civilization what it is?' the founders of CSICOP asked in their promotional literature. Their own behaviour sometimes suggests to me that we are indeed.

Randi is at his most accurate when describing himself. 'I'm an actor playing a part, and I do it for the purpose of entertainment,' he said in the *PM Magazine* television interview of 1 July 1982. His role as scientific investigator was not one of his successes.

If I were to adopt the research methods of the psi-cops, I would have no difficulty in producing the following scenario, most of which is untrue and based on smears and assumptions:

As is well known, one of the purposes of the Soviet Committee for State Security (KGB) is to undermine Western society. It has frequently done this by infiltrating legitimate protest or dissident groups and using them for its own purposes, often without the knowledge of group members. What would be a more obvious target for penetration than the Humanist Association, many of whose members are known Marxists? What would be more convenient than to set up a publishing house to publish the propaganda of the Humanists and their CSICOP sub-agents? (Sample titles: *Atheism – The Case*

*Against God, Ethics Without God, The Problem of God, Sex Without Love.*)

Why go to so much trouble and expense to discredit the whole field of parapsychology? To distract attention from the real work that is going on at somewhere like the tightly-guarded Institute for Cosmic Biology at Khodinsk airfield just outside Moscow, of course. Or one of those off-limits laboratories in Akademgorodok in Siberia, or Alma-Ata in Kazakhstan.

The above scenario (which, I repeat, is malicious non-sense) could be rewritten to 'prove' that the Central Intelligence Agency and not the KGB is calling the psi-cops' shots. A well-known parapsychologist recently announced in public that eight years after one of his projects was completed, he learned that the money had originated from the CIA. The Company is just as good at this kind of thing as its Soviet counterpart, both of which know that anybody suggesting anything like the above will be denounced as a paranoid witch-hunter.

Allegations of CIA or KGB involvement would be denied in all good faith by CSICOP officials, as they were in the 23 June 1985 issue of the *Sunday Times* after columnist Henry Porter had mentioned them. If CSICOP was being manipulated by any intelligence organization, it would be the last to know.

Again, let me repeat that most of the above four paragraphs is nonsense. I include it merely as an example of how 'careful investigation' of the kind favoured by CSICOP could be used against them.

When criticizing Geller, anything goes. Even *Reader's Digest* prefers magicians' allegations to scientists' testi-mony. In its book *Mysteries of the Unexplained*, we are told that Uri's feats 'have now been largely dismissed as fraudulent'. Tracking this unsupported statement to its sources, I found them to be a pair of magicians. One was quoted at second hand (from *The Humanist*), while the other, Milbourne Christopher, claimed that Uri used a palmed magnet to *stop* watches – something he has never attempted to do. Why should we believe anything else Christopher (or any other magician) alleges?

Fortunately, the entire case for the existence of useful and hitherto unexplained faculties in human beings does not rest solely on Uri Geller. As William James put it, these are both common and typical. Everything Geller has ever claimed to do has been done by others, although nobody has yet claimed to do all of them, or to do any of them with quite as much panache. So, before presenting some evidence and conclusions of my own, I will devote a chapter to the recent activities of some of the others.

# 15

## *The State of the Art*

On 30 November and 1 December 1983 a symposium was
held in Leesburg, Virginia, on 'Applications of Anomalous Phenomena'. It was organized by Kaman Tempo, a
division of the Kaman Sciences 'think-tank' in Santa
Barbara, California, and its stated purpose was 'to provide a venue where outside-of-government researchers
could present government managers and scientists with
details of their research and an assessment of the potential
of applications of this research'. There were nineteen
speakers, several of them heads of major university
departments, and the guests were described as 'senior
scientists and civilian and military managers'. No guest
list was published.

In all countries meetings are frequently held at which
scientists brief members of governments and intelligence
communities on recent developments in their fields. This
one was somewhat unusual. Its purpose, in the plain
language of the host, Dr Scott Jones of Kaman Tempo,
was: 'to bring a group of senior researchers to Washington
to share their assessments of where we are in 1983 in
ability to apply psychic phenomena, and what they project
the 1990 position to be'.

Subjects discussed ranged from telepathy, clairvoyance,
precognition and psychokinesis to 'human/equipment
interaction systems' (i.e. people affecting computers) and
'the continuity of life'. There was also a discussion of the
military applications of 'anomalous phenomena'. To fly
nineteen people from all parts of the country and put

them up for two or three days must have cost a good deal, and it should be noted that they were not asked to discuss the *possible* existence of psychic phenomena, but to describe what was being done with them.

No mention was made of Geller in the published Proceedings of the Leesburg symposium, but there was plenty of discussion of almost everything he has ever claimed to do, from bending spoons and reading minds to finding objects and missing persons, locating natural resources and making computers go wrong. I will summarize it here in two sections:

1 Anomalous mental phenomena: telepathy, clairvoyance, precognition and remote sensing (dowsing).
2 Anomalous physical phenomena: psychokinesis, or interactions between mind and matter on all levels from the microscopic to the macroscopic.

The first type of mental phenomena discussed was clairvoyance, or 'remote viewing' as they prefer to call it at SRI International, where Project Scanate got under way on 29 May 1973. The experimenters on that occasion were Harold Puthoff and Russell Targ, the two laser physicists who had begun to look into anomalous matters the previous year with Uri Geller. Their subject was a New Yorker named Ingo Swann, an artist and writer by profession who was widely read in parapsychology and had plenty of ideas of his own as to how his abilities should be tested. He deserves the credit for launching Project Scanate in the first place, for it was his idea to try to obtain useful information at long distance – any distance – with nothing more to go on than the geographical co-ordinates of the site. By scanning those co-ordinates (hence the word Scanate) he hoped to provide a description more detailed than any available map of the site in question would show.

Swann did not go into a trance, beat drums, or jump into an isolation tank. He simply made himself comfortable, lit a cigar, took a sip of coffee and began to reel off very precise descriptions of locations thousands of miles away about which Puthoff and Targ knew nothing except their exact longitude and latitude. One of these, of which Swann drew an accurate map, was the remote Pacific island of Kerguelen, site of what is officially described as a weather research centre. It is in fact the site of a Soviet missile-tracking installation.

The co-ordinates for Project Scanate, in which six other subjects later took part, were provided by a source identified by reporter Ron McRae as a case officer from the Central Intelligence Agency who had been assigned to check out the psychic scene. In his book *Mind Wars* (1984), McRae describes how the agent later took part himself in a Scanate test as a subject, and found his impressions to be as accurate as those of Swann and the others. His reaction, after three successful runs, was: 'My God, it really works!'

More than a hundred tests were carried out during the life of Project Scanate, which ran for two years. Targets chosen by the CIA, in association with the National Security Agency, included a number of very sensitive military locations in the Soviet Union. Descriptions of these provided by Scanate subjects were later confirmed, in some cases very precisely, by satellite observations. Other targets selected were nearer home: one was an installation in the Washington area of which the subject provided not only a general description, but such fine details as contents of locked file cabinets.

Summarizing the SRI research in remote viewing, Puthoff pointed out that several other laboratory teams had successfully replicated it, notably the Princeton University group headed by Dr Robert G. Jahn, dean of its School of Engineering and Applied Sciences. He had been particularly successful in what he described as 'precognitive remote perception'.

'The percipient', Jahn explained, 'performs his perception and fills out his check sheet hours, and in some cases even days, before the target is visited by the agent – indeed, in most cases, before the target has even been selected.' What passed through the minds of some of the military members of his audience when he told them that has not been recorded.

There have been some intriguing spin-offs from the work at SRI and Princeton. One is that it has been found that almost anybody can do remote viewing, and another is that it is possible to get better at it, like most other things, by practising and learning to avoid simple mistakes. The most common of these is trying too hard to interpret what is picked up by the viewer in the form of shapes. As Puthoff explained during his presentation: 'A viewer will say, "I see one of those things that, you know, flies around and has got wings, but isn't a bird. It comes out of a worm, but I can't think of the name of it."' Told it sounds rather like a butterfly, the viewer agrees at once.

There are some striking similarities between the findings of the remote viewing researchers and those of the scientists who pioneered the study of the workings of our two brain hemispheres. Roger Sperry, who won a Nobel Prize for his split-brain research, found that when people had their brain hemispheres forcibly separated in order to suppress major afflictions of epilepsy, their two brain-halves responded to external information in quite different ways. Using only their left hemispheres, they could describe things in words, but they could not identify them by shape or touch. Using only their right hemispheres, they could recognize shapes and general impressions, but could not put names to them.

It is quite wrong to assume, as some have, that normal people with intact brains make use of one half independently of the other. Our brains are designed to operate as single integrated entities. All the same, it is common experience that we all have two modes of thinking, one logical and analytical, the other intuitive. In my book *If This Be Magic* (1985) I suggested calling them left-mind and right-mind modes for convenience, and pointed out that while the normal brain must make full use of both, there are times when one is a hindrance rather than a help. We often feel our intuitions contradicting our sense of logic, for example. There are also times when we suppress an intuition (or, more often, somebody else's intuition), act logically, and find we have made a mistake and that it was the intuitive channel, or right mind, that picked up the correct information.

This is precisely what has been found to happen again and again during remote viewing experiments. Some viewers could perceive targets with remarkable accuracy, but they would describe them in words or on paper quite wrongly because of what Ingo Swann called 'analytical overlay', or what I would call left-mind swamping of the right-mind channel.

One way round this problem is to use more than one viewer at a time, and this was the approach developed by Stephan Schwartz and his Mobius Group, based in Los Angeles. He assembled a team of clairvoyants of widely differing backgrounds, including a photographer, an investment banker, a retired hunting guide and a housewife, and he soon found that two brains were better than one in the psychic detection business, while three were better still. On some projects he used as many as eleven.

He described one of his most successful assignments at the Leesburg symposium. He had been approached by a district attorney from Lancaster County, Pennsylvania, to see if he could help on a case of a missing fourteen-year-old girl. He was given a photograph of the girl, but no further information except that she had disappeared. Having a daughter of his own of the same age, Schwartz felt strongly motivated to help, but was only able to reach two of his pool of clairvoyants on this occasion.

Both of them announced that the girl was dead. One said that she had been struck on the head, the other that she had been suffocated. Both thought that there had been a sexual assault, and both agreed that the killer was a man known to the girl. All of these could be said to be reasonable guesses for a case of this kind. However, the two Mobius psychics went on to build up a picture of events that was detailed enough to persuade the police to search the area they described.

'The description of the area where the body was found', Schwartz reported, 'was perfect. So they found the body.'

A man was later tried and convicted. He had been under suspicion, but without a body there was little the police could do. With the help of Schwartz's team, which the police were good enough to acknowledge in writing, they found the body and solved the case. The girl, incidentally, had been both struck on the head and suffocated.

Next to describe progress in the field of psychic detection was Dr Karlis Osis, research director of the American Society for Psychical Research in New York. While Uri

Geller was working on the Son of Sam case, as he has described in this book, Osis was doing the same independently using a group of six. It was one of his most frustrating cases, for five of the group produced no useful information at all, while the sixth provided specific details that, looked at with hindsight, could have led to an early arrest if they had been co-ordinated with Geller's information and acted upon. She stated that the killer was an employee of a certain post office, and even provided part of his car licence-plate number.

Osis tried to follow up the post office lead, but was denied access to staff records. Yet he remained optimistic about the potential application of psychic sensing to the detection of criminals.

'We know what to do, which hypotheses to test, how to optimize procedures, select and train talented persons, and what equipment and software are necessary to facilitate our efforts,' he told his audience at Leesburg. 'When methods of applying ESP become operational, there will be no walls for the criminals to hide behind.' All that was now needed, he concluded, was 'a will to proceed'.

I came across one example of such a will myself at about this time. One day, I was doing some reading in the library of the Society for Psychical Research in London when a young woman police cadet turned up, asking if we could provide her with source material for her research project: the use of psychics in police work. I hope that, by now, all police college libraries have a copy of W. S. Hibbard and R. W. Worring's *Psychic Criminology: an operations manual for using psychics in criminal investigations*, published in 1982 by Charles C. Thomas of Springfield, Illinois.

I have also met a member of the Royal Canadian Mounted Police, together with a lady who, he assured me, had been able to provide him with accurate and useful information concerning major crimes, including murder. She had never solved a case on her own, he added, but he reckoned that psychics had a useful part to play as just one of several types of specialist who can contribute to the solution of crimes.

A will to proceed is to be found here and there.

The 'civilian and military managers' who spent the weekend at Leesburg must have concluded that anomalous phenomena of the mental kind were not only quite common and potentially very useful, but not all that difficult to induce. If any of them went on to look into the history of research in telepathy and clairvoyance, they would have found no shortage of textbooks in the libraries in which all the basic rules are spelled out in plain language. Upton Sinclair's *Mental Radio* (1930) and René Warcollier's *Mind to Mind* (1948) would have provided enough teaching material for a trial course in applied telepathy for civil or military purposes. This, they may have decided, is something we can work with.

Psychokinesis, or anomalous physical phenomena, is an altogether different matter. Nobody is quite sure what all the rules are, and its unpredictable nature has made it something that many scientists would rather not allow into their well-ordered laboratories, as the following example illustrates.

Uri Geller was not the first person in whose presence expensive equipment began to act strangely on the SRI premises. That honour belongs to Ingo Swann, and the experiment in which he was involved was more scientifically acceptable than the incident with Geller and the D-ARPA computer, because Swann did exactly what he was asked to do. The scene was the basement of the Varian

Physics Building at Stanford University (of which SRI International is now independent) and the scientist in charge of the experiment was Harold Puthoff. It was June 1972, and Russell Targ had not yet joined him for the Geller research.

The first thing Puthoff asked Swann to do was to pit his wits against a machine that had been designed specifically to be impervious to external influences of any kind except those it was supposed to measure: extremely weak magnetic fields. It was known as a Squid, or superconducting magnetometer, and it was buried under the concrete floor. Swann's own version of what happened was given at a lecture to the Society for Psychical Research in London in April 1978, and is hitherto unpublished. It is not only very amusing, but it gives a good idea of the psychological conditions needed for successful experiments in psychokinesis. It also gives some idea of the problems these tend to cause.

When Swann learned that the thing he was supposed to influence was out of sight under a slab of concrete, he felt he had been tricked. His first impulse was to thump Puthoff in the face and fly home to New York. Then he thought: If it doesn't work, I'm finished, but if it does, it might be interesting. So, having worked himself into 'a real tizz', as he put it, he asked icily what he had to do.

'Float down there and interfere with the magnetic field,' said Puthoff, explaining that this would show up on the chart recorder that had already been running normally for an hour, showing a steady trace on the paper.

Swann set to work. Earlier, he had demonstrated his ability to travel 'out of the body' in a series of well-observed experiments in New York, but this was the first time he had been asked to perform physical work on one of his astral trips.

'I don't know what I did,' he said, 'except that I knew I was going to get these guys if it was the last thing I did.' He then startled the three scientists present, who included the designer of the Squid, by announcing that he could actually see the workings of the instrument. He promptly made a sketch to prove it.

'Oh my God,' said one of the scientists. 'That's the thing I just took out a patent on. Nobody is supposed to know about that.' Then followed a period in which 'the frequency of the oscillation doubled for about thirty seconds', as Puthoff described it. This is plainly visible on the chart recording published in *Mind-Reach*, the section in question being signed by Swann, Puthoff and physicist Dr Martin J. Lee.

There was some nervous laughter. Swann asked if he had done anything convincing.

'Well, yes,' he was told. 'If you can do it again.' Psychics are always being told this, and it understandably annoys them.

'Let's get this straight,' said Swann through clenched teeth. 'If I do it again, you'll have to say I really did it?'

The designer of the Squid, Dr Arthur Hebard, suggested that there might be something wrong with his machine, but agreed he would be impressed if Swann could stop the signal altogether.

Five seconds or so later either the magnetometer or the chart recorder – it was not possible to establish which – entered a period of mechanical brain-death that lasted for three-quarters of a minute. Instead of moving up and down in a steady and symmetrical sine-wave pattern, the recorder's pen ran in a straight line. One of the observers went into a compulsive nervous laugh, and Swann himself began to giggle. 'I knew I had them,' he recalled.

All 'they' wanted to know, though was: could he do it *again*?

With commendable patience, Swann tried but failed. 'I'd achieved what I wanted,' he said, 'which was to teach them a lesson.' Having done so, he found his psychic powers had 'receded' from him. He remarked that his best results were always obtained when he was trying to get his own back on his investigators.

Puthoff noted that the forty-five-second period of flat chart trace coincided exactly with the time during which Swann was trying to do what he had been asked. He then distracted Swann's attention by discussing something else for a few minutes, during which the sine-wave returned to its normal shape and stayed put. However, when he steered the conversation back to the magnetometer, the chart instantly showed a most anomalous burst of high-frequency activity. Then, after the experiment was over, the machine continued to run normally in the presence of its inventor for a further hour.

Ten years later, there had been a total of 281 laboratory experiments in psychokinesis. Much of the best work came from SRI, where Puthoff and Targ were joined in 1976 by nuclear physicist Dr Edwin C. May, and from Robert Jahn's engineering department at Princeton.

As both May and Jahn reported to their audience at Leesburg, there had been much progress since the early days in which star subjects such as Geller and Swann had threatened the well-being of expensive pieces of modern technology, not to mention that of their owners and designers. The trend now was to use specially designed random number generators (RNGs) that enabled physicists to study something with which they felt more at home: the decay of a radioactive substance. It was known that a chunk of rock of a certain composition would decay to emit a stream of particles that could be made to switch on a light or generate a digit, but there was no known way of predicting exactly when the machine would choose 0 or 1, or ON or OFF.

Scientists reckoned that if a mind could bend a spoon it should be able to control the movement of a single atomic particle, which could easily be measured and recorded. The pioneer in this field was Dr Helmut Schmidt, a physicist with Boeing in Seattle, who published his first results in 1969, and before long the RNG replaced the parapsychologists' playing cards and dice as the standard apparatus for testing PK.

The Princeton group carried out a series of experiments, some running for weeks or even months and using eight different operators as subjects. Some of them were able to shift the scoring rate in either direction on request, to register what Jahn called PK-plus or PK-minus, and the overall result of the series was statistically highly significant. There was one probability in about 10,000 that it was due to chance alone. Some of Edwin May's subjects at SRI were able to do even better than that, and he too was able to present results for which pure chance seemed an unconvincing explanation.

Wait a minute, some of the military and civilian managers must have been thinking. If people can move particles around at a distance, they can snarl up computers.

They can indeed. Take, for example, the case of 'the man who bugs micros without really trying', described in the April 1985 issue of *Computing with the Amstrad*, the house journal of a well-known computer manufacturer.

Peter Strickland is a textile technician who has an unusual problem. 'If it involves a computer, you can almost guarantee it will malfunction if I'm around,' he said. On a visit to a factory, he had caused chaos on the production line because the computer that was controlling it 'went berserk' every time he approached it. He only had to move a few feet away, however, and it would return to sanity and normal operation. The poor fellow could not even use his own microchip-based calculator. It would work perfectly well for anybody else, but for its owner it could not get the simplest sums right. He was now the proud but nervous owner of his first home computer. 'I'm still expecting my CPC464 to malfunction any time now,' he concluded.

Electric fields, especially when they are pulsed at very low frequencies, certainly can affect people, whatever the spokesmen for the Central Electricity Generating Board prefer to tell us. I have spent a couple of very uncomfortable weekends in the Dorset village of Fishpond, where the locals have been campaigning for ten years to have their overhead power lines re-sited after experiencing a wide range of most unpleasant symptoms. These could have something to do with the high rate of fatal heart attacks and accidents caused by drivers blacking out there. I felt some of the same effects at the Greenham Common airfield, the NATO missile base that has been the target of a prolonged camp-in by anti-nuclear women protesters. There is a rather odd radar installation there which is not pointing up in the air, as radar dishes used to do in my RAF days, but straight along the ground. When I approached the fifteen-mile chain-link fence that surrounds the base, I felt a peculiar loss of focus, as did a colleague who was with me. Many of the campers to whom we spoke had suffered even worse effects. Whether these were produced accidentally or on purpose we were not able to establish.

There must be normal explanations for such effects of electricity on people and I wish more research could be done into them. The effects that some people have on electricity is quite another matter, and a more mysterious one. It was discussed at the Leesburg meeting by Dr Robert Morris of Syracuse University (now Koestler Professor of Parapsychology at Edinburgh University). In his well-documented presentation, he did not need to remind his audience that if there was a psi component in the ever-increasing interactions between human and computer in the 1980s, they should know about it.

He began by pointing out that although it was quite common to describe certain people as accident-prone, little had ever been done to study the personalities of those who always seem to be having accidents of all kinds for no obvious reason. The most famous example was the theoretical physicist Wolfgang Pauli, of whom his fellow physicist George Gamow wrote that he only had to walk into a laboratory and 'apparatus would fall, break, shatter or burn'.

Morris mentioned a recent episode of the apparent opposite of the 'Pauli Effect', in which a magnetometer had begun to malfunction but had started up on its own as soon as the repairman arrived to fix it, and before he had touched it. When the man left the room, it promptly shut down again. An alert observer persuaded the repairman to come in and out of the room three more times, and each time he did so, the same thing happened. 'It started up every time he got close, and shut down every time he went away,' said Morris. The eventual solution: 'They got someone else to repair it.'

Morris then described an experiment he had carried out himself to test a hypothesis that did not seem to have been adequately tested before: that anomalous equipment malfunction could be related to stress on the part of its operator.

Using thirty-two undergraduates as subjects, he divided them into two groups, one consisting of those who enjoyed sports and competition in general, and the other of those who did not. He then prepared two sets of written instructions, labelled 'striving' or 'non-striving'.

All subjects were asked to do the same thing: to sit and stare at a computer display unit on which a randomly generated line of dots was moving down the screen, each dot being one step to the left or right of the preceding one. Subjects were asked to make the trail drift over to one side.

Half of them were given 'striving' instructions, which meant they were to try to 'beat' the computer at all costs, waving their arms and yelling at it as if they were at a football game if they felt like it. The other half was told to 'non-strive' by relaxing, taking their shoes off, not trying hard at all but just helping the computer do what they wanted it to do.

Morris was testing two hypotheses at once. Would the competitive types do better than their easygoing colleagues? Would the kind of instructions each individual was given make a difference? He had shuffled the instruction sheets so that he had no way of knowing if a 'striving' student received one or the other.

When results were added up, his first hypothesis was laid to rest, for there was no significant difference between the scores of the strivers and the non-strivers. The second hypothesis, however, needed a closer look. Of the sixteen students given striving instructions, thirteen scored below chance level, whereas of the sixteen given non-striving orders, fourteen scored above it. Those who had tried hardest, in fact, had been the least successful.

This called for immediate replication, so Morris ran a second test using twice the number of students. This time, he added some 'relaxation enhancement' in the form of light hypnosis to the group given the non-striving instructions.

The result: no statistical difference between the two groups.

However, as most people involved with PK research know only too well, experiments of this kind tend to produce unplanned spin-offs. On this occasion, what happened was that the computer broke down. And it kept on breaking down.

'We realized we had a natural experiment in front of us,' said Morris. Looking at his subjects' personality questionnaires, he noticed that the majority of his computer-crashers had a sceptical attitude towards their task and tended to be 'more inclined to anxiety in performance situations' than their less crash-prone colleagues.

'Our computer system seemed to be crashing in the presence of people who didn't value what they were doing very highly, and were inclined to be anxious about their performance,' Morris concluded.

Looked at in the light of this evidence, Geller's performance in Tokyo is of particular interest. It might be said that on that occasion he was definitely a striver rather than a non-striver. Indeed, most people who know Uri well would probably agree that he always is a striver, with his daily routine of punishing physical workouts and his generally exuberant and competitive personality. However, the picture on the screen at Tokai University froze the very moment he stopped striving. Close observation of his spoon-bending technique, supported by my own photographic evidence, shows that the same switching-off process applies here. He begins with a period of intense striving and metal-rubbing, and he then relaxes into the non-striving mode. That is when the spoon bends, frequently continuing to do so after it has left his hands.

It may turn out to be that non-strivers are most successful in PK tasks if they have previously been through a period of striving, while strivers will only succeed if they change modes. I hope this approach will be explored further.

There is another approach, and by way of a surprise bonus, the Leesburg symposium delegates were given a brief course in do-it-yourself metal-bending! Their instructor was the pioneer of what has come to be known as the PK party, an aerospace engineer from the McDonnell Douglas Astronautics Co. named Jack Houck. He has combined a lighthearted approach to his subject with a serious scientific one, with the help of his colleague Severin Dahlen, a professional metallurgist.

The purpose of a PK party is not to sit around and discuss PK, but to do it. The first one was held in Houck's California home on 19 January 1981, and involved twenty of his friends from all walks of life. At that time, he had never met Geller, or witnessed any of his live performances. Nor was he familiar with the research of Kenneth J. Batcheldor, who had been demonstrating since 1964 that PK can be generated to order in small groups, using the traditional Victorian table-tilting procedure, without any a priori belief in spirits. (His work was described in detail in my book *If this Be Magic*.) From his base in the heart of the high-technology establishment, Houck worked it all out for himself.

The first PK party was, he told me in 1985, an experiment designed to test a conceptual model he had devised the previous year. He continued:

I had selected the PK metal-bending phenomenon simply because people had laughed during several briefings of my conceptual model, where I had indicated that I thought all of these mind phenomena worked in a similar way. In those briefings, I basically predicted that if you create a peak emotional event at the current time, you would get the phenomena at the current time, and thus, immediate feedback.

According to his model, any ordinary non-mystical person could achieve the kind of state described by mystics for centuries and experience one of the paranormal powers, or *siddhis*, that can be acquired in this state. They include the ability to see at a distance, to make contact with other minds, and to achieve identity of mind with physical objects.

Houck and his guests sat around in a circle, clutching their spoons, while Dahlen read out the simple instructions:

1 Get a point of concentration in your head.
2 Make it very intense and focused.
3 Grab it, and bring it down through your neck, down through your shoulder, down through your arm, through your hand, and put it into the silverware at the point you intend to bend it.
4 Command it to bend.
5 Release the command and let it happen.

These instructions, I must emphasize, have to be experienced in a group setting and not merely read in printed form. As Batcheldor has found, it is only in a group that the essential state of instant faith and expectancy can be achieved that leads to the manifestation of PK. This is an experiment in which everybody has to participate, with total and uncritical commitment.

The trainee spoon-benders were told to feel for 'warm-forming' signs that their spoons were beginning to heat up or become sticky. When they appeared, a little normal physical force could be used to bend the spoon. This is what Houck calls 'kindergarten' bending. It is of no scientific value since the bending is done manually, at least in part, although much less force is used than would normally be needed. Its value is that the bender can feel the spoon becoming pliable and warm, and can bend it into shapes that would be impossible to produce by conventional means.

'Everyone felt pretty silly sitting there holding the silverware, until the head of a fork being held by a boy (aged fourteen) bent over all by itself,' Houck told the Leesburg audience. The boy had managed to skip the kindergarten stage altogether. This led to an 'instantaneous belief system change' among the others, most of whom had seen it happen. As soon as they knew for certain that metal could be bent, and bent right now, they found their spoons and forks going soft for periods of up to twenty seconds during which they could be twisted around as if they were made of Plasticine.

By the end of the party, everybody had bent something, with two exceptions: a lady who had remarked beforehand that she could not see the point in bending spoons, and Houck himself, who was too busy observing what was going on to be able to obey his own instructions. As I found for myself at the two PK parties I attended, at Cambridge in 1982 and Basle, Switzerland, in 1983, you cannot observe and participate at the same time.

Looking back on his first PK party, Houck recalled:

Little did I know that four and a half years later I would have conducted 128 PK parties, with over 5,000 people in attendance at them. Anyone can conduct a party if they have enough courage to stand up in front of a group. There are now at least 35 people conducting PK parties around the world. These parties provide an environment where everyone can experience psychokinesis, if they allow themselves to have the experience.

One of these party-givers is New York television executive Diana Gazes, who claims that the success rate among first-time metal-benders at her weekly workshops is around eighty per cent. Just about anyone, she reckons, can learn to do it. She herself learned from Eldon Byrd, who in turn learned from Geller. Byrd was in fact the first scientist to publish a positive report on Geller's laboratory PK, and has become an accomplished bender himself, his speciality being the crunching of spoon-bowls as if they were rose petals.

After one of her 1985 workshops, the president of a business publishing company had this to say to her:

I had a very surprising evening at your metal-bending seminar. It's mind-expanding, indeed, to see how possible the impossible is. Metal-bending changes all reference to 'It can't be done.' Metal can't be bent, but you said it could be done easily, and it was done. If that can be done, it gives one confidence that so much more can be done.

Dennis Stillings, whose journal *Archaeus* has published several technical papers by Byrd, Houck and Dahlen, has also found metal-bending to be a fairly simple business once the psychological preparation for it is understood. His reply to the die-hards who insist it is all trickery is a simple one, 'People acquainted with these phenomena find they are so common and easily accomplished, that cheating is silly.'

A twelve-year-old girl who attended one of Byrd's parties, at which three-quarters of the guests managed to bend something, put her finger on the crucial feature of the psychological preparation. After she had, according to writer Elizabeth Fuller, 'crunched a spoon with one hand like a female Oddjob', Byrd remarked that children tend to be best at this kind of thing.

'Yeah. Because nobody's told us we can't do it. Right?' the girl asked.

'That's exactly right,' Byrd replied.

The connection between spoon-bending and world peace may not be obvious, yet there is one. In 1983, a graduate student from John F. Kennedy University in Orinda, California, sent questionnaires to 800 people who had been to a PK party hosted by Houck and Dahlen. She received replies from 311 of them, nearly three-quarters of whom said that they had felt what Houck calls the 'warm-forming effect' after following the instructions mentioned above. An even higher percentage believed that PK existed even if they had not managed to produce it themselves.

Those who had succeeded found that they were able to use their newly discovered powers to control their environments, their health and their futures. Once somebody has found that the mind can alter the structure of a spoon (or, in the case of the Batcheldor groups, levitate a table), the logical step is to use the same mind – or better still a group of like minds – to alter more complex structures, whether physical, social or political.

Jack Houck has carried out some interesting experiments using seeds instead of cutlery at his parties, the object being not to bend them but to make them sprout. He first tried this at the suggestion of Eldon Byrd, who was present when Geller demonstrated his seed-sprouting skill on Japanese television. Houck's pupils have been able to make soyabean seeds sprout by applying much the same technique as the one already described for bending spoons. In this case, they are, of course, only making something happen that would have happened eventually on its own, but if it is possible to use applied PK to speed up a natural process, the implications for healing are fairly obvious.

Mesmer's pupil, the Marquis de Puységur, who discovered the hypnotic trance state in 1784, described healing by what was then called animal magnetism as 'the action of thought upon the body's vital principle'. Healers, he said, should place their hands on patients' bodies 'in order to induce heat there'. Sudden bursts of heat are still a widely reported feature of the hand-healing technique. I have experienced them myself while being treated by Matthew Manning, an expert healer who for a short time in the early 1970s was also a very proficient metal-bender.

There are now many who would argue that the 'anomalous' phenomena of telepathy, clairvoyance and PK are anomalous no longer. They are here to stay and are being put to practical use, and a great deal of the credit for this breakthrough is due to Geller.

'I think Uri Geller has done a tremendous service to the world,' Houck told me, 'by opening up the minds of many to the possibility of psychokinesis.' Which, as he has said so often, is what he always intended to do.

# 16
## Close-up Magic

There was always something different about Uri.

When he was four or five, his mother and his god-mother, Mrs Susan Elisabeth Korn, were on one of their regular visits to the Tel Aviv coffee-house where they liked to sit on the pavement, watch the world go by, and bring each other up to date on the local gossip. Neither of them took much notice, at first, when Uri picked up a spoon, held it in the palms of his outstretched hands, and began to stare at it.

Before long, it was Mrs Korn's turn to stare, in complete amazement. More than thirty years later, she was able to recall for me what happened next as vividly as if it had taken place the previous day.

'He just looked at it,' she told me, 'and it started bending.' Uri's hands had not moved. Wondering how on earth he had done it, Mrs Korn reacted as hundreds of others were later to react in similar situations, and asked if he could do it again with another spoon.

Uri could and did, as he did on several subsequent occasions in front of his godmother, who was probably the earliest witness outside his immediate family to any of his paranormal demonstrations. His mother had already become accustomed to them, as mentioned in Chapter One, and more were soon to follow. One day as she and Mrs Korn were playing cards, which they did regularly, she noticed that her watch had stopped, so she took it off her wrist and put it down. Uri promptly picked it up and began to rub the glass with his finger, whereupon almost at once the watch began to tick again.

At about the same time, Mrs Korn became aware of her godson's uncanny telepathic ability. 'He used to say things as if he could see through your soul or your brain,' she told me. 'He always seemed to know what we were going to do, or where we were going.' Having a son of her own a few months younger than Uri (her son is now a high-ranking officer in one of the Israeli armed services), she reckoned she knew what was normal child behaviour and what was not.

Playing card games when Uri was around became slightly unnerving. He always seemed to know who was going to win, and Mrs Korn suspected that he could see through the backs of the cards in her hand. (Many years later, Uri admitted that he could, though only when she was holding a joker.) One day, she decided to put his strange powers to the test.

'He told me to draw something,' she recalled, 'and said he would tell me what it was. So I sent him out of the room and drew a picture of a dog. I put it in an envelope and sealed it, and then I gave Uri the envelope and asked him what was inside it. He just held it in his hands and said "You've drawn a dog".' (Uri's present dog, like one of its predecessors, is named Joker.)

'You have to watch this boy,' Mrs Korn told his mother. 'I don't know how he's going to grow up.' Uri, on the other hand, seemed to know exactly how. Mrs Korn clearly remembers him assuring her that she would hear more about him later on, and when she read his book *My Story*, more than twenty years later, her immediate reaction was: 'My God, it really happened, just as he predicted.'

* * *

Mrs Korn is not the only witness who can testify that Uri was not quite like other boys.

Donald Wood is a successful entrepreneur whose interests range from electronics engineering and computer software to property development and his own think-tank, which specializes in the invention of new technologies. He is one of two ex-pupils of Terra Santa College in Nicosia, Cyprus, now living in England that I was able to locate without much difficulty in 1985. Although he was two years junior to Uri, he remembers him very well.

'Uri was a very daring fellow, very much a leader,' he told me. 'If there was anything to be done, he could do it very well.' He remembers Uri teaching him to shoot with an air rifle, training him on the basketball court, and leading regular expeditions around the maze of underground caves near the school, a task none of the other boys was willing to undertake. Once, the two of them climbed to the top of the tallest building in Nicosia close to the 'green line' that divided the Greek and Turkish sections of the city. As they peered over the parapet, they were spotted by a Turkish guard who promptly opened fire on them. Donald was terrified, but Uri calmly led him out of the line of fire to the safety of a doorway. In quieter moments, he remembers them collecting stamps and making model aeroplanes together. His most vivid memory is of Uri's skill on the basketball court:

He used to throw the ball from a long, long distance and get it into the net every time, even when he was looking the other way. I have no doubt that his psychic powers are real, and I think scientists should apply their minds to them instead of arguing about them.

Joseph Charles spent the whole of his six years at the college in Uri's class and knew him very well. With the minimum of prompting, the memories flooded back:

There was a circle below the basketball net, and we thought we were pretty good if we could score from the edge of it. Uri would get the ball and pause for a bit, then he would throw it with one hand and get it in, every time, even from the half-way line.

There were many unusual things about Uri. Those caves, for instance – there were sixty or seventy of them running for miles, deep down, in all directions, and they were pitch dark. We'd never go down there on our own. But we always felt confident with Uri – he would always be our leader, and he would lead us right to the end and get us back out again.

Uri's classroom-break demonstrations of his unusual abilities soon became a regular feature of school life, both on and off the basketball court:

He would tell me to do a drawing and fold the paper while he was out of the room. We'd make sure he wasn't peeping through the keyhole or the window. Then he'd come back in and draw exactly what I'd drawn. He did that several times, and always got it right.

He'd throw a pack of cards on the floor, face upwards, and tell me to think of one, without touching it. When I said I was ready, he would grab my hand and go over them, and find the exact card. I didn't believe it the first time, and thought it was just a coincidence, but he did it many times. That was brilliant.

Then he had this watch – he could make its hands go forwards or backwards without touching anything.

Joseph joined the merchant navy after leaving school and later worked as a courier before starting his own transport firm in the East End of London. He recalled a memorable visit to Uri in New York in 1974:

We went out for a meal, and were talking about the old times. He was eating his fruit salad with a normal restaurant spoon and it just started to bend. 'You see, Joseph, this is the problem I get even when I'm eating,' he said. He threw the spoon on the table, and it went on bending on its own, and then it broke without either of us touching it. I've still got it – both parts – at home. I also gave him a very short and thick key to bend, which he did. I'm fairly strong, but I couldn't straighten it out again.

Uri a fake? Nothing of the kind!

For every report that Geller is a fake psychic, there are dozens of accounts of incidents like these, both from people who have known him well for many years and from those who only met him once. Is it possible, I soon began to wonder, that anybody could fool so many people for so long and so often?

In theory, it is. Magicians frequently fool each other as well as the public. Sometimes they pay a lot of money for the secret of a new trick – there being no other way they can figure out how it is done.

I have been totally fooled myself on several occasions. The late Milbourne Christopher put on a spectacular display of close-up sleight-of-hand when I took him along to visit the site of the Enfield poltergeist, which I described in my book *This House is Haunted* (1980). He did things with a single piece of torn newspaper that were as impressive as anything Geller has ever done on a stage, and if he had claimed to have psychic powers I would have found it difficult not to believe him. The piece of paper seemed to move around the room on its own while I was standing right beside him. I have still not worked out what he did with it.

This is simply because, like any skilled magician, Christopher knew exactly what he was going to do, and when, and I did not. I could only see what he wanted me to see. Neither I nor anybody else can prove Geller to be genuine (or false, for that matter) solely on the basis of what we see him do, or think we see him do. We have to approach the question from several different directions.

I have already established that Uri's unusual abilities were well witnessed long before he met Shipi and Hanna Shtrang, and that almost everything he has ever claimed to do has been done by numerous other people. This increases the probability that his abilities are genuine, though it does not constitute proof. This will only be achieved when a sufficient number of ordinary people have found they too can bend things or receive telepathic information. In this high-strangeness area, proof has to be reached on an individual basis.

In my Introduction, I described the first of several intriguing incidents that I was to witness over the following months in Uri's London apartment. I will now give an account of some of the others, in approximate order of strangeness, beginning with some examples of what may have been his normal, rather than his paranormal, powers.

One day, I arrived to find Uri lying flat on the floor beside a large-scale map of an area he visited later in 1985 to look for minerals. One corner of it was weighted flat with a ship's compass which, I noticed, was not orientated in the same direction as the map.

'What's that for?' I asked.

'Oh, it's a kind of good-luck thing,' said Uri casually. 'I use it to get in the right mood. Look, I'll show you.'

I sat on the floor beside him, noticing as I did so that the fat compass needle did not move at all when I gave the concrete floor a good thump a few inches from it. Uri clenched his fist lightly and waved it in the air a good six inches above the compass. Immediately, the needle began to rock to and fro, quite slowly.

'You try it,' he said. I did, tensing the muscles in my hand and wrist as hard as I could without making any impression at all on the needle. Muscles do generate tiny magnetic fields, I knew, but I could not manage to affect the compass with mine.

Satisfied with the feedback he was getting from the compass, Uri put it aside and ran the flat of his hand over the map, on which he had already drawn several circles in pencil, and one or two in coloured ink. These were the spots over which he had felt reactions in the palm of his hand of the kind he has already described. In November 1985, he showed me a tiny strip of gold, about a centimetre in length, that he had personally fished out of the rock-crusher and separator that had been placed on one of the spots he had selected.

Some time after this, I brought along my own pocket compass, and asked Uri to show me how he made needles move. 'I'm not asking you to do it,' I said, 'I just want to see how you go about it.'

'I never tried with a cheap one,' he said, rather disdainfully. His own ship's compass was a high-precision model, its needle suspended in oil. Mine had cost me about one pound and its needle was balanced on a small spring. It had one advantage over his expensive model, however: when a magnetic field was applied to it, the needle would shake up and down in response to the pulse rate of the field. The same thing would happen if it were physically disturbed by knocking the table beside it. Therefore, if, as I originally suspected, Uri's needle-moving routine was a purely magnetic one, caused by his unusually powerful hand and wrist muscles, my cheap little instrument would register the effect better than his, for when its needle shook, it made a clearly audible sound.

'This is what I do,' he said. He clenched both his fists and brought them to within six inches of the compass, moving his head towards it at the same time.

'It could be a magnetic effect,' I said. 'Muscles do create small magnetic fields, and you're fairly muscular.'

'No, you're wrong,' he replied. 'Look – I can't clench my left fist completely and I can't stretch out my left arm fully, either.' He showed me the large scar where he had been operated on after being wounded in the Six Day War. It was close to his left elbow joint, and the stitch marks were easily visible.

'I'm not strong in this arm at all,' he added. 'I can't even lift a heavy suitcase with it.' I and many others had assumed Uri to be stronger than most. There went that myth, debunked by Uri himself. 'Anyway, I do it with my mind, not with my hands. I can do it with no hands at all. Watch.'

He knelt on the concrete floor, resting both hands on the carpet, concentrated hard for a few moments, then brought his head sharply towards the compass as if he were a dog about to bite it, letting out a sharp grunt as he did so. I watched the needle from a distance of a few inches.

'Yes,' I said. 'It moved a little.' It had not, but I felt that some false feedback would encourage him, as indeed it did.

He tried again, and this time the needle swung quite slowly through at least fifteen degrees, without wobbling. From where I was watching, I could see that he did not touch the table. Anyway, even if he had, the needle would have wobbled up and down and not moved sideways as I had seen it do.

Later, I tried to do what he had done with much effort and no success at all. I could more or less repeat the effect with my small nine-volt magnetic pulse generator, bringing its probe to within four or five inches of the compass – about the same distance as when Uri had zapped it with his head-power. So it may be that there is some human magnetic field involved in his case, which is of interest in itself if true. How it could turn itself on or off to order is quite beyond my understanding.

Uri himself insists that the power involved is not a magnetic one, even if it can produce results similar to those of a normal magnetic field. He believes it originates from the centre of the forehead, site of the pineal gland or 'third eye' long believed to be associated with mysterious human powers. All I can say is that Uri can unquestionably make a compass needle move by bringing his head close to it. He can also make the same motion and not cause it to move, which would seem to rule out the 'hidden magnet' in his hair, neck or mouth theory.

Another example of what could have been either normal or paranormal ability took place in the summer of 1985. One day, Uri telephoned me to ask if I could contact somebody in one of the security or intelligence services. To shorten a long story of which I cannot give any details at present, he had met a man whom he felt to be up to something illegal, and he wanted it to be on record that he had no connection with the business involved. I did what he asked, and in due course I was telephoned and told that the man in question had been arrested and charged with a serious offence. (He was subsequently sent to prison.) I was thanked for my help, but told no more. As Uri has pointed out, in cases of this kind you never are told any more.

The first of many informal experiments in telepathy between Uri and me took place at his kitchen table, where much of the work on this book was carried out. We were talking about the transmission of simple drawings or single words.

'Think of a letter of the alphabet,' Uri said suddenly. I closed my eyes and immediately saw the letter R, with several parallel lines running through it. As I opened my eyes, Uri scribbled on a newspaper and passed it to me. At the bottom of the page he had written the letter Q and circled it. Above it, he had written R and crossed it out. I had neither written nor said anything at all.

'Now, think of a city,' he said. I thought of Bratislava in Czechoslovakia, which I had visited in 1983. I recalled a delightful evening at a pavement restaurant that I had spent with friends from the conference I had attended. Then I remembered that the meal had not been in Bratislava but in Vienna, where we had all stopped on our way home. The two cities are only forty miles apart, and are linked by the winding, muddy (not blue) River Danube, the image of which popped uninvited into my mind. I decided that I had messed up the experiment, and was about to suggest we try another when Uri handed me my notebook, in which he had been scribbling.

He had drawn two parallel wavy lines across the page, which could be said to resemble an aerial view of a river. However, underneath he had written 'Wall? China.' What he had done fitted a well-established pattern noticed by almost everybody who has ever done experiments of this kind: he had reproduced the shape of what I had been visualizing very accurately, but had misinterpreted it, for which I could hardly blame him, since my thoughts had been very muddled. I was also interested to see that he had not mentioned or written the name of a city, which he had asked me to think of and which I had failed to do properly.

Our next spontaneous experiment arose at my suggestion and not his. I had received a postcard showing a very dull-looking hallway in Sigmund Freud's house in Vienna, and one evening I took it along with me to show him. I held it up several feet away, and gave him a generous clue.

'There's a connection with you,' I said. This was the name Freud, his mother's maiden name. Uri looked at the picture intently, but said nothing, so I put the card away. Later in the evening I produced it without warning and held it up again, now in a very dim light and still several feet away from him. I visualized the grim features of Freud as hard as I could.

'All I'm getting is an old man with a beard,' said Uri, scribbling something on a piece of paper. I leaned forward and read the words 'Freud. Vienna'. That, I decided, could as well have been guesswork as telepathy. Or he might have visited Freud's house, for all I knew. I said nothing, not wishing him to think I was putting his powers to the test – he had already given me his views on scientific experiments. I was putting them to the test, but in my own way: by letting them manifest themselves naturally and spontaneously.

The best of my informal experiments of this kind, carried out several months later, also involved a man with a beard. Again, I managed to spring it on Uri without warning. While he was making a long telephone call, I drew what was meant to be a portrait of Father Christmas on my pad, holding the pad parallel with my chest as before. I was about to add Santa's traditional nightcap when Uri rang off. At the same time, I decided the cap was too complicated to draw so I left it out.

Uri noticed that I was up to something. 'What are you drawing?' he asked.

'You tell me,' I suggested.

In less than a minute, he had drawn a face with thick and straight lines for the eyebrows and nose, exactly like mine. He omitted the beard, but added some straight lines very similar to mine at the top of his face. Underneath, he had written: 'Hat on head.'

'I just thought of a hat,' he said as I showed him my drawing, but before I said anything about my thought of the night-cap.

This was rather uncanny, as was the fact that each of our drawings was precisely twenty-seven millimetres in height.

On 5 August 1985, there was an incident of a slightly different order. I telephoned Uri in the morning and said I would come and see him in mid-afternoon, when I had been to my bank. At least a week previously, I had asked him if he could discover the number of a Swiss bank account belonging to the father of a friend of mine, who had died without telling it to her. She was hard up and needed the money she knew to be there, but Swiss bankers are Swiss bankers and would not let her have it without the number. Uri said he did not think that was something he could do and I said no more about it.

On my way to his apartment building, I thought of asking if he could read my bank account number instead. He had never met my friend, but he had met me, which might make a difference.

He was taking a shower when I arrived, so Hanna brought me a coffee and some biscuits and left me in the living-room for a few minutes. Then Uri came in, rubbing his hair with a towel.

'I just got a flash while I was washing,' he said. 'Guy's bank account, and the number 88. Do you want me to see if I can read your account number?'

I was just about to ask precisely that. The number 8, incidentally, is not in either of my two account numbers, though the last two digits of my bank code number are 86. It could be said that Uri had remembered my earlier mention of my friend's father's bank number, plus the fact that I had just been to my bank, and come out with a lucky guess. Even so, the precise timing was impressive.

So was the demonstration of instant telepathy by Uri's lively son Daniel. By the age of four and a half, he had already flown with several different airlines, and could reel off the names of at least twenty of them on demand. Uri told me to write down the name of an airline and ask Daniel to guess it.

I wrote down SAS, the line I was due to use a week later, and visualized it as well as I could. Daniel got it wrong with his first two guesses.

'No, you're doing it wrong,' said Uri to me. 'Look.' He turned to Daniel. 'Which airline would you like me to give you for your birthday?' he asked, when I had shown him what I had written. Daniel was the other side of the large dining table.

'SAS,' he replied at once.

'You have to make it very direct,' Uri explained. 'You have to put it in a way he can understand.'

I suspect we shall be hearing more from Daniel Geller in due course.

None of these incidents struck me as a perfect example of the kind of mind-reading for which Geller is famous. I mention them merely to illustrate the sort of thing that seems to happen more often in the Geller household than elsewhere in my experience. There were three others, however, that gave me a good deal to think about, and I am still unable to provide any normal explanation for any of them. One of them remains in my mind as the nearest I have yet come to witnessing an anomalous event in perfect conditions. I will describe them in order of strangeness.

On 17 October 1985 at about 6.50 P.M., I was sitting in the living-room and talking about nothing in particular with Uri and Shipi when we all heard what I can only describe as a quiet thud coming from the adjoining toilet, which I had been the last person to use.

'That was something,' said Shipi, without much interest. We all got up, opened the door of the toilet and switched the light on. A plastic hairbrush was lying in the middle of the room, which was about eight feet by six. There had definitely not been anything on the tiled floor when I had left it a few minutes earlier.

I asked Uri to stay there, close the door, and drop it again when I had returned to the chair in which I had been sitting. He did so, and the sound was identical. The hairbrush, we all agreed, had been on the shelf beside the basin the last time we had seen it. I was unable to suggest any possible normal means by which it could have travelled three or four feet on its own, as it unmistakably had.

On 20 August 1985, Uri and I were sitting at the small table in the kitchen having a snack. Shipi was between us, and Hanna was standing at the worktop preparing some cooking. Uri mentioned that he had found a pen in his bathroom that he could not remember buying, and this led me to describe various instances of 'apports' in my experience, in which unfamiliar objects had simply turned up without explanation. I embarked upon a long account of one of the most intriguing cases of this kind that I knew of, which involved my colleague Maurice Grosse.

Several years previously, and long after the Enfield

poltergeist case which he and I investigated in 1977 and 1978, Maurice's wife had mislaid a treasured ring. She had taken it off one night and left it in the usual place on her dressing-table, and the next morning it was not there. They searched the room, and indeed the entire house, repeatedly, and even turned out all the rubbish sacks. They took everything out of all the drawers in the dressing-table and combed every inch of the bedroom, but no ring appeared. Finally, and reluctantly, Maurice wrote to his insurance company to put in a claim for compensation. This was about three months after the ring had been lost.

He posted the letter on a Friday, and on Saturday morning both he and his wife were baffled to find that the ring had appeared in its usual place on the dressing-table.

While I was telling this story, Shipi was making a shopping-list on an old paper bag he had fished out of the kitchen waste bin, having failed to find anything to write on within reach.

As I was saying the words 'he wrote to the insurance company', I noticed an odd expression on Uri's face. He was staring at the table in front of him with his eyes bulging out of their sockets, as if he had just seen a ghost, or perhaps a worm crawling out of the packet of crisp-bread in front of his plate.

'Are you all right?' I asked.

It was some time before he said anything. He just sat and stared at the table. Finally, he picked up a folded sheet of paper and handed it to me. It was a cover note from an insurance company, dated 1 May 1985 and referring to a more recent claim, announcing the enclosure of a cheque in payment for the policy belonging to Mr M. Grosse, whose home address was written beneath his name.

Maurice, I knew, had been to visit Uri about a week previously. He told me later that he had definitely not been into the kitchen. He agreed it was possible that the piece of paper had been in his briefcase at the time, but he had no reason to take it out.

Eventually I managed to get a coherent account from Uri. 'When you said "insurance", I looked down and there it was,' he said. 'It was between the plate and this packet of biscuits, and part of it was underneath the packet.'

The kitchen table, as usual, was fairly cluttered with packets, jam pots and plates. I thought I would have noticed the paper when I came in, but could not be sure. I was more certain that Uri had been sitting back in his chair while I was telling the story, and had not made any movement towards the table.

Even assuming that he was playing an elaborate practical joke on me, I could not understand how he persuaded me to embark upon a story concerning an insurance policy belonging to Maurice Grosse. Moreover, if he was inclined to play practical jokes, I thought it likely that he would have tried something similar again, but although I visited him three or four times a week throughout several months in 1985, he never did.

This was one of those frustrating incidents that do not lend themselves to thorough investigation. Uri insisted that the piece of paper had simply appeared in front of him, and I had to take his word for it. As the incident to be described next had already taken place just over a month earlier, I had to admit that sudden materializations of things in Uri's apartment were not only possible but also reasonably probable.

\* \* \*

The incident I shall always think of as The Big One took place on 18 July 1985. It was a quarter-past three in the afternoon of a cloudless summer day, and bright light filled the living-room. Uri was sitting motionless on his exercise bicycle, reading a draft of one of the chapters of this book. I was sitting about four feet from him, with the back of my chair at about forty-five degrees to the window, which meant that I was looking along the room towards the hallway and front door and Uri was well within the limits of my right visual field.

I just sat there and waited for him to finish reading the draft, looking in front of me and thinking of nothing at all, as is my habit when I have to take a short break during working hours. I was certainly not in any kind of altered state of consciousness, though. I had drunk nothing all day apart from coffee and water. I had not been sitting in silence long enough to fall into a state of reverie.

The object appeared, in mid-air, directly in my line of vision at a height of about eight feet from the floor and two feet below the ceiling. It seemed to hover there for an instant, and then it fell to the thickly carpeted floor, making only the softest of sounds. It did not fall straight down, but at an angle of seventy-five degrees as measured from the floor.

I said nothing. Uri seemed not to have noticed it. He went on reading the draft, holding it in front of his face and concentrating all his attention on it as I had noticed he tended to do, whatever he was engaged in doing.

I thought to myself: did I see what I think I just saw? I decided I did. There was the object, which looked like a small shaving mirror, lying on the floor just under the edge of the coffee table. So it could not have fallen straight down. It landed about five feet from me, and at least nine or ten feet from Uri. It also fell slightly towards us.

He had definitely not thrown it, I could be sure. He had not moved a muscle for several minutes, and in any case the falling angle was wrong. It fell as if it had come from a good distance in a wide arc.

I kept quiet for long enough to satisfy myself that Uri was not going to say anything about this unexpected apport. Then I cleared my throat.

'Excuse me, Uri,' I said. 'What's that?'

He looked up and saw where I was pointing. 'Oh, that's my shaving mirror. What's it doing there? Perhaps the children . . .'

'They're out in the park, with Hanna and Shipi,' I said. 'It wasn't the children. It just dropped from the ceiling.'

'That's funny,' he said. 'I didn't hear anything. Drop it again and see what sound it makes.' I did so, from about the height where I had first seen it. It made a much louder sound and did not land anywhere near the table. (Later, I found that it measured two-and-a-half by three-and-a-half inches, and weighed forty-eight grams.)

Uri was mildly intrigued by the incident, though nothing like as much as he was after the discovery of the piece of paper described above. He seemed to accept the fact that this kind of thing happens now and then. We went to the main bathroom, opening two doors to get there, and he showed me the travelling toilet case where the mirror was normally kept. There were two very solid walls in between it and the spot where I had seen the mirror appear.

'It's the first time this has happened since that silver coin turned up in the kitchen,' he commented. That had been about three months previously. 'Sometimes it happens five or six times in one day, like when the writer from *Esquire* magazine came to see me in New York. Then it doesn't happen for maybe half a year.'

In my book *The Haunted Pub Guide* (1985) I described the 'Was It Something I Said?' Effect, whereby things fall off walls or shelves at the precise moment when somebody makes a remark, usually a disparaging one, about the traditional ghost of the establishment. It has been frequently reported, and there is good first-hand testimony for it, including some of my own.

In 1980, for example, reporter Barry Leighton and photographer Bob Naylor of the Wiltshire local newspaper the *Evening Advertiser* were visiting the supposedly haunted Crown pub in Pewsey, where a number of odd incidents had been reported. The landlord's daughter had been clouted on the nose by a mustard pot that had taken off from its rack in full view of both her and her mother, who in turn narrowly avoided being struck by a flying frying pan. A bundle of five-pound notes went missing from the till and turned up in the bedroom, laid out like a pack of cards, and so on.

While the landlord was describing all this action and excitement, Bob Naylor was taking a picture of an antique pistol hanging on the wall.

'It's annoying sometimes,' said the landlord, 'especially when an ornament crashes to the floor without warning.' The pistol immediately did so, followed by another of the bar's decorations.

'It happened in front of our eyes,' Barry Leighton wrote in his story (3 January 1980). 'There was no trickery involved. It was unnerving.'

I managed to unnerve a BBC radio reporter myself while recording an interview late one night in the highly haunted Seven Stars pub in Robertsbridge, Sussex. We were on our own in an upstairs room, and I was holding forth on my theories of how ghosts tended to do things in a certain order, for reasons known only to them.

'You always start,' I began, 'with either knocks . . .'

Before I could add 'or loud banging noises', there was an almighty thump on the floor a few feet from us. The timing could not have been more precise, as listeners were able to hear for themselves in the *Colour Supplement* programme on 13 October 1985. My trusted fellow ghost-hunter Andrew Green, who was downstairs at the time having a quiet cup of coffee with the landlord and his wife, and the programme's producer, assured me that he had not heard the noise, nor had he or any of the others done anything that could have caused it. I reckoned I had good evidence on tape for the 'Was It Something I Said?' Effect.

Immediately prior to the mirror-materialization epi-sode, however, neither Geller nor I had said anything at all for several minutes. I wondered if what he had been reading might have been responsible, but this did not seem possible. He was reading the page numbered 7/4 (page four of an early draft of Chapter Seven, now Chapter Eight) in which he mentioned his work at SRI International, and noted that seven plus four is eleven – his 'magic' number. I found this somewhat far-fetched, although I had to admit that Uri's magic number certainly seems to produce results. This was about a week after he had won both the raffle prizes at Clement Freud's party with tickets numbered 111 and 121.

There was another possible connection. During one of the many videotapes and films shot while Uri was at Stanford, a very similar incident took place in which a watch is said to have materialized in mid-air and fallen in front of the camera. I have not been able to see this piece of film, but I have been assured by somebody who has that the watch appears complete from one frame to the next. The mirror would, I am sure, have done the same had I been able to film it.

Going through my notes later, I found that three days before this incident I had been discussing such phenomena with Byron Janis, who had witnessed a good many of them since he and Uri first met in 1972.

'They happen in three ways,' he told me. 'Sometimes they shoot across the room as if they'd been thrown, or they can just appear in place without any sign of how they got there, or they can drop from just above your head.' He gave me several examples of all three categories that he had witnessed.

'I've never seen anything like that,' I said, referring to the third category. I had witnessed several examples of the first two during some of the cases of the poltergeist type that I had investigated. 'Hope I do one day,' I added.

Had it, after all, been Something I Said?

Six months later, I was to ask myself the same question. On 18 January 1986 I was kneeling on the floor looking at some of the maps Uri had used while working on the Bronfman kidnap case. The map of New York City reminded me of another of his early cases.

I put my finger on the Yonkers district. 'That's where the Son of Sam lived,' I said. As I spoke the word 'Sam', there was a loud noise behind me. Uri was seated on his exercise bicycle in front of me. Neither of us had seen anything move, but we found the shaving mirror on top of a box beside the mirror-wall in the dining area. There was a large scratch on one of the strips of plastic that covered the mirror-wall, and the shaving mirror itself was cracked on one side. It was the same one that had materialized in front of my eyes the previous July.

We went into the bathroom to see if anything else was missing from the shelf beside the basin. All seemed to be in order. I was last out of the bathroom and shut the door behind me. Uri went back towards the living-room, and I followed. As I shut the door of the corridor, there was a very loud thud almost under my feet. A large plastic bottle of bath foam was lying on the floor beside a cardboard box opposite the bathroom door. The box had been there when I came out of the bathroom. The bottle had not. If it had, I would have trodden on it.

On another occasion, in the same month, there was a more direct connection between something I said and an unusual incident. We were sitting in the kitchen, and I was describing some of Maurice Grosse's many experiences of objects moving around in mysterious ways. I remembered that the last time I had mentioned them the insurance form had appeared on the table, and I wondered what would happen this time. What did happen was a sound that caused me to look under the table, where beside my feet I found a toothbrush that had apparently travelled there on its own. It was still damp, and an Israeli house guest later assured me that it was hers, and that she had last seen it in the bathroom, where she had used it that morning. She had known Uri for a long time, and was not particularly surprised.

Once again, on 15 February 1986, I noticed that something I wrote could have the same effect as something I said. I had shown Uri what I hoped was the final draft of this chapter and asked for his comments. He had none, except 'Okay', and after handing it back to me he went into his bedroom, leaving me alone in the living-room with Shipi, who was making a telephone call.

While the call was going on, with Uri still in the

bedroom, there was one of those now familiar noises. I investigated it at once, and discovered two small golden objects that looked like marble-sized ball-bearings. While I was searching the floor, there was a very loud noise beside my feet, and another of the ball-bearings appeared on the carpet about a foot from where I was standing. At the same time, Uri came out of the bedroom saying that 'something' had just shot past him. Whatever it was, neither he nor I could find it.

I showed him the three ball-bearings. (Shortly afterwards I discovered a fourth on the floor.) 'Where do they come from?' I asked.

He looked at them for a moment. 'They're part of one of Meir's devices,' he replied. 'The last time I saw them they were in his factory – in Israel.'

He immediately telephoned Meir and asked him to open the safe where the bearings were kept and count them. There should have been one hundred of them. Meir called back soon afterwards to say that there were six missing. Several months later, the remaining two had still not been found.

One way and another, I became convinced of something that many had learned before me: inexplicable things do happen in the presence of Uri Geller.

# 17
## Whatever It Is

Who is the real Uri Geller? Is he a complete fraud, a very clever magician who has fooled much of the world into hailing him as the greatest psychic of all time? Or is he the greatest psychic of all time, despite all the denunciations and allegations? Surely he must be one or the other, but how are we going to find out which?

For some, there is no difficulty at all. There are no such things as 'psychic powers', they say, so anybody claiming to practice them must be phoney. Any kind of action at a distance or exchange of information beyond the limits of our known senses is impossible. People certainly have hunches and intuitions, to be sure, but there is no need to dream up words like telepathy and clairvoyance to account for them. As for psychokinesis, we know enough about the human brain to say that any kind of 'mind over matter' outside the body is nonsense. There is no known natural force that could account for it. If there were, we would have been able to measure it by now. All so-called psychic phenomena can be ascribed to one of three well-known factors: coincidence, faulty observation, and lies.

If you take this view, as many do, then Geller must be a magician. He began in show business, and he has never left it. Nowadays, instead of performing to large audiences he performs to single individuals, who should know better than to take him for what he claims to be. He has a great act, and he has perfected it in fifteen years of constant repetition. But, say the magicians, he's one of us. We rumbled him the minute he set foot on the stage.

We gave him the chance to confess and to be welcomed into our secret brotherhood. He turned it down, and went on to fool most of the people most of the time, but not all of us. He's a magician all right – it takes one to spot one, and we spotted him right at the start.

If Geller's 'powers' were ever to be the subject of a court case, this is probably how the prosecution would summarize its claims. The defence would object, waving handfuls of papers and protesting that numerous eminent scientists had shown that the accused had unusual powers. Had he not demonstrated them over and over again in the laboratory just as convincingly as on the stage or in the television studio?

The prosecution would have none of this. Scientists are the easiest of people to deceive. They are not trained to deal with professional deceivers. As for all those deluded businessmen who have paid Geller millions to find gold, they would be better off hanging their maps on the wall and throwing darts at them . . .

So the arguments would go on. By the end of the case the jury would be too confused to reach a unanimous verdict, and everybody would go home still believing what they had always believed.

It is very difficult to prove anything nowadays, even in a court. I have sat on a jury myself and taken part in two cases, one of which went on for several days. On both occasions, the accused was found not guilty, and our verdict is now on the record. In one case, I am proud to say that it was probably due to my vigorous arguments with my fellow jurors, in which I pointed out that the prosecution case was all based on assumptions, hearsay and testimony from the police, who were obviously hoping for a conviction although they had somehow managed to 'lose' the only piece of evidence that would have settled the matter.

The case for the prosecution sounded quite reasonable, as did the case for the defence. Both were argued eloquently and at great length. Choosing which of them to believe was not easy for some of us. The defendant was an Asian immigrant, which complicated matters. One juror assured me privately that 'they're all a bunch of crooks', but did not say so in the jury room in front of the five non-white members, each of whom might well have had some fellow-feeling for the defendant (as might I also, having been born in India). We all had our own views about crime in general, and the way it should be dealt with, and some of these were quite extreme. However, when I managed to concentrate the minds of my colleagues on the case in question, and pointed out that we were supposed to reach a verdict solely on the evidence, we all had to agree that the prosecution case just was not good enough to send a man to prison. So, much to my relief, we let him off.

Uri Geller went on trial in 1970, when he was first publicly denounced, and the case continues. The prosecution has claimed that he must be a magician, for two reasons: everything he does (well, most of it) can be replicated by conjurors, and there are no such things as psychic powers in the first place. Even the scientists who have studied him most closely, with one or two exceptions, have not come out and endorsed his powers unconditionally. They have pointed out correctly that science is not about what people believe, but about repeatable experiments and explanatory theories, and they have neither of these to report.

On the other hand, millions of people all over the world

have no doubt at all that Uri is a genuine psychic. Strange things have happened in their own homes just as he has predicted: clocks and watches have started ticking, spoons and forks have twisted out of shape for no obvious reason, and messages have been received from some distant television studio or newspaper office, after being beamed out without the help of any known form of radio or electronics. Is it possible to fool so many people for so long? And can we dismiss the testimony of Uri's closest friends, each of whom can reel off a list of very odd things that they have seen happen in his presence?

The case for Geller is just as reasonable as the case against him. The reason why neither has yet been accepted to everybody's satisfaction is very simple: there are too many vested interests and preconceptions involved on both sides. Many have already reached their own verdicts, and nothing said by either side is going to make them change their minds. Little that I say will make any difference either, so I will say nothing to those whose minds are made up except that the evidence on which they base their opinions may not be as good as it seems. From now on, I will address myself only to those who, like me, are genuinely mystified by Uri Geller and are equally prepared to believe that he is genuine or that he is not. That is exactly how I felt when I began to work on this book. The fact that I already had plenty of experience of other people's psychic powers made me all the more anxious to arrive at the right verdict. Like any collector, I had no wish to acquire a fake.

Let me return to my court case for a moment. I spent a good deal of time during the trial watching the defendant, who was only a few feet from me. He did not say much when he was spoken to, answering questions quietly and politely and often looking very bewildered.

'You can see he's got something to hide,' my anti-Asian fellow juror muttered one morning during the lunch break, to which I replied that in my opinion he just looked terrified.

'Wouldn't you be?' I asked. We had both been looking at the same person, yet we had reached very different conclusions about him. If you are suspicious about somebody, anything he says or does is going to look suspicious.

So it has been, right from the start, with Geller. Magicians, who think they know how he does his tricks, watch for the misdirections and the rapid hand movements they think he must be using. And they see them! At least, they think they do, and they assure us that they did.

However, two points must be considered. One is that magicians can be deceived just like anybody else. The Amazing Randi was taken for a ride with no difficulty at all by the non-magician Dennis Stillings, who proved his point by doing it again at once. The other is that magicians are professional deceivers, and are the most suspect of witnesses, although it is hard to imagine what could have motivated magicians such as Dickson, Zorka, Cox and Leslie to come out in favour of Geller other than a simple desire to speak the truth. It should also be remembered that these four observed him rather more carefully than the majority of his detractors have ever done. On the whole, the evidence from the magicians is inconclusive, but weighted strongly in Geller's favour.

The same is true of the evidence from the scientists, whose positive findings far outnumber their negative ones. They may not have come up with final proof of any kind, but most of them are quite sure that something very odd went on while Uri was in their laboratories. As for the evidence from the general public, this is overwhelmingly in his favour. There are millions of people all over the world who may not understand what psychic power is, and may not even be very interested in it, yet they have experienced it for themselves. Like Uri, they have lived a little of the mystery. They may since have banished it from their conscious minds, but for a brief moment they have known that there is more to human nature than finds its way into science magazines and textbooks.

There have been too many snap judgments both in favour of Geller and against him, and some of the more extreme examples of each strain belief. For example, some of those who accept his powers without question find Puharich's extraterrestrial-control theory too much to swallow, and I have not yet managed to swallow it myself. Nor have I spat it out, however, for, improbable as it may seem, it cannot be ruled out. Puharich has an impressive track record in many areas of scientific research, and if we accept some of his findings why should we reject others? We may complain that some of his theories about Uri only added a further complication to a subject that was quite complex enough already, but I for one am not prepared to assert that they are wrong.

It is much easier, as both Uri and I have shown, to debunk some of the misleading material that has been published about him. To list all the cases would be a very tedious task. To give just one of many possible examples: Brendan O'Regan wrote in the *New Scientist* (20 November 1974) that the feature on Geller published in the 17 October issue of the magazine contained no less than forty-two erroneous statements, seventeen of them 'blatant errors of fact' and the rest either 'unsupportable innuendo' or 'gross misrepresentation'.

If science magazines cannot get their facts straight, what can we expect from the popular press? In September 1985 I was interested to read in an Israeli magazine called *Bul* (issue dated 13 September 1986!) that yet another anti-Geller opus was on the way, subtitled 'The Crook from Outer Space'. Among its sensational revelations: the 'Israeli comedian of the past' was now living in a state of terror, 'like a hypnotized mouse', having been placed on an unnamed person's hit-list, and was guarded around the clock by 'a team of frightening gorillas'. Uri translated this extraordinary article for me with surprising good humour, and readily allowed me to dig through his vast files of anti-Geller material, of which I am sure he has more than anybody else. After visiting his home several times a week for more than six months, I saw nothing more frightening than the children's collection of toy monsters, and it was some time before I became aware of his security arrangements, which are as discreet as they are effective.

I will now try to scrape off both the mud and the whitewash and reach my own conclusions about Uri Geller.

It cannot be disputed that he has had an impact upon his time such as we have not seen since the days of the Victorian medium Daniel Home (1833–86) and the escapologist Houdini (1874–1926), both of whom became household names, though for very different reasons. Home baffled and astonished London society and several European royal families for more than twenty years, producing most of the standard phenomena of the seance room from table-turning and materialization of 'spirit' forms to the levitation of himself, and a hundred years after his death his reputation remains intact. Houdini spent much of his life crusading against Spiritualist mediums and imitating their performances on stage, yet such was his skill at escaping from handcuffs, strait-jackets and jails, that some suspected him of having psychic powers, and there is reason to believe that he seriously considered this himself. Ironically, it was Houdini and not Home who was accused of fraud, and he had to fight a court case in 1902 to clear his name as an 'honest' deceiver of the public.

Geller has made a reputation that can be seen in two ways depending on your point of view. To some he is the second Home, to others he is the Houdini of his time. His act may be unlike either of theirs, yet he has combined something of what would seem to be two incompatible careers: demonstrator of psychic phenomena and purveyor of entertainment to the masses. Like Home, he has produced so many apparently genuine psychic phenomena for so long that to some he must be a magician. Like Houdini, he has mystified audiences large and small so consistently that others believe he must have genuine psychic powers.

Comparisons cannot be taken too far. Geller is not the second Home or the second Houdini. He is the first Geller, and by any standards he is an original. He has extended his fields of operation far beyond the stage, studio and laboratory. He has put his talents to work in those areas where we would expect psychic powers, if there are such things, to be most useful, and he has literally struck gold. It should be remembered that he has done so not on his own initiative but on that of his employers, some of whom he has named.

There is plenty of evidence that people have risen to the top of many professions by making use of what they would call 'hunches', 'gut feelings' or simply 'intuition'. In 1962, three members of the Industrial and Management

Engineering Department of Newark College of Engineering in New Jersey began to look more closely into this matter. Two of them, Douglas Dean and John Mihalasky, later co-authored a book entitled *Executive ESP*, and by the time this was published in 1974 they had statistical evidence to show that successful company presidents scored better at computerized number-guessing tests than less successful ones. Their results, they concluded, 'show that the probability of getting a superior profit-maker is much increased by choosing a man who scores well in precognition'. Curiously, few of their subjects professed to have much interest in psychic matters. 'I do not know any psychics,' said one. 'I believe in ESP for one reason – because I use it.'

In December 1974, the magazine *Psychic* published interviews with nine American business leaders who described numerous instances in which they had made their own mind-power work for them. They included the founder of the Ampex Corporation, a former director of Phillips Petroleum, the owner of a steel company, a publisher, a management consultant, and the head of a large property development firm. Their comments included this revealing one (from the steel man) on the subject of parapsychology, 'I've experienced it, felt it, seen it – whatever it was!'

If top people speak in this vague way about psychic powers (or whatever they are), can we expect somebody who earns a living by claiming to use them to be any more precise. Geller is in fact considerably more articulate than many concerning his own powers and the way he uses them. He has told us here all he can about how he bends his spoons, receives and sends his telepathic messages, and finds things. He makes it all sound quite easy, but unfortunately most people who follow his instructions as given here will find that they cannot do the same. For the use of psychic power is far from easy to explain. It depends not so much on what you do but on who you are.

Who do you have to be, then, in order to become a Uri Geller? There are some clues to be found in his life story that may be worth examining for a moment. First, let us take the incident in which a spoon he was using during a meal when he was about four years old bent and broke in front of his eyes. This was witnessed by his mother, who has assured me that it happened just as he described it. She has also confirmed to me that Uri was able to read her mind from a very early age. So it seems that he grew up accepting that this kind of thing was quite possible.

It is well known that children do not develop a sense of logic and critical ability until both hemispheres of their brains are fully formed, which is usually around the age of eight. Before then, as any hypnotist knows, they are very highly suggestible and will accept whatever comes along as part of their view of reality.

It is also well known to the new generation of parapsychologists, who are interested in how psychic phenomena occur spontaneously rather than in how they would like them to occur in their carefully controlled experiments, that the essential first condition for their occurrence is a complete absence of resistance to them. Once this resistance is allowed to build up, it is very hard to break down. Psychic functioning is not a question of learning how, but of avoiding being told that this or that cannot be done.

Psychic functions are not really as mysterious as they are often made out to be. The American psychiatrist Jan Ehrenwald has shown that such human 'hyperfunctions' as telepathy, clairvoyance and psychokinesis are the exact mirror-images of the 'functional deficits' of the hysterical conversion syndrome. The latter lead to a restriction of human abilities, usually in the form of 'hysterical' blindness, mutism and paralysis; the former expand the reach of the ego by enabling it to transmit or receive information at a distance, or to create motion of physical objects without contact. Writing of the features of the 'psi syndrome' in his book *New Dimensions of Deep Analysis* (1954), he noted that:

We have seen time and again that despite their apparently capricious, haphazard nature they are governed by the same laws which apply to the dream, to the neurotic symptom and to unconscious processes in general. In short, they are subject to established psychodynamic principles.

So we can look upon psychic powers as extensions of normal powers rather than as something supernatural only bestowed on people who come from outer space. When we describe somebody as having been born psychic, what we really mean is that he, or more often she, was born with abilities we probably all have, but which are educated out of most of us. It has become socially acceptable for women to have 'intuition', but less so for men. All the evidence indicates that women have no more intuition, or any other psychic powers, than men, but that they have much less resistance to them. The majority of 'mediums' therefore tend to be women, but this does not reflect the distribution of psychic gifts between the sexes. (In the magazine article mentioned above, only one of the top executives interviewed, publisher Eleanor Friede, was a woman.)

Ehrenwald has come across many examples of telepathy and precognition in his own consulting room, and speculates that the doctor-patient relationship is similar to the 'symbiotic' relationship of mother and child. Symbiosis, in this context, means a close and mutually beneficial relationship between two living beings. This is naturally strongest between a mother and child, but it can also occur later in the child's life whenever its interests are closely associated with those of somebody else, whether or not personal emotions are involved. It is a relationship that can be quite independent of sexual or intellectual attachment.

As an only child, whose father was often away from home on military service, Uri was inevitably in his mother's company relatively more than he would have been as a member of a larger family with a father in permanent residence. This did not lead to the unnaturally prolonged dependence of child upon mother that is sometimes found in families in similar circumstances. Indeed, Uri's childhood seems to have been perfectly normal in every way. What interests me is that his early psychic experiences, most of which involved his mother, were allowed to remain undisturbed in his forming mind. He grew up accepting them, and has never found any reason to reject them.

I often wonder if that bending spoon in the hand of four-year-old Uri actually fell apart by entirely normal means? It could have been a spoon of poor post-war quality that had reached the end of its useful life, implanting as it did so an image in Uri's mind that was to remain there for good.

The psychologist Kenneth Batcheldor has studied the psychological conditions necessary for the manifestation of psychokinesis for more than twenty years, and as I described in my book *If This Be Magic* he has put his theories into practice with remarkable success. One of his most important discoveries is that inexplicable phenomena, such as the tilting of a table, can be expected to occur once those concerned believe, even wrongly, that they are already occurring. He calls this process 'induction by artifact', and I demonstrated it myself when I told Uri that he was making the needle of my compass move by mind-power. As I have already described, he did not in fact do this until after I had told him (wrongly) that he had. He then made it move at once. A naturally disintegrating spoon would be the ideal artifact to induce a belief in the possibility of spoons bending by less normal means.

An important feature of the symbiotic relationship is what Ehrenwald calls 'doctrinal compliance', whereby patients produce what they believe the doctor, analyst or hypnotist expects. This, he says in the book mentioned earlier, can be in the form of 'unintended suggestion emanating from the therapist who is usually unaware of its operation'.

Something like this seems to have taken place when Andrija Puharich arrived in Israel in 1971. For the first time in his life, Uri found himself being taken seriously by an experienced research scientist, who also happened to be a skilled hypnotist. Uri has described how ever since he can remember he has been interested in space travel and the possibility of distant civilizations. Puharich spelled out his own interest in such matters very plainly in the preface to his book *Uri*:

I had suspected for a long time from my researches that man has been in communication with beings not of this earth for thousands of years. This personal opinion comes from a close reading of the record of ancient religions and from my own observations and data.

The latter included some remarkable information from an Indian named Dr Vinod, obtained during a self-induced trance and supposedly originating from the intelligence source called The Nine.

The very day after Puharich first met Geller, they discussed space matters, and Uri gave a detailed account of his longtime interest in this area. At one of their first hypnosis sessions, Puharich asked outright, 'Are you one of the Nine Principles that once spoke through Dr Vinod?' The answer was 'Yes'. Doctrinal compliance had been established, and what followed was inevitable: a sudden and dramatic elaboration of all the space-fantasies that had been in Uri's mind throughout most of his life.

It must be made clear that those fantasies were genuine. We have the independent testimony of Mrs Agrotis and Joseph Charles, and no doubt there are other pupils and teachers from Terra Santa College in Nicosia who remember being entertained by Uri's spontaneous end-of-term recitals of them. Neither Puharich nor Geller made them up. They were there, and as we would expect they grew and blossomed in the favourable climate of the hypnotic trance. They may not have been literally true, any more than a dream need be literally true, but they were unquestionably in Uri's mind. As I have said, how they got there is a question I cannot answer.

Once rapport had been established between researcher and subject and strengthened by this common interest in matters extraterrestrial, Uri's psychic gifts developed rapidly. So did his already considerable self-confidence. He was all set for a career as a psychic superstar.

However, Uri made it clear right from the start of his association with Puharich that what he really wanted to do in life was become rich and famous. This is not a surprising ambition for an only child of a family of very modest means who already had more than a year's experience as a professional entertainer, and a very successful one.

Whatever we choose to think of Puharich's extraterrestrial theories, we must give him the credit due to him. It was almost entirely through his efforts that Geller ever set foot in a scientific laboratory, which he never really wanted to do. And why on earth should he? Would it be reasonable to have asked, say, Itzhak Perlman to take part in a series of laboratory experiments in sound production instead of playing his violin on concert platforms all over the world?

Since 1971, Geller's whole career has been a succession of responses to challenges and the suggestions of others. Although his stage routine has not changed much in fifteen years, he has never been able to resist a challenge in the form of a suggestion or an offer, rather than the now-or-never confrontation favoured by hostile critics. It was not even his own idea to become a public performer in the first place – his original stage career evolved gradually, from private demonstrations for Shipi and Hanna Shtrang, through similar spontaneous shows in the homes of others to the school performances arranged by the enterprising Shipi (who was fourteen at the time) and finally to the public stage, where he might have remained for some time if Puharich had not steered his career in other directions.

It was Sir Val Duncan of Rio Tinto-Zinc who suggested that Uri should apply his talent to such serious matters as finding oil and minerals. This suggestion was later reinforced by a number of hard-headed businessmen of whom two, Clive Menell and Peter Sterling, have allowed their names to appear on the record. I have met a third, who flew several thousand miles to London in 1985 for the sole purpose of securing Uri's services, and flew home as soon as he had done so. He was not prepared to let me quote him on anything at all, except that he had not informed even his fellow directors of his plans. He gave me the impression that he knew exactly what he was doing, proving Uri's observation that people at the top do not question his abilities, but often simply arrange to put them to work.

It was the man known as Mike who tried to entice Geller into the intelligence community, and it was various American customs, narcotics and FBI agents who on their own initiatives asked him to look for kidnap victims, corpses, and assorted villains. His success in all these areas was limited for reasons that are easily understood: he is a public performer by nature, and not an undercover agent, and he has good reason to fear for his personal safety if he becomes too widely known as the psychic detective or the super-dowser who cannot fail.

Credit for the original suggestions that he should expand his horizons is due to two influential Israelis: Amnon Rubinstein, who was to become minister of communications, and the defence chief Moshe Dayan. Rubinstein, in whose home Uri gave one of his first demonstrations, originally acted as adviser and guide and has remained on friendly terms up to the present. As for Dayan, we can assume that he passed on his impressions to those he reckoned to have a need to know. The only service Uri will admit to having performed for him was helping locate a piece of pottery during a late-night archaeological dig. I would be surprised if Dayan had failed to make any further use of skills of this kind.

Richard Deacon, a well-informed writer on espionage matters whom I know personally, devoted a chapter of his book *The Israeli Secret Service* (1978) to the controversial subject of 'psychic espionage'. He makes it clear that this is something on which the Israelis are considerably more up to date than any other Western nation. According to one of his sources, Geller's activities were closely monitored by Soviet-bloc observers from shortly after his arrival in the USA, and it is known that they were monitored by the Mossad long before then.

The idea of psychic espionage is an exciting one, and has led to a good deal of wild speculation but very little hard evidence. The only area in which it has been well established that there is a useful role for psychically talented spies to play is that of remote viewing. In 1984, columnist Jack Anderson published a series of articles on a CIA project codenamed Grill Flame, a development of the work already mentioned at SRI begun in 1972 by Ingo Swann, Harold Puthoff and Russell Targ. This project, Anderson said, had produced information later verified by satellite about a very sensitive nuclear test site at Semipalatinsk in Soviet Kazakhstan, and had led to the location of a crashed Soviet Tu-95 'Backfire' bomber somewhere in Africa.

Targ, together with his colleague Keith Harary, visited the Soviet Union in 1983, returning in October 1984 to carry out an experiment in remote viewing between Moscow and California, with the Georgian psychic healer Dzhuna Davitashvili as subject. During the experiment, which was videotaped, she produced accurate information about two target sites in San Francisco selected by a random number generator and visited by Harary. The experiment, which was witnessed by a member of the Soviet Academy of Sciences (whom I have met), demonstrated the possibility not only of remote viewing of a site 10,000 miles away, but also of precognition, for the targets were not selected until six hours after they had been described.

The military applications of this kind of experiment would seem to be potentially considerable. However, if I were in charge of a team of psychic spies, Geller is the last person I would want to be involved. Not only is he too well known and too accessible to the media, but he has always refused to co-operate on any test that could lead to negative or destructive use of psychic powers. Psychic warfare is quite feasible in theory, but the problem in practice would be finding subjects willing to take part.

A psychic peace campaign, of the kind described in Uri's Chapter Twelve, is another matter. Here, the prospects are promising. In the course of several visits to Eastern Europe, I have constantly been given urgent pleas for helping research the peaceful uses of psychic powers. I do not think this would have happened unless those concerned were well aware that research into their less peaceful uses is going on.

Recent events have shown that an individual's change of attitude can have far-reaching effects. Barely three years after the Yom Kippur War of 1973, Egypt's President Sadat made his historic visit to Israel, changing the minds of millions simply by stepping off an aeroplane. There followed the longest period of peace between Israel and Egypt since the creation of the former. The Geneva meeting in 1985 between the chief executives of the USA and the USSR was another occasion on which the states of mind of Ronald Reagan and Mikhail Gorbachev may have achieved more effect than anything they said to each other. The same may be true of the ostensibly unsuccessful 1986 summit meeting in Iceland. The idea that an individual like Uri Geller can help shape world events simply by shaking hands with Adnan Khashoggi is less far-fetched than it might appear. Events are caused by minds, and minds can be changed both by their owners and by others.

There is a place for real magic in the modern world. Indeed, it is much needed, although the distinction must be made between co-operative and autocratic magic. If the magician seeks to dominate his environment, in the manner of Dr Faustus, he will be destroyed by the forces he creates or invokes. If he seeks to alter his environment by invoking an already existing creative force and collaborating with it for the common good, he will work apparent miracles.

'Magic is not, as so many wrongly believe, merely a collection of rites, ceremonies and supernatural feats. It is much more than that. In a few words, it is *a way of looking at the world*. In its very essence it implies *a mental state*.'

I apologize for taking this perceptive comment, by one of the harshest critics of the paranormal, out of its context: a review of Professor Lynn Thorndike's eight-volume *A History of Magic and Experimental Science* by Eric J. Dingwall in the first issue (1959) of the *International Journal of Parapsychology*. Thorndike's monumental work, which took him fifty years to write, is, in Dingwall's words, not only a history, but 'an illustration of the dangers inherent in the magical way of looking at the world and . . . an indication of the apparently enormous difficulties that mankind has in escaping from such conceptions'.

That such dangers exist is undeniable. Nor can we challenge Dingwall's assertion that 'it is where there is ignorance, as Montaigne pointed out in the sixteenth century, [that] imposture has free scope'. Yet this is only one side of the picture.

The 'slow escape from magic', to use Dingwall's term, coincided with the emergence of modern science and the triumphs of such demystifiers of nature as Newton, Descartes and Galileo. Yet magic has refused to go away, partly because modern science, for all its achievements, has not yet answered any of the questions most of us really want answered. In many areas, such as the limits of the human mind and its possible survival of physical death, it has preferred not to look for answers. Meanwhile, it has been our scientists and not our occultists who have found ever more efficient ways of harming and killing us and of systematically destroying the natural environment. Scientists have much less cause for self-congratulation than some of them appear to think.

The idea that medieval magic evolved into or was replaced by modern science is a myth. If mankind still believes in magic, it is because there is a widespread and very deep-rooted awareness that there is some truth in it. The psi phenomena of today are, as Ehrenwald has pointed out, 'derivatives of magic that have been dehydrated, deboned and filleted to make them digestible for scientific consumption'. The term 'psi', he says, is 'an antiseptic, expurgated or sanitized version of magic'.

The extraordinary reactions provoked by Uri Geller's appearance on the scene, both favourable and hostile, show that today both the desire for magic and the fear of it are as widespread as they have ever been. Here was a talented and personable young entertainer claiming to be performing real magic in the context of the dehydrated and sanitized profession of conjuring. By doing so, he infuriated the professional magicians by suggesting that he could do what they could only pretend to do. He also upset many scientists, who operate in a different reality, by showing that psi phenomena cannot be studied in terms of science as currently understood.

'Is Chaos Necessary?' is the title of the chapter in Targ and Puthoff's *Mind Reach* in which they discuss their SRI research with Geller (whose name they seem to have done their best to avoid mentioning ever since). To be fair to them, they were no more prepared, despite their impressive scientific backgrounds, for a laboratory subject like him than he was prepared for scientists like them. Chaos is necessary, Geller knows it, and he has a remarkable instinctive ability for producing it in almost any conditions. The real magician cannot operate in everyday reality; he must destabilize it and replace it with his own.

One criticism often made of Uri is that he is inclined to see mysteries where others do not. If there is a thump on the ceiling while he is talking to a reporter he will suggest that it was something 'strange'. Or if somebody mentions a certain person or a place, he might claim 'I was just going to say that – I'm reading your mind!' and so on. This can easily be mistaken for 'fraud', but it is an essential part of the destabilization process, one that has been fully validated by Kenneth Batcheldor's theoretical and practical research into the psychology of paranormal physical phenomena. Uri knew all about 'induction by artifact' long before Batcheldor gave it a name.

'Once the belief in a supernatural world is established and the conviction that, by appropriate methods, this world can be explored and brought into a kind of subjection to the operator's wishes, then magic follows as night follows day,' wrote Dingwall in the article mentioned above. 'But,' he continued, 'once the belief in a supernatural order of things is weakened, then doubts as to the correct interpretation of obscure events arise and the scientific way of looking at the world begins to make its appearance.'

As I have seen for myself time and time again, psi phenomena do not take place until those concerned either expect them to do so very soon, or believe that they already are taking place. This has been my experience on several cases of the poltergeist type, at experimental table-sessions with the Batcheldor group, and on many occasions in Uri's company. His ability to induce psi by artifact is unrivalled.

It may be asked why, if this is so, stage magicians do not occasionally perform real magic by mistake, as it were, after inducing belief in it in their audiences. The answer is that there is good reason to believe that now and then they do. Houdini, for example, spent much of his life tormented by the question of whether this had happened to him, and he had private conversations on the subject with a number of mediums as well as fellow magicians. Unfortunately, he never found the answer, or if he did he kept it to himself. This side of Houdini's complex and contradictory personality is well discussed by his sympathetic biographer Raymund FitzSimons in his book *Death and the Magician*.

David Berglas, one of Britain's best-known magical entertainers, has been both president of the International Brotherhood of Magicians and acting chairman of the British branch of the Committee for Scientific Investigation of Claims of the Paranormal. He has told me that many of his professional colleagues do believe in psi and that all of them (himself included) cannot always fully explain how they produce their own effects.

After following Geller's career closely for more than twelve years, and becoming one of the very few magicians to establish friendly personal relations with him, Berglas had this to say In *Psychic News* (13 December 1986): 'If he is a genuine psychic, and genuinely does what he claims to by the methods he claims to use, then he is the only person in the world who can do it. He is the only one to have demonstrated consistently. He is a phenomenon, and we must respect that. If, on the other hand, he is a magician or a trickster or a con-man, he is also phenomenal – the best there has ever been. So, whichever way you want to look at him, we must respect him as one or the other.'

When I asked Berglas which way he wanted to look at Geller, he made the enigmatic comment: 'I can do what he does. Whether I do it in the same way that he does, I really don't know.'

Uri Geller is a magician. That is, he practises what appears to be real magic as defined by Dingwall. If he were to use a few simple tricks in order to induce the real stuff, this would not affect the validity of the final product. (He has repeatedly assured me that he does not.) In my opinion, his instinctive grasp of the conditions – usually chaotic – necessary for the manifestation of psi is the best evidence in favour of his genuineness. Others argue that it is precisely this ability to control his surroundings that points to his non-genuineness. How, then are we ever going to settle the matter one way or the other? I can argue that Uri has satisfied me that genuinely inexplicable things take place in his presence – the episode of the shaving mirror would be enough to establish that. Others, however, can claim that since even professional magicians can be fooled, who am I to distinguish between a real psychic and a fake one?

I can only testify that on the evidence of my own senses,

I have no reason to believe that he has ever tried to deceive either me or anybody else. The case against him is founded on the shakiest of evidence, not to mention several often repeated lies. His detractors have done a very poor job, preferring the innuendo, the assumption and the smear of dispassionate observation and careful study of facts. They have rejected evidence that would be considered acceptable in any other field of scientific inquiry, and they have used methods that would be considered unacceptable in them. I am wholly unimpressed by both their case and their methods of presenting it. Kangaroo courts should not be mistaken for courts of law. On the evidence I have seen and examined, of which it has been possible to summarize only a small part in this book, there is only one possible verdict: Geller is not guilty as charged.

The witch-hunters have been chasing after the wrong target. They have failed to grasp the obvious: if there are such things as what are generally known as psychic powers, they must be available to observers as well as to those under observation. If somebody can demonstrate them positively, others can demonstrate them negatively and suppress the very effect they claim to be trying to observe.

Deciding for yourself whether there are such things as psychic powers or not is really quite easy. What is difficult, and impossible for some, is accepting the fact that they might exist. The late Sir Alister Hardy once designed an experiment whereby an agnostic or even an atheist can test the efficacy of prayer, which can be summarized like this: 'Whether you believe in it or not, try it for yourself, on the assumption that it might work. Obey the rules scrupulously, then see if you get results.' Prayer, he said, is a 'formula for generating religious experience' – whether you are already 'religious' or not.

The same type of experiment can be carried out by anybody interested in finding out whether there are such things as telepathy, clairvoyance or psychokinesis. Expecting them to happen under your conditions and when you are ready for them is no use at all. They happen under their conditions and in their own time. The sensible researcher will re-create those conditions and then allow them to occur.

The history of psychical research is full of frauds, con-men, con-women and assorted nuisances who have wasted the time of a lot of well-intentioned people. Uri Geller, in my opinion, is not one of them. Nor is he just one more 'medium' in the Home-Palladino-Schneider category, which is reserved for those very rare individuals who demonstrate unusual and inexplicable powers and are not found to be fraudulent.

What is he, then?

He has two firsts to his credit. He is the first professional entertainer to bring ostensibly genuine psychic phenomena into the homes and lives of millions. He is also the first to put psychic powers to work successfully on a large scale in the 'real' world of big business.

In the process, he has unnerved us all. He has given us a tantalizing glimpse of what might be. Some of us have taken a quick look at this and backed away in fear and confusion. Others have denounced it as something that should not be allowed to exist. A few have looked more closely.

What they have seen has forced them to question their assumptions about the way the physical world and the human mind are supposed to behave. Scientists have done their best to return to normal work after a brief visit to their calm laboratories by the travelling Geller show. Millions of television viewers have sat and watched this enigmatic and mischievous fellow going about his business of reorganizing reality.

The bent spoons may be locked away in filing cabinets. The face may have faded from the screens. But the subversive idea has remained buried in the collective subconscious: *things are not what we have been taught they are.*

It will not, I suspect, remain buried for long.

# What Scientists say about Uri Geller

*Wernher von Braun* (NASA scientist) 'Geller has bent my ring in the palm of my hand without ever touching it. Personally, I have no scientific explanation for the phenomena.'

*Dr Wilbur Franklin* (Physics Department, Kent State University) 'The evidence based on metallurgical analysis of fractured surfaces [produced by Geller] indicates that a paranormal influence must have been operative in the formation of the fractures.'

*Dr Harold Puthoff* and *Russell Targ* (Stanford Research Institute) 'As a result of Geller's success in this experimental period, we consider that he has demonstrated his paranormal, perceptual ability in a convincing and unambiguous manner.' (The results of these experiments were published in the respected British journal *Nature*, Vol. 251, No. 5)

*Dr Friedbert Karger* (Max Planck Institute for Plasma Physics, Munich) 'Based on preliminary investigations of Uri Geller, I cannot establish fraud. The powers of this man are a phenomenon which theoretical physics cannot yet explain.'

*Dr Albert Ducrocq* (Telemetry Laboratory, Foch Hospital, Suren, France) 'The bends in metal objects [made by Geller] could not have been made by ordinary manual means.'

*Professor John B. Hasted* (Birkbeck College, University of London) 'The Geller method of breaking steel is unlike anything described in the [metallurgical] literature, from fatigue fractures at −195 degrees to brittle fractures at +600 degrees C. Why is metal bending important? Simply because we do not understand it.'

*Eldon Byrd* (US Naval Surface Weapons Center, Maryland) 'Geller altered the lattice structure of a metal alloy in a way that cannot be duplicated. There is no present scientific explanation as to how he did this.' (This is the first research related to parapsychology conducted at a US Government facility to have been released for publication by the US Department of Defense.)

*William E. Cox* (Institute of Parapsychology, Durham, North Carolina) 'I have failed to conceive of any means of deception in the static PK tests with Geller, nor have magicians I have consulted.'

*Dr A. R. G. Owen* (New Horizons Research Foundation, Toronto, Ontario) 'Metal objects were bent or divided [by Geller] in circumstances such as to prove conclusively . . . that the phenomena were genuine and paranormal.'

*Dr Thomas Coohill* (Western Kentucky University, Physics Dept., Bowling Green, Kentucky) 'There is no logical explanation for what Geller did here. But I don't think logic is what necessarily makes new inroads in science.'

*Dr Walter A. Frank* (Bonn University) 'The Geller Effect is one of those "para"–phenomena which changed the world of physics. What the most outstanding physicists of the last decades of this century could grasp only as theoretical implication, Uri brought as fact into everyday life.'

*Professor Helmut Hofmann* (Department of Electrical Engineering, Technical University of Vienna, Austria) 'I tested Uri Geller myself under laboratory-controlled

354 *The Geller Effect*

conditions and saw with my own eyes the bending of a key which was not touched by Geller at any time. There was a group of people present during the experiment who all witnessed the key bending in eleven seconds to an angle of thirty degrees. Afterwards we tested the key in a scientific laboratory using devices such as electron microscopes and X-rays and found that there was no chemical, manual or mechanical forces involved in the bending of the key.'

*Professor Erich Mittenecker* (Professor of Psychology, University of Graz, Austria) 'Uri Geller is extraordinarily gifted in telepathy.'

*Professor Charles Crussard* (Professor of Metallurgy, School of Mines, Paris and Scientific Director of Pecheney, France) 'Uri bent a strong heat-treated alloy bar held by myself and my assistant at each end. There was absolutely no pressure exerted by Uri while the bar was bending. All the controlled experiments I conducted with Uri Geller have been described in *Sciences et Avenir*, no. 345, pp. 1108–1113.

# Books about Uri Geller

*Uri*, Andrija Puharich, Doubleday/Robson
*The Magic of Uri Geller*, James Randi, Ballantine
*The Amazing Uri Geller*, Martin Ebon, New American
   Library
*Uri Geller: Fup eller Fakta?*, Leo Leslie, Samlerens
   Piccoloboger
*The Strange Story of Uri Geller*, Jim Colin, Raintree
*In Search of Superman*, John Wilhelm, Pocket Books
*The Geller Papers*, Charles Panati, Houghton Mifflin
*The Geller Phenomenon*, Colin Wilson, Aldus Books
*Superminds*, John G. Taylor, Macmillan/Picador
*The Metal Benders*, John Hasted, Routledge and Kegan
   Paul

# Acknowledgments

My thanks to the following, for helping both me and this book in many ways: Uri Avneri, Moshe Ben-Haim, Michael Bentine, Robert Bolt and Sarah Miles, the Bulgari family, Aurelia and Dr Heinz Bundschuh, Eldon Byrd, Joseph Charles, Ron and Nicola Collin, Luis Conde, Yacov and Shoshi David, Iris Davidesco, Philip J. Donnison, Lady Mary Fairfax, Paul Fenton, Wolfgang Foges, Clement and Jill Freud, Matthew Freud, David Frost, John and Elizabeth Fuller, Ilonka Fullop, Eva Geller, Margaret Gero, Meir and Anat Gitlis, Beverly Gordey, Tony Hammond, John Hasted, Ron Hawke and family, Rany Hirsch, Volgyes Hugone, Brian Inglis, Byron and Maria Janis, Yasha Katz, Prince and Princess Michael of Kent, Betty Kenworthy, Adnan Khashoggi, Walter Klapper, Ulrich Kohli and family, Susan Elisabeth Korn, Richard Kuttner, Stuart Kuttner, Anita Lagercranz, Jesse and Pat Lasky, Beniamino Levi and Roberta, Larry and Gloria Lighter, José López Portillo, Carmen Romano de López Portillo, Tom Maschler, Jeff Mishlove, Edgar Mitchell, Brendan O'Regan, Gönczi Palne, Charles Panati, Ian Paten, Gideon and Ofra Peleg, Lea Peleg, Princess Luciana Pignatelli, Guy Lyon Playfair, Santiago Pollarski, Andrija Puharich, Hal Puthoff and Russell Targ, Aliza and Martha Rosenberg, Michael and Jackie Rosenberg, Amnon, Roni and Tal Rubinstein, Yboi and Denes Schner, Dick and Joaney Seaver, Avi Setton, Dani Shalem, Arie and Hava Shtrang, Shipi Shtrang, Eli Tavor, Dennis Thomas, Barrie Thompson and family, Tibor, John Tishman, Walter and Mary Jo Uphoff, Margaret van Hatten, Bob Warth, Ezer Weissman, Sir John Whitmore, Bob and Candace Williamson, Colin Wilson, Donald Wood, Jun-Ichi Yaoi, Hezi and Tali Zakai, Artur Zorka. And to all my friends around the world.

And to Hanna, for keeping my feet on the ground.

1987                                        URI GELLER


I would like to thank the following for their help: David Bolt, Anthony Colwell, Mandy Greenfield, Maurice Grosse, Jack Houck, Dr Marcello Truzzi and Professor Robert Van de Castle. Special thanks are due to Uri, Hanna and Shipi for their co-operation, patience and hospitality throughout the writing of this book.

GUY LYON PLAYFAIR

# Picture Credits

The publishers would like to thank the following for permission to include photographs: the Marquess of Bath, Longleat House; Gamma Liaison; *News of the World*; Guy Lyon Playfair; RTZ Limited; Shipi Shtrang; US Embassy; UPI Ltd; John Rigby.

They are also grateful for permission to reproduce the following cartoons: Keith Waite cartoon (no. 1), Syndication International Ltd; Dick Teresi/Frank Cirocco cartoon (no. 2) reprinted by permission from *Science Digest*. Copyright © 1976 The Hearst Corporation. All rights reserved; *Omni* cartoon (no. 3) reprinted courtesy *Omni Magazine* © 1985; Paul Sellers cartoon (no. 4), United Feature Syndicate; Dry Bones cartoon (no. 5) reprinted by permission from the *Jerusalem Post*. Copyright © Y. Kirschen; Mark Boxer cartoon (no. 6), *The Times*; Heath cartoon (no. 7), *The Sunday Times*; Ray Rigby cartoon (no. 8), *New York Post*.

# Epilogue
## *Mind Over Missile?*

I was as surprised as anybody else to open the 4 May 1987 issue of *US News & World Report* and read the following on the 'Washington Whispers' page:

Senate Foreign Relations Chairman Claiborne Pell last week reserved a vault in the attic of the Capitol – a room often used to examine top-secret documents. Purpose: Assemble government officials to hear Israeli psychic Uri Geller reveal what he has divined of Soviet strategic intentions. Geller, who claims to be able to bend spoons with mental force, once briefed former President Jimmy Carter.

I was not surprised by yet one more untrue story about me in the press. This one was true. What surprised me was seeing it in print.

I do not know who leaked the story. I only know that it was not me. As many eminent people in all walks of life could testify, when I am asked to keep quiet on a sensitive matter, I keep quiet.

There was no indication in the brief item of why anybody would have thought I had anything useful to say about Soviet strategic intentions. Not surprisingly, the world's media decided to find out for themselves. First off the mark was *Newsweek*, which sent a reporter to my home in England, where I had only just returned after a very tiring three-week promotion tour for the hardcover edition of this book in the US, and where I was hoping for some days of recuperation in the spring sunshine.

I had no such luck. By the time the 11 May issue of

*Newsweek* was on the stands (several days before the cover date) there had also been a full-page feature in the *News of the World* (3 May) and even a fifteen-column-inch story on the front page of Britain's leading Sunday newspaper, the *Sunday Times*. Again, all three of these major stories were substantially accurate, though again most of the information they contained did not come from me.

The truth was gradually emerging: that I had met the head of the Soviet arms negotiating team in Geneva and also his US counterpart, Ambassador Max Kampelman, in addition to the highly respected five-term US Senator Claiborne Pell, plus quite a distinguished cast of supporting characters.

I was even given the honour of an item in the weekly BBC radio satirical programme 'Week Ending' (1 May) in which I was supposedly introduced to President Reagan as the fellow who was going to use 'his awesome psychic powers against the Soviets'. Sample dialogue:

*Reagan*: Baloney! I bet you can't tell what I'm thinking right now.
*Me*: You're thinking, 'Bet you can't tell what I'm thinking right now'.
*Reagan*: That's good. This guy's genuine. OK, Geller – you're on!

It was all good fun, although the actor playing my part did not sound like me. (I also never met President Reagan and I never use my 'awesome powers' against anybody or anything except maybe spoons.)

The *New York Post* published the cartoon reproduced opposite, with its row of contorted Soviet missiles.

I enjoy a good joke, including those made at my expense. World peace and nuclear disarmament, how-

8 Cartoon from the *New York Post*, May 1987.

ever, are serious matters, and now that a good deal of the story of my brief involvement in this area has been made public by others, let me tell you what really happened. I particularly want to set the record straight in order to avoid speculation that might harm the careers of some of the finest public servants of the United States – and maybe also of the Soviet Union.

I do not know how it all started. I do not know who said what to whom, when or where, so I cannot tell you the whole story. I can only put on record what I know.

With the first publication of this book in Britain in October 1986, I soon learned that there was a sudden revival of interest in me. Scraps of information coming my way from friends, and from friends of friends, led me to believe that some of my former colleagues in the US

defence and intelligence communities were asking themselves why they had let me go, and why they no longer
asked me to do anything for them.

Then, late in December 1986, I received a most unusual
telephone call. The dialogue, to the best of my recollection, went like this.

'Mr Geller? My name is Casey. You may have read
about me in the papers lately. I've known about you for
many years.'

Somebody had to be kidding me. The only Casey I had
been reading about was the newly appointed director of
the Central Intelligence Agency, the late William Casey.
I forget what I replied, but my voice must have betrayed
my suspicions.

'If you're psychic you'll know this isn't a joke,' said the
caller. He sounded to me like an elderly man of some
authority. He could well have been the CIA chief, so I
decided to go along with him and see what developed.

'OK,' I replied. 'I believe you. How can I help you?
I'm quite astonished and flattered that you're calling me
out of the blue like this. Did anybody tell you to get in
touch with me?'

'No, no, Mr Geller. I just wanted to ask if you could do
something for me over the 'phone, just for my personal
satisfaction?'

'Well, I've done it in the past, but I don't know if it'll
work.' I gathered he wanted to do some kind of telepathy
test, and I remembered that my first contact with the CIA
had been very similar to this one.

'I'm looking at something,' he went on. 'Can you
describe it for me?'

I closed my eyes and went through my usual visualization method. Then I drew what I had picked up and
described it to my caller. I told him I had seen a dagger

with an ornamental tortoise-shell or ivory handle.

There was a long silence. I wondered if we had been disconnected. Then came the reply.

'I'll – be – darned! You got it. OK, OK, that was enough for me. It was nice talking with you, Mr Geller.' And that was that.

I had already met Senator Claiborne Pell socially. He and I turned out to have close friends in common, so there was nothing unusual about our initial meeting. It came about when an old friend of mine, Princess Luciana Pignatelli, introduced me to a member of the British Royal Family, the German-born Princess Michael of Kent.

During my conversation with the Princess (which was private and as far as I am concerned will remain so) she mentioned the Senator as an old friend who not only had a very distinguished public career – he was now chairman of the US Foreign Relations Committee – but was also very open-minded towards psychic and spiritual matters. Although I did not know it at the time, the Senator's interests were on the record back in 1984, when an article in the *New York Times* (10 January) quoted him as having 'discussed the parapsychology field with Soviet research- ers during a visit to the Soviet Union in August . . .'

We got along very well from the start. I found Senator Pell to be a man of great dignity and wisdom, and although he could be described as a member of the old school of politics, he also struck me as one of the most forward-looking and open-minded statesmen I had ever met. What especially impressed me was that he wanted above all to know if I thought psychic power could be used for peaceful purposes.

We had a very pleasant meeting. I bent a spoon for him and reproduced a drawing he had made out of my sight, of a smiling face. Nothing specific was arranged, and I never imagined that we would meet again so soon or in such sensitive circumstances.

Not long after that mysterious telephone conversation with a man who claimed to be the head of the CIA, another call came out of the blue into my home. The caller was secretary to Ambassador Kampelman, who told me very formally that the ambassador would like to meet me, and could I suggest a suitable venue?

I assumed he would not want our meeting to be too public, to put it mildly, so I hastily arranged to borrow the boardroom of a London company owned by a friend I could trust to keep quiet, and that was where we duly met – just the two of us.

Max Kampelman was one of the few people who have asked to see me and then *not* asked me to bend a spoon or read his mind. He struck me as a man not fond of wasting time, and I believe he had been well briefed on what I could do. He was particularly keen to know if I thought that a human mind could influence others at a distance in a positive way, and as with Senator Pell I found him to be a person of great warmth and constructive intentions. Our talk lasted about an hour, during which we also touched on the question of Soviet Jews, which was naturally of interest to us, and when we shook hands out on the pavement nothing was said about any further meeting.

By February 1987, the German-language edition of this book had been published by Ariston, a publisher with its headquarters in Geneva. They arranged an extensive promotion tour for me in Germany, Austria and the German-speaking areas of Switzerland, and it was while I was in Zurich that I received yet another of those out-of-the-blue 'phone calls inviting me to come at once to Geneva.

The US/Soviet disarmament talks were already under way, and I was to attend a function at the US Mission. The date was 27 February, and the invitation came from Ambassador Kampelman's aide. (Whether the invitation originated with the ambassador, I do not know.) It was agreed that if the press spotted me I was to be described as an entertainer, although whoever heard of entertainers at disarmament talks?!

So, almost as soon as I stepped from the plane at Geneva, I found myself on centre-stage in a real-life drama that could have had immense international consequences.

The formal business of the day was over (I had not been invited to that) and a reception was held at the US Mission for American and Soviet delegates and their wives. It may have been no more than an informal social event on the surface, but as any diplomat will know these affairs are not held just for fun. The serious business continues at them, and I did not have to be psychic to know that I had walked into a room where some very heavy stuff was going on amid the social chatter and raising of glasses.

I was delighted to spot two familiar faces, those of Senator Pell and Ambassador Kampelman, and to be introduced to no less than five other senators: Ted Stevens, Richard Lugar, Arlen Spector, Don Nickles and a man who could well be a future US president – Albert Gore. I was even more honoured and pleased then to be presented to the First Deputy Foreign Minister of the Soviet Union and head of his mission, Yuli M. Vorontsov.

I had come a long way in a short time, for the man I was meeting just a couple of months after that enigmatic telephone call from somebody claiming to be William Casey (I still have no proof that it was) was one of the three most influential men in Soviet foreign affairs, together with his minister, Edward Shevardnadze, and party secretary Mikhail Gorbachev.

I liked Mr Vorontsov at once. I felt no trace of hostility from him, and we soon began a pleasant and informal conversation, ranging over world affairs in general and the abilities of individuals to alter the course of events by no more than the state of their minds and their real desire for peace.

I was sure he had such a desire. For all their history of wars, revolutions and massacres, I feel that there is a peaceful side to the Russian personality (though not perhaps to all nationalities in the Soviet Union), together with an energy and enthusiasm for life not often found in other peoples.

Vorontsov knew who I was, and since I had been brought along as an entertainer, I thought I had better do some entertaining. I began by making a seed sprout, and then picked up a spoon and began to bend it in my usual way, handing it to Vorontsov and telling him it would go on bending while he was holding it. To his delight, and my great relief, it did.

His manner towards me after my little show became even more cordial. He smiled, and said, 'I know these powers are real', then went on to tell me about the Soviet healer Dzhuna Davitashvili, who is thought to have treated the late Mr Brezhnev – though this was not the time to ask about that alleged incident.

After the reception, I was invited to join a group for dinner at Roberto's restaurant, where I was seated opposite Vorontsov at the table that also included Kampelman, Pell and two other senators.

Like the reception, the dinner was more than a purely social affair, and I will not repeat any of the dialogue that buzzed around my ears during the meal. It soon became clear to me – by perfectly normal means – that both sides had come to Geneva to bargain, negotiate and discuss, not to present previously established fixed positions, as might have been the case under earlier Soviet administrations. History was being made all around me, and the well-being of tens of millions of people would depend on how well my fellow-diners got along with each other.

Throughout the meal, I kept up a steady bombardment of my own form of negotiation: intense images of peace. The previous year, I had only had a few minutes with the first 'victim' of my peace campaign, Adnan Khashoggi, and, as I have described, I am sure he received the message. With Vorontsov I had three or four hours, and I really let him have it. I am convinced that he too got the message.

I signed a copy of my book for Vorontsov and his wife, telling him he would have a good laugh when he read it, because he was going to think, 'How come the US is still using him, because the book is fairly derogatory about the CIA?'

Vorontsov laughed. 'Don't worry,' he said. 'They never read books!'

Three days later, on Monday 2 March 1987, the story hit the world's headlines. 'West Welcomes Gorbachev Nuclear Weapons Proposal' (*Financial Times*) and 'Urgent Missile Talks Today on Soviet Offer' (*The Times*) were two typical ones from the British press. In a front-page column headed 'Soviet Offer is Genuine Article', *The Guardian*'s Jonathan Steele summarized two explanations of what he called 'Mr Gorbachev's dramatic U-turn' in the form of a no-strings-attached offer to remove all medium-range nuclear missiles from Europe, East and West.

The 'hard-line' version was that it was a clever Soviet ploy to lure President Reagan into an unwise deal at a time when he faced difficulties in other areas. The 'optimistic' theory was that 'Gorbachev is making an important concession', and Steele commented: 'I accept the second theory . . .'

I would love to claim all the credit for this, but I should point out that Gorbachev's surprise offer was made the very day after my dinner party at Geneva. It is true that when I said good-bye to Vorontsov, I told him to tell Mr Gorbachev what had happened, which he assured me he would and I have no doubt that he did. However, there were many indications that the Soviet leader had been planning a major initiative of this kind ever since the 1986 Reykjavik summit with Reagan – and I had nothing to do with that!

Even so, the *Sunday Times*' headline in its 3 May issue was: 'Did Uri Bend the Will of Gorbachev?' Maybe I did? Who knows? Only Vorontsov and Gorbachev, and they are not telling.

Back home after my brief plunge into international affairs, I had plenty to do. The French edition of my book came out, calling for more promotion, and I had little time to prepare myself physically and psychically for my three-week tour of the US in April.

On 7 April, less than a week after the start of my US tour, I found that the authorities had not finished with me. I received a very high-powered invitation to a dinner party at the house of a prominent and influential industrialist in the Washington area, whose other guests included such prominent political figures as Milton Friedman,

House Speaker James Wright, Representative Charlie Rose, and a handful of senators including Alan Cranston. It was a private and informal affair, and I was sure I had not been invited just to bend the spoons.

I took the opportunity to say my piece on world affairs and the ability of individuals to influence them for the general good. My little peace lecture was pretty well rehearsed by now, and I already had reason to believe that it had opened quite a few minds in recent weeks. I hope it opened one or two more that evening.

Perhaps it did, for towards the end of my coast-to-coast tour I received yet another of those invitations of the kind you cannot refuse. This was to the meeting at the Capitol at which, as *US News & World Report* put it, I was asked to reveal to US government officials what I had 'divined' of Soviet strategic intentions.

I flew in from Minneapolis, and was met at the airport by Senator Pell's aide, who drove me straight to the Capitol. As we rolled into the parking lot, I realized I was still in my usual sports clothes, and felt I ought to change into something more suitable for a top-level meeting with some of the leaders of the world's most powerful nation. Time was running short, so I stripped right down there in the Capitol parking lot and managed to get my suit and tie on, hoping a curious cop would not stop by and wonder exactly what was going on!

The meeting was not an unqualified success for me. The audience, according to *Newsweek*, consisted of 'forty government officials, including Capitol Hill staffers and Pentagon and Defense Department aides, gathered in a high-security room to hear Geller hold forth on his abilities'. That was not quite correct – I did not hold forth on my abilities, but on my usual theme of world peace and the need to invest more in the development of mental abilities. I reminded the officials that I now knew what I was talking about from first-hand experience when I said that top Soviet officials were aware of the psychic dimension. I had only recently spent an evening with the Number Three man in the Soviet foreign affairs hierarchy, and I had, I thought, left him with something to think about.

So far, so good. Then, as *Newsweek* reported quite correctly, 'the psychic tried guessing – unsuccessfully – the shapes that the assembled guests had drawn on bits of paper'. I just had a bad day as far as telepathy was concerned. I was really worn out after barnstorming around the country. I had been on the promotion bandwagon since October, with very few rest breaks, and on top of that I had suddenly been hauled into a major international affair. All I could concentrate on by then was getting back to my wife, my children and my home.

Shortly after the start of my April promotion tour in the United States, I was contacted by an Israeli. He did not tell me who he was, and I did not ask him.

He was very well informed about my recent activities in areas other than those for which I am best known, and his message to me was very brief. What it amounted to was this: I could be in serious trouble, and I should watch my step.

Maybe he overstated his case, but knowing the people I assume he was working for, I would not bet on it. I became paranoid. Was somebody out to kidnap me, or to 'terminate' me, as they say in intelligence circles? It seemed ridiculous, but . . .

These things do happen. My good friend John Lennon was gunned down outside his own home by a mentally disturbed young man. That great man of peace Terry

Waite disappeared in the labyrinths of Lebanese political intrigue after setting out on another of his brave one-man peace missions. What really happened to those three British scientists working in a sensitive defence-related industry who were all found dead in most unusual circumstances? People do get kidnapped. They do disappear. They do get terminated. There are some really sick people out there. There are also some powerful and well-financed individuals who have vested interests in preventing world peace. The victims of these perverts and warmongers always seem to be those most dedicated to peace, love and spiritiual progress.

As soon as I got home, I wrote three short letters, put them in an envelope and had this delivered to the Soviet Embassy in London. I enclosed a covering letter to the ambassador asking him to pass on the letters. One was to Secretary Mikhail Gorbachev, one was to Yuli Vorontsov, and the third was to the director-general of the Soviet Committee for State Security, better known as the KGB. The contents of the letters were identical, and this is what I wrote:

After my demonstration at the US Mission in Geneva for the US and Soviet delegations, I heard rumours that the KGB might be planning to either kidnap me or kill me.

I am just a good showman and an entertainer, and I am harmless. I do hope the rumours are false.

My best wishes,
Peace
Uri Geller

Was I over-reacting, or was that cryptic message from the nameless Israeli genuine? Knowing how people in Israeli security circles operate, I would doubt that he was wasting either his own time or mine.

Had I written to the right people, though? Did some-body else want me out of the way? I could not think of anybody, but all the same I carried out a thorough check of my security and improved it in a number of ways, making use of the best advice available anywhere.

I tried to visualize the scene when Vorontsov reported back to his government after the Geneva talks. Maybe he really did believe that the US had signed an arms deal with me? There must have been some confusion in the Kremlin – entertainers do not normally show up at disarmament talks. What was the US up to? Did they have a secret weapon: me?

To add to their confusion, I had made it perfectly clear what I was up to. I told Vorontsov more or less what I told all the other people mentioned in this chapter – that the mind is mightier than the missile, and instead of spending billions on missiles, we should put some real money into minds.

It is already clear that I am not the only one to believe this, for when the story of my visits to Geneva and the Capitol hit the headlines, there was an interesting devel-opment: I received official invitations from no less than four major countries. All of them wanted me to visit them in order to discuss ways of achieving peace with top government officials including heads of state.

When I received these invitations, I accepted them all and included a selection of articles and items about my recent activities from the press. I also included a fair selection of derogatory material written by my detractors and other sceptics.

All four countries replied to the effect that after care-fully studying the material I sent them, they would still like me to visit them. Previous 'peace conferences' have focused on ways of reducing war. We are now putting the emphasis on ways of increasing peace, which is not quite the same thing.

Looking through my file of anti-Geller articles, I cannot help feeling once again that I have come a long way. For instance, here is the 1977 issue of *The Humanist* with the cover story entitled 'Psychics Debunked'. I was one of them. of course, And here is the *New Scientist* (16 April 1987) admitting just ten years later that 'despite CSICOP's attempts to discredit Uri Geller, the spoon-bending psychic from Israel, Geller has earned up to $250,000 a day telling mining companies where to look for oil and gold.' In 1978, you may remember, the same magazine described me as a 'fake'. Now, at least, I have been promoted to the status of a 'psychic'!

The issue today is no longer whether Uri Geller is real or not. It is one of much more importance: whether a wider understanding of the real power of the human mind can make for a better world.

I am proud of what I did at Geneva, and I am grateful to those courageous public figures who invited me there regardless of the ridicule they knew they could expect from their own press (although as it turned out, the episode was very objectively and fairly reported). Two of them, incidentally, wrote to thank me for my services after the story had become public.

I do not know who was ultimately responsible for getting me to Geneva, and it will be some time before we can say what effect, if any, I had on the minds of the Soviet officials I met.

My guess is that they went home with plenty to think about, and that as soon as they were back at their desks quite a number of urgent messages flew around the country, from Moscow and Leningrad to Minsk, Kharkov, Kiev, Pushchino, Krasnodar, Novosibirsk, Alma-Ata,

Taganrog, Yerevan and Tbilisi – in fact, everywhere that 'bioelectronics' (their word for psychic functioning) is already being studied. A research budget would be increased here, a new laboratory added there, more staff taken on somewhere else . . .

The next peace summit talks could be really interesting.

# Index